Forging Gay Identities

Forging Gay Identities

Organizing Sexuality in San Francisco, 1950–1994

ELIZABETH A. ARMSTRONG

The University of Chicago Press / Chicago & London

The University of Chicago Press, Chicago 60637
The University of Chicago Press, Ltd., London
© 2002 by The University of Chicago
All rights reserved. Published 2002
Printed in the United States of America

11 10 09 08   2 3 4 5

ISBN: 0-226-02693-0 (cloth)
ISBN: 0-226-02694-9 (paper)

Library of Congress Cataloging-in-Publication Data

Armstrong, Elizabeth A.
    Forging gay identities : organizing sexuality in San Francisco, 1950–1994 /
Elizabeth A. Armstrong.
        p.   cm.
    Includes bibliographical references (p.   ) and index.
    ISBN 0-226-02693-0 (cloth) — ISBN 0-226-02694-9 (pbk.)
        1. Gays—California—San Francisco—Identity. 2. Gays—California—San
Francisco—Political activity—History—20th century. 3. Gay liberation
movement—California—San Francisco—History—20th centuty. I. Title.

HQ76.3.U52 S263 2002
305.9′0664′0979461—dc21

                                                        2002006413

To my parents

CONTENTS

Part III. Conclusion

TABLES AND FIGURES

Tables

Figures

PREFACE

Forging Gay Identities examines the dynamic growth of the contemporary lesbian/gay movement in San Francisco from the 1950s through the mid-1990s. While covering events documented by a variety of popular and scholarly accounts, this book is unique in several ways. It draws on unique data—a comprehensive data set of San Francisco's lesbian/gay organizations—that allowed me to trace the development of the community in a systematic way. Both my description and explanation of the transformation of the movement in San Francisco depart from conventional understandings. My description of the changes in San Francisco's gay world, developed through analysis of the organizational data, focuses on the crystallization of a gay identity movement as the New Left declined in the early 1970s. In contrast, other accounts focus either on the emergence of gay liberation or the political ascendance of Harvey Milk in the later 1970s. The encounter between early homophile organizing and the New Left produced gay liberation and its signature contribution—coming out. The sudden decline of the New Left reduced conflict between radical and moderate strands of gay liberation by eliminating the viability of the more radical agenda. It was at this moment in the early 1970s that gay activists integrated identity politics, interest group politics, and a growing commercial sexual subculture into a gay identity movement. These potentially contradictory projects were held in dynamic tension by defining the central goal of gay politics as the expansion of possible ways to express gay identity. By privileging identity politics in this way, even blatant political contradictions were defused. The collection of the organizational data set, data analysis, and the construction of the argument were guided by a cultural-institutional approach to social movements. This approach integrates cultural approaches to social movements and institutional sociology. I developed this approach as I discovered that neither was able to fully account for the development of this particular social movement. Social movement theory, in particular, could not account for the integration of the cultural, political, and commercial within the lesbian/gay movement. How-

ever, this cultural-institutional approach can be used to develop explanations of the transformation of other movements as well as other nonmovement fields.

While writing this book I encountered questions about the origins of my
interest in the lesbian/gay movement. I sometimes sensed that this curiosity
was fueled by interest in my sexual identity. Underlying this curiosity was the
presumption that if I identified as a lesbian, my curiosity made sense, but that
it was mystifying if I did not. While my sexual biography is relevant to my interest in the topic, it was not the only or even primary source of my curiosity.
My fascination with this case grew out of the recognition that the transformation of the lesbian/gay movement in San Francisco raises challenging
questions for our understanding of American political culture and for several sociological literatures.

My hope is that this book conveys the general importance of the emergence of lesbians and gays as a political and cultural force in the United States
in the second half of the twentieth century. Analyzing the remarkable
growth of the lesbian/gay movement in the late twentieth century provides
insight into changes in the ways Americans think about identity and how
Americans assess the costs and benefits of participating in civic culture. The
contours of this movement challenge the capacity of sociological thinking
on social movements to explain it. The rapidity and success of this institution
building project demand explanation by those who endeavor to explain institutional transformation. The dramatic revision in the meanings associated
with same-gender sexual experience illustrate the fluidity of these meanings,
their vulnerability to rapid reconstruction, and the processes through which
these meanings have and can be changed.

My interest in this set of intellectual questions grew out of an intersection of generation, gender, sexuality, geography, and intellectual milieu. I am
a white, post–baby boom woman, born and raised in the Midwest. I attended
college at the University of Michigan in Ann Arbor and graduate school at
the University of California at Berkeley.

At the University of Michigan in the late 1980s my friends and I learned
about the events of the 1960s (not part of the standard high school social
studies curriculum in Kansas) and developed the distinct sense that we
missed out. I was mesmerized by a course by Alice Echols on the women's liberation movement in which we read women's liberation movement documents. My friends and I flocked to Jeff Paige's political sociology course,
where we were first exposed to Marxism. Too studious to throw myself
wholeheartedly into political movements on campus (which, at that time,

were primarily about issues of racism and sexual assault), my fascination with the New Left became an intellectual one. The men that I shared my college experience with gravitated to the study of political economy. As a young woman trying to manage the painful contradictions of coming of age in the midst of an unfinished gender revolution, my interests turned to issues of gender and sexuality.

These interests pulled me into graduate school in sociology. With Nancy Chodorow, Arlie Hochschild, Kristin Luker, Todd Gitlin, and Ann Swidler on the faculty, Berkeley was an obvious choice for someone interested in studying gender, culture, and the New Left. My experiences in graduate school and living in the Bay Area only intensified my interest in these issues. As a community, Berkeley celebrated its role in the events of the 1960s. I took graduate seminars with Todd Gitlin and listened to fellow graduate students tell of their experiences in the movements of the 1960s. Everyday life in the Bay Area brought issues of lesbian/gay politics to the fore. Wonderful work being done by faculty and students in the Berkeley sociology department on sexuality illustrated the richness and complexity of the area. Steven Epstein, Arlene Stein, Joshua Gamson, and Tomás Almaguer were all at Berkeley at this time writing essays and books that would become classics in the field.

As I struggled to make connections between the lesbian/gay movement and existing theories of social movements, I found that existing theory could not fully account for the growth and transformation of this movement. Political process theories were limited in some ways, while new social movement theories were limited in others. Observations of the San Francisco Lesbian/Gay Freedom Day Parade suggested that the movement cohered, even as theorists predicted that the diversity of identities evident in the parade should have been paralyzing, as they were for the women's movement. Reading the organizations literature (at Ann Swidler's insistence), it became evident that I was interested in a phenomenon of general interest to organizational theorists: the formation and transformation of organizational fields. Thus, I started this project with an eye to using the tools of organizational sociology to account for a case that social movement theory seemed unable to fully explain. Along the way I found that the tools available in institutional sociology also needed to be reworked in order to account for the transformation of this field.

While I was motivated primarily by the theoretical questions raised by the case, it is unlikely that I would have embarked on this project if I had not found the conventions governing mainstream heterosexuality unsatisfying. I am drawn to a sexual sensibility evident in gay men's public sexual culture, which is at odds with the monogamous and romantic sensibility defining mainstream heterosexuality.

This book is intended both for those who have a particular interest in the forging of contemporary gay identities in the United States and for social scientists interested in other cases of political, cultural, or institutional change. Chapter 1 presents an overview of the argument, an elaboration of the theoretical perspective, a description of the dramatic change in San Francisco's lesbian/gay world, and a more detailed introduction to the rest of the book. Each chapter begins with an introduction that summarizes the theoretical and empirical contributions of the chapter. Chapters 2 through 9 are loosely chronological in organization. The first part (chapters 2 through 5) explains the forging of a gay identity movement. Each chapter addresses a crucial development necessary for the crystallization of a gay identity movement. Chapter 2 analyzes the development of homosexual organizing before 1969; chapter 3, the emergence of gay liberation; chapter 4, the decline of the New Left and its effects on the gay movement; and chapter 5, the consolidating of the gay identity movement. The second part (chapters 6 through 9) addresses the consequences of the gay identity movement. Chapter 6 describes the explosive growth of the movement in the 1970s. Race and gender exclusions are examined in chapter 7, while chapters 8 and 9 explore how the gay identity movement influenced and was influenced by AIDS and queer politics. Chapter 10, which concludes the book, illustrates the ways the specific arguments highlight the strengths of a cultural-institutional approach to movements and suggests how it might be used to explain the development of other movements that participated in the New Left. Chapter 10 also examines how the findings of this book intersect with ongoing debates about civic engagement in the United States.

Sociologists may find chapter 1, the chapter introductions, and the conclusion particularly useful, as these develop the general theoretical contributions. Readers primarily interested in the case may want to skim the theoretical section of chapter 1, "A Cultural-Institutional Approach to Movements."

ACKNOWLEDGMENTS

Institutions make the writing of books such as this one possible. Not only do they provide the material resources necessary for such projects, they also provide the contexts in which the intellectual relationships crucial to such work can be formed.

First and foremost, I would like to thank my advisors in the Berkeley sociology department. This project was birthed in discussions with Ann Swidler, whose able guidance nourished it from a fledgling idea to a completed manuscript. Her ability to home in on what is interesting steered me away from many dead ends, while her absolute confidence in the project convinced me it could be done. The influence of Ann's theorizing on the nature and working of culture are so deeply embedded in this book as to be difficult to excavate. Discussions with Neil Fligstein, over many a lunch and cup of coffee, shaped my thinking in fundamental ways. I am also indebted to comments and advice from Kim Voss. In the process of translating the manuscript from a dissertation into a book, Laura Schmidt and Dan Dohan read and reread the entire manuscript, providing comments as encouraging and as incisive as any I have ever received.

While this project was started at Berkeley, it was finished at Indiana University at Bloomington. I am grateful for the warm welcome and enthusiastic interest of colleagues and graduate students in my new departmental home. Thanks to Clem Brooks for stimulating discussion of the central arguments of the book. Brian Powell arranged for Emily Fairchild to assist with the preparation of the references. Her quick, good-natured, and conscientious work is much appreciated. I am grateful to the faculty and graduate students who commented on a presentation of the work at a session of the Political and Economic Sociology workshop, including Patricia McManus, Maurice Garnier, Art Alderson, and Pam Walters. Thanks also to Kent Redding, Marty Weinberg, Tom Gieryn, Indermohan Virk, Donna Eder, Jason Jimerson, Eliza Pavalko, Alicia Suarez, Sharon Adams, and Emily Childers for cites given, books loaned, and conversations shared. Scott Long and Rob Robinson, outgoing and incoming chairs, have made the transition smooth. On my arrival, the office and computer staff got me working instantly. Thanks to Susan Platter, Mark Zacharias, Reed Nelson, Melinda Martin, Kevin Hawkins, and Jack Thomas. Special thanks to Paula Yocum for cheerfully handling the duplication and delivery of the manuscript.

This work could not have been done without support by fellowships and research awards. Particularly critical, both because of the timing and the generosity of the funding, was a Sexuality Research Fellowship from the Social Science Research Council (funded by the Ford Foundation) in 1996. A Doctoral Dissertation Improvement Grant from the National Science Foundation (award number SBR-9400895) supported data collection and coding. With the NSF grant, I was able to hire assistants to help with the coding of research guides and directories. I would like to thank Will Rountree, Maren Klawiter, and especially Yong Lee for their work. I am honored to be a recipient of the American Sociological Association's Martin Levine Dissertation Award. I also received a grant from Phi Beta Kappa of Northern California. A National Science Foundation Graduate Fellowship and a Berkeley Fellowship supported the development of my thinking earlier in graduate school. Neil Fligstein provided me with an informal postdoctoral arrangement with the Center for Culture, Organization, and Politics at the Institute of Industrial Relations at the University of California, Berkeley.

Thanks to Jean Six for copyediting work done on the dissertation manuscript, and to Susie Hull, Christy Williams, and Tom Armstrong for their work on the figures for the book. Photographic Services at Indiana University and Susan Everett of Coudal Partners in Chicago helped prepare the photographic images for publication.

David Valentine and Gina Gatta provided me with access to back issues of *Gaybook* and *Damron's*. Bill Walker assisted me in navigating the archives of the GLBT Historical Society of Northern California. Eric Garber allowed me access to his manuscript on Bay Area commercial establishments. Thanks to Yong Lee for visiting lesbian/gay archives in both Los Angeles and New York in search of difficult-to-locate resource guides.

Thanks to Susan Stryker and Kim Klausner of the Gay, Lesbian, Bisexual, Transgender Historical Society of Northern California for providing research assistance, photographs, and contact information for the photographers whose work is published here. Thanks to Joan E. Biren (JEB), Rink Foto, Daniel Nicoletta, the Gay, Lesbian, Bisexual, Transgender Historical Society of Northern California, the *San Francisco Chronicle*, the *Oakland Tribune*, and the San Francisco AIDS Foundation for permissions to publish the photographs in this book.

Conversations with colleagues around the country have provided an important backdrop of this work, helping to refine my thinking and maintain my enthusiasm. Thanks to Mitchell Stevens for attentively listening to long explanations of my arguments and for great comments on the first chapter of the book. Marc Ventresca and Mike Lounsbury showed early and consistent interest in this work and put me in conversation with others engaged in related work. Conversations at Northwestern University at the Institutions, Conflict, and Social Change Workshop with Doug Creed, Bryant Hudson, Naomi Olson, Amin Panjwani, Marvin Washington, and Kelly Moore were particularly useful. In visits to the Stanford Department of Sociology, Dick Scott, Mike Hannan, and Susan Olzak expressed early interest in the project. I received extremely helpful comments from Dick Scott's medical organizations research group. John Mohr provided great comments at an ASA roundtable early in the project. Conversations and correspondence with Steve Murray, John D'Emilio, Gayle Rubin, Susan Stryker, Steve Epstein, Paul Halsall, David Frank, and SSRC fellows helped clarify the contribution of this work to research on sexuality. Myra Marx Ferree and Joane Nagel provided useful insights into the similarities and differences between this movement and others. Discussions with Bethany Bryson, Orville Lee, Nicki Beisel, Mary Bernstein, Amy Binder, Debbie Gould, Wayne Brekhus, Lionel Cantu, Wendy Griswold, Dan Chambliss, Mark Gould, John Campbell, John Martin, Nancy Latham, Aziza Khazzoom, J. Schiao, Rich Wood, Paul Lichterman, Lissa Bell, and Elizabeth Rudd also contributed to my thinking.

This project has also been influenced by the advice and comments of others who were on the faculty at Berkeley while I was there, including Jorge Arditi, Claude Fischer, Kristin Luker, Michael Rogin, Arlie Hochschild, Nancy Chodorow, Tomás Almaguer, Bob Blauner, Chris Ansell, and Todd Gitlin, and by the work of Josh Gamson, Steve Epstein, and Arlene Stein.

I thank Doug Mitchell of the University of Chicago Press for his early and continuing interest in this project. Doug began discussions with me about this project years before it even reached fruition as a dissertation. He understood what I was trying to accomplish and seemed to find it as interesting as I do, inspiring my immediate confidence and loyalty. Doug selected wonderful reviewers. The comments of Frank Dobbin and an anonymous reviewer proved to be invaluable in revising the manuscript. Thanks to others at the University of Chicago Press, particularly Robert Devens, Leslie Keros, and Mark Heineke. Thanks to Michael Koplow, freelance copyeditor for the press, for his meticulous eye.

Friends around the country have sustained me throughout this writing process. Thanks to Alice Burton, Marcus Kurtz, Karen Licavoli Farnkopf,

Mike Green, Sara Austin, Kathy Fox, Karen Aschaffenburg, Karin Martin, Elizabeth Rudd, Barbara Littleford, Denise Nolan, Kate McKean, Dan Dohan, Tree Stuber, Sherry Reinhardt, Judy Salpeter, Susan Everett, Rosemary Busher, Fiona Redwood, Elizabeth Boling, Christy Kendrick, Marc Goulden, Deepak Gupta, Maresi Nerad, Renate Sadrozinski, Myan Baker, and Adam Malson.

I owe a great debt to Sean Stryker for accommodating his life to my dogged insistence on completing this book and continuing with academic sociology. He made it possible for me to be rigidly uncompromising by exhibiting enough flexibility for the both of us. He turned his facile, creative intellect from academic sociology to the realm of computer programming, transforming himself from sociologist to software engineer. My son Aaron, blissfully unaware of this book-writing process, has loved, entertained, distracted, and exhausted me throughout this process. Without the wonderful child care provided by Robin Fetisoff, Lakeshore Children's Center, and Bloomington Developmental Learning Center this book could not have been written.

My greatest debts are to my parents, Tom and Jeanette Armstrong, to whom I dedicate this book.

NOTE ON USE OF
IDENTITY TERMS

Sexual identity labels are highly political. During the last fifty years, the communities that now call themselves "lesbian, gay, bisexual, and transgender," "LGBT," "lesbigay," or "queer" have used a variety of different terms. The continually evolving and highly contested nature of this movement means that there exists no term to accurately apply to it for the entire period from 1950 to 2000. Throughout the book, I use identity terminology as precisely as possible, trying not to introduce contemporary terminology into discussions of earlier events. In the 1950s and 1960s, activists referred to the movement as "homosexual" or "homophile." In the 1970s, "gay" was assumed to refer to both men and women, while actually describing a mostly male community and movement. Women referred to themselves as "lesbians" or "lesbian feminists." In the early 1980s, activists developed the now familiar concatenation of "lesbian and gay" or "lesbian/gay." In the 1980s, "bisexual" and "transgender" were added to the list. When I refer to the whole time frame, I use the terms "gay" or "lesbian/gay" because these terms dominated between the years 1970 and 1990. Historians of sexuality sometimes now use "queer" as a way of signaling awareness of the historical specificity of gender and sexual meanings systems. I chose not to refer to the development of the "queer" community in San Francisco because the term evokes a political sensibility critical of the solidification of identity categories. Such a sensibility does not accurately capture the enthusiastic, celebratory, and uncritical elaboration of lesbian and gay identities that characterized the center of the gay political project in the 1970s and 1980s.

ONE

The Transformation of
the Lesbian/Gay Movement

Every year in San Francisco, the last Sunday in June is devoted to the Lesbian/Gay/Bisexual/Transgender Freedom Day Parade and Celebration. The parade brings several hundred thousand people into the streets to participate in a collective contemplation of contemporary lesbian and gay life. It is impossible to absorb the entire spectacle. Parade contingents represent the diversity of lesbian and gay organizations and display myriad variations on lesbian and gay identity. Onlookers read the banners with organization names and the signs that designate individual identities. As the contingents pass, people's comments range from amusement to erotic appreciation, from deep respect to downright disgust. The community relishes the spectacle—an enacted, moving list—a literal field of organizations and identities. The parade's public display of identity is powerful although, of course, ephemeral. But the organizations that participate in the parade are not so fleeting. Most are permanent. This is an annual celebration of the organizational infrastructure that grounds the life of San Francisco's lesbian/gay/bisexual/transgender communities.

Neither the parade nor the organizations in it existed before 1970. Thus, the parade reflects the proliferation and diversification of lesbian/gay organizations in the last thirty years. Since 1950, such organizations in San Francisco have evolved from a tiny underground bar subculture of uncertain legality into a sprawling, interlocking set of visible organizations that influence virtually every aspect of life in the city. From 1964 to 1994 the number of nonprofit homosexual organizations in San Francisco increased from 6 to 276.[1]

This book examines this evolution in gay life, gay organizations, and gay identity. The story of this evolution is not a tale of smooth, gradual development. Instead, it occurred in two historic ruptures. Throughout the 1950s and 1960s, public homosexual organizations were limited to a tiny number of organizations that thought of themselves as "homophile." Homophile organizations modeled themselves on interest group politics and hoped to improve life for homosexuals by educating the mainstream public. They had names that conveyed little explicit information about sexual identity, such as the Society for Individual Rights, the Daughters of Bilitis, and the Mattachine Society.

The first rupture occurred in 1969, when gay liberation made its dramatic appearance. Gay liberation defined itself in opposition to the existing homophile project. Like other parts of the New Left, gay liberation was complex and contradictory. The most radical strand of gay liberation, which I refer to as "gay power," sought a total transformation of society.[2] Sexual liberation was defined as merely one aspect of a broader social transformation. Building gay identity was seen as a step toward eliminating social categories altogether.

The second rupture, which occurred in the early 1970s, was less dramatic but even more significant. At that point, affirming gay identity and celebrating diversity replaced societal transformation as goals, marking the origins of a *gay identity movement*. This shift in logic sparked the rapid proliferation of a vast diversity of new gay organizations. These new organizations had more specific titles, reflecting a continuously unfolding variety of new identities and subidentities, such as Affirmation Gay/Lesbian Mormons, Gay Asian Pacific Alliance, Straights for Gay Rights, and Gay American Indians.[3] Organization names now included elaborate identity information and represented specialized subidentities. This turn toward identity building was accompanied by rapid political consolidation and the explosive growth of a commercial subculture oriented around sex. For the first time, gay organizations agreed upon a national gay rights agenda and moved aggressively to pursue common goals in the political arena.

These vast changes in the gay community present a fascinating puzzle for those wishing to understand the social forces that hold social movements together. In the lesbian/gay movement, which scholars have referred to as the "quintessential identity movement," we find a paradox.[4] Contrary to the assumptions and expectations of many experts on social movements, the focus on identity building and identity elaboration has not proved to be paralyzing or divisive for the gay movement. Paradoxically, the unity and diversity of the gay community seem inextricably interconnected. Therefore, by looking closely at this "quintessential" identity movement we can better understand a phenomenon that is common to many contemporary social movements.

IN THIS BOOK, I argue that the key to understanding the paradox of gay identity lies in its historical origins. The ability of the gay movement to balance commitment to a group identity with the protection of individual differences was built into the movement as it crystallized in the early 1970s. The movement would not have coalesced when and as it did without the development of homophile politics before 1969, the cultural innovations made available by the New Left, the sudden decline of the New Left in the early 1970s, and the efforts of activists in the early 1970s to ensure that the gay movement survive. Each of these processes contributed in a crucial way to the movement that formed in the early 1970s. In isolation, these processes would have been insufficient. Only because they all happened in sequence did they lead to the forming of a gay identity movement.

Homophile organizing in the 1950s and 1960s began the process of transforming homosexual identity from a private group consciousness into a public collective identity. It established the legitimacy of creating public organizations of homosexuals and the notion that homosexuals were a group deserving rights that could be won by engaging in interest group politics. But homophile politics could not have generated the visible public identity needed for truly effective use of interest group politics, nor could it have justified a proliferation and diversification of organizations. The encounter between established homophile organizing and the New Left produced gay liberation and provided homosexual activists with the cultural tools that made "coming out" possible. The decline of the New Left reduced the plausibility of revolutionary socialist ideas and cleared the way for an identity-focused "gay pride" movement.

By defining the primary goal of gay politics as the expansion of the range of ways to express gay identity, the gay movement was able to balance interest group and identity politics. This way of understanding the goal of gay politics highlighted the most individualistic aspects of identity politics. Other movements understood identity politics as endorsing the creation of communities of similarity. In contrast, the gay movement focused on freedom of individual expression, making it hypocritical to exclude any form of gay political expression. Gay interest group politics—pursuing gay rights—was defined as one possible way to express gay identity. Activists were thus able to reframe a potential liability as an advantage, redefining the community's diversity as strength. "Difference" was defined, paradoxically, as a point of similarity. Gays and lesbians were all individuals in search of freedom of expression. Instead of extrapolating from "what we share is that we are all different from straight people" to the notion that "we must all be the same," the gay identity movement acknowledged, "yes, together we are different from straight people, but as individuals we are also different from one other." Individualism, which one would expect to hamper collective action, in this case structured and motivated it.

The vision of a unified but diverse movement was further reinforced by the discovery that a common, well-understood kind of cultural event, a parade, provided experiential evidence for the claim that unity and diversity were not in contradiction. Lesbian/gay freedom day parades provided an articulated structure linking gay organizations while allowing an unfettered display of diversity. Unlike a march, which requires agreement on a set of political demands, a parade needs only the willingness of participants to be associated with each other.

This book tells the story of how, in the early 1970s, a tiny group of gay activists created a new understanding of same-gender sexual experience that would have far-reaching implications. This model of identity influenced the ways people all around the country and the globe make sense of same-gender sexual desires, practices, and relationships. It enabled the spectacular cultural, political, organizational, and commercial successes of the gay movement in the 1970s and 1980s. The movement was culturally generative; its very logic challenged members to produce more variants of gay identity. The new framework shaped what was possible and what was not possible for the gay movement to accomplish. Movement claims to universality and diversity made it difficult for those excluded to identify the ways the movement reflected the particular experiences of a cohort of white, middle-class American men. The gay identity movement enabled an impressive gay response to the AIDS epidemic, which led to the emergence of a competing set of AIDS organizations. Internal contradictions embedded in the movement at the moment of founding continue to shape debates in gay politics today and provide the fissures that may lead to the possible demise or transformation of the movement.

I focus on San Francisco because it, along with a few other major urban centers in the United States, served as the birthplace of what has become a national (and even international) lesbian/gay movement. The frameworks forged in these core cities diffused to smaller cities and towns around the country. Evidence of this diffusion can be seen in the proliferation of freedom day parades, the ubiquity of the language of coming out, and the spread of gay rights politics. Those who have studied lesbian and gay life in smaller towns might argue that the assumptions of the urban-centered gay movement do not describe gay life outside of big cities. This lack of fit does not negate the reality that, in the early 1970s, a hegemonic understanding of same-gender sexual experience crystallized in a few urban centers in the United

States and that others, even those whose experience it describes less well, have now to contend with it.[5] The chapter proceeds by outlining a cultural-institutional approach to social movements, followed by a description of how lesbian/gay San Francisco changed over time, and concludes with an overview of the arguments presented in the book.

A Cultural-Institutional Approach to Social Movements

I developed this explanation of the evolution of the gay movement in San Francisco through applying a cultural-institutional approach to social movements. This approach integrates the insights of cultural theories of social movements with the analytical power of field approaches to institutional change developed by organizational theorists. I review cultural approaches to social movements, showing how they developed in response to weaknesses in political process and resource mobilization (PP/RM) theories of social movements. I argue that cultural approaches to movements continue to rely on concepts steeped in the resource-rationalist assumptions of political process and resource mobilization theories. I then show that contemporary organizational theory has developed in ways compatible with a cultural approach to movements. This makes it possible to address limitations of the cultural approach to movements through drawing on concepts from contemporary organizational sociology, particularly the concept of "field." I conclude the section by showing how a cultural-institutional approach enabled a description of lesbian/gay movement development impossible within political process and resource mobilization approaches to social movements.

Cultural Approaches to Social Movements

Cultural approaches to social movements are diverse, ranging from European new social movement theories to historical scholarship on the role of culture in political change.[6] The thread that unites this work is a critique of the resource-rationalistic assumptions shaping the PP/RM theories that have dominated social movement scholarship since the early 1980s.[7]

It is often noted that resource mobilization theory "rescued social movement activity from the irrational world of the psychologically needy, and placed it in the intellectual world of rational politics."[8] Arguing against collective behavior and mass society theories, resource mobilization theorists asserted that social movements are rational, goal oriented, and organized rather than spontaneous and pointless. Movements succeed or fail depending on access to resources and political opportunities.

Less remarked upon is that the argument for the rationality of movements relied upon claims about the nature of society, particularly American society.[9] In *Political Process and the Development of Black Insurgency,* Doug McAdam argued that social movements were rational because society was organized around an unjust set of political and economic rules that excluded many from access to legitimate channels of influence.[10] Thus, it was only rational for those excluded to conduct politics through "noninstitutionalized" channels. Political process theory focused on change efforts initiated by the powerless and designed to redress economic and political inequalities through noninstitutionalized channels. This view limited attention to movements that seek the redistribution of economic or political power. Other kinds of collective efforts to achieve social change fit uneasily, or not at all, within this definition of the object of study.

A number of scholars, such as Steven Buechler, have argued that "theoretical development never occurs in a socio-political vacuum."[11] Scholars developed resource mobilization and political process theories in order to explain the civil rights movement and other 1960s movements.[12] However, as scholars became interested in other movements, such as the women's, environmental, and lesbian/gay movements, they found that PP/RM theories did not adequately describe or explain these movements. As Mary Bernstein observed, PP/RM theories were "unable to explain social movement action that seems to be working at cross purposes to achieving policy change."[13] The cultural goals of identity movements appeared "nonpolitical" from within PP/RM frameworks. Not only were these movements pursuing the "wrong" goals, they were also composed of the "wrong" people. Some participants, such as white middle-class gay activists, were privileged in many ways. The expressive methods sometimes used by these movements seemed pointless within PP/RM theories. Rational theories of individual motivation did not explain why people participated. In short, these movements were not acting the way PP/RM theories suggested that movements were supposed to act.

Scholars responded to failures of PP/RM to account for "new" social movements in several ways. One response was to dismiss these movements as "apolitical" and to berate contemporary movements for "selling out" by turning to dead-end identity politics.[14] A second response was to modify PP/RM theory in order to account for these new movements. This approach attempted to interpret the cultural motivations and goals of new movements within a resource-rationalist view of social movements. For example, resource-rationalist understandings of individual motivation asserted that people participate when offered material incentives.[15] PP/RM theorists developed the notion of "identity" or "solidary" incentives to explain why some people participated even without material incentives.[16] Francesca Polletta and James Jasper have responded by arguing that "arguments like these, designed to show that cultural meanings and emotions are not logically incompatible with rational-actor models, yield convoluted causal pictures. . . . Why not simply admit the emotional satisfactions of collective identity?"[17]

The third response to the failures of PP/RM theories was to develop new theories to understand and explain these new movements. New social movement (NSM) theory devoted itself to describing what was "new" about post-1960s movements.[18] These scholars, who were predominantly European, saw a focus on identity as "the most distinctive feature of NSMs."[19] NSMs were also seen to differ fundamentally from earlier movements in terms of tactics, structure, and participants. This literature claimed not only that NSMs were "fundamentally different from the working class movements of the industrial period," but also that these movements were the "product of the shift to a postindustrial economy."[20]

In contrast, historical scholars argued that identity was not new in contemporary movements, but that the role of identity in earlier movements was not fully understood.[21] Historical scholarship on the role of culture in political change built on William H. Sewell Jr.'s work on revolutionary France. He showed that in moments of "collective creativity," the cultural constitution of interests and identities could change abruptly and profoundly in ways that could not be predicted from changes in political and economic institutions.[22] Scholars engaged in historical work on collective action have developed a rich body of scholarship showing how meaning construction contributes to collective action.[23]

"Framing" and "collective identity" literatures have also contributed to an emerging critique of resource-rationalist perspectives on movements. Frame analysis of movements, developed by David Snow and colleagues, assumes that meaning does not "grow automatically out of structural arrangements, unanticipated events, or existing ideologies. Rather, movement actors are viewed as signifying agents actively engaged in production and maintenance of meaning for constituents, antagonists, and bystanders or observers."[24] Similarly, work on the role of collective identity in movements argues that analysis of collective identity produces insights into why groups form around an issue, how interests emerge, why people participate in movements, and why groups choose the forms of protest they do.[25]

These cultural approaches all treat interests and identities as politically constructed, define social movements broadly, see the state as one among many possible targets for social movement action, see the instrumentality of cultural strategies and the culturally constituted character of instrumental action, attend to the cultural creativity of movements, and understand that while movement action is "meaningful," it is not always "rational."[26]

Cultural approaches to social movements build on and contribute to a widespread interest in the role of culture in sociology more generally. However, these approaches still rely on concepts embedded within resource-rationalist theories that trivialize and obscure social processes in which they are interested. For example, the term "social movement" remains laden with meaning associated with political process theories. While scholars have redefined the concept to refer to all collective efforts to accomplish social change,[27] the term still evokes the sense that the more directly a movement seeks to change state policy, the more legitimate it is as an object of study. Phenomena such as denominational challenges within the religious sector, efforts within the corporate sector to extend partner benefits to lesbian/gay couples, and challenges to the organization of medical care or education tend to be seen as peripheral to the central concerns of social movement scholarship.[28] A cultural approach to movements needs concepts that legitimate the study of the full range of collective efforts to accomplish social change while providing analytical tools for scholars to make finer distinctions among different kinds of collective action.

Social Movement Approaches to Organizations

Contemporary scholarship in organizational analysis has developed concepts that can address the weaknesses of a cultural approach to social movements. To show how organizational sociology can contribute to a cultural approach to movements, I first discuss the development of field theory within organizational sociology.

Turning to organizational sociology in order to enrich social movement theory is not new. Resource mobilization theory was founded by applying 1970s organizational theory to social movements. In the early 1970s organizational theorists assumed that formal organizations acted rationally, in pursuit of goals, and that their success or failure depended upon resources. Resource mobilization theory applied this reasoning to social movements, arguing that social movement organizations were like *any other organization.*

In the intervening years organizational researchers have developed approaches to organizations critical of these resource-rationalist approaches.[29] Organizational ecology called into question the usefulness of thinking of organizations as acting rationally, but placed a heavy emphasis on the importance of environmental resources in determining organizational survival.[30]

Population ecology contributed to a shift in organizational analysis from examining individual organizations to a focus on populations of organizations.

With the emergence of neoinstitutional theory, organizational theory developed an approach critical of both resource and rationalistic assumptions. Neoinstitutional theory argued that the structure and survival of organizations could be explained as much by how well they resonated with their symbolic environment as by their technical efficiency.[31] Paul DiMaggio and Walter Powell used the term "organizational fields" to refer to the organized arenas that exert influence over the structure of individual organizations.[32] In contrast to "populations of organizations," defined by population ecologists in terms of shared location in an objectively defined competitive niche, the concept of organizational field referred to culturally and politically constructed arenas. Field members share understandings about the goals of an enterprise, about who can participate, and about how the enterprise is to be pursued. Fields crystallize around institutional logics, which define the taken-for-granted rules structuring goals, strategies, and members of the field. Within established fields, identities and interests are institutionalized.[33] A practice, structure, or arena of social life is institutionalized to the extent that it is "stable and self-reproducing."[34] By establishing the "rules of the game," fields limit the strategies of action that can be pursued. Some forms of action are defined as appropriate and possible, while others are not. The rules of the game in established fields tend to benefit some actors more than others. The limiting of appropriate and possible organizational forms tends to produce organizational homogenization.[35] The more structured the field, the more homogeneous the organizations.

In its original formulation neoinstitutional theory was of limited interest to social movement scholars, as it explained the reproduction of institutions, not institutional change. By the time Powell and DiMaggio's edited collection *The New Institutionalism in Organizational Analysis* was published in 1991, institutionalists were beginning to address the inability of their theories to account for agency, power, and institutional change.[36] In their search for tools to help them explain institutional change, scholars turned to social movement theory for theoretical resources, thus reversing the flow of ideas from organizational to social movement scholarship.[37] Organizational theorists have found social movement theory to be a theoretical treasure trove and have borrowed liberally from all parts of social movement scholarship from resource mobilization to NSM theory.[38]

Research at the intersection of social movement and organizational scholarship has the potential either to reinforce resource-rationalist assumptions or to extend cultural approaches. Kelly Moore and Michael Young have expressed concern that work at this intersection seems to be relying more on social movement theories based on resource-rationalist assumptions. They argue that these approaches

> don't go far enough: they remain tied to theories of social movements that were themselves heavily indebted to studies of profit-making firms and rely on an instrumental-resource view of organizational action. The distinctiveness of collective oppositional action is underplayed in their propositions. . . . Continuing down the road signposted by resources and instrumental action will not allow us to develop greater understanding of the significance of social movements as crucibles of dissent, creativity, and audaciousness.[39]

It would be a mistake for organizational sociology to return to an approach that takes rationality for granted. As Frank R. Dobbin persuasively argues, cultural approaches to organizations have energized organizational sociology.[40] Scholarship at the intersection of organizations and social movements is likely to be advanced by integrating the insights of cultural approaches in both areas. Michael Lounsbury and Marc Ventresca, in their introduction to an analogy of current research in organizational sociology, concur when they recognize that "a focus on cultural processes can reorient and renew a broader social structural approach to organizations. . . . Cultural approaches to social structure provide particularly fertile ground for the development of novel theoretical insights."[41]

A Cultural-Institutionalist Approach to Social Movements

The current round of cross-fertilization between social movement and organizational theory has occurred almost entirely within organizational sociology, in the service of advancing organizational theory. A few scholars, such as Neil Fligstein, Elisabeth Clemens, Debra Minkoff, Doug McAdam, and W. Richard Scott, have begun to articulate the implications of this new intersection for social movement scholarship.[42]

I develop the contributions of contemporary organizational theory for social movement scholarship, focusing on how a field approach contributes to cultural approaches to social movements. I show how incorporating the concept of field allows the study a broad range of collective action projects, makes visible processes of institutionalization obscured within PP/RM theory, and provides new tools for sharper analytical distinctions among types of collective action.

While the shift in level of analysis introduced by the concept of field is important to social movement scholarship, that the concept of field is premised on a social constructionist understanding of reality is even more important. As discussed above, fields are defined by the existence of shared understandings about the rules of the game structuring an arena. Institutionalists do not restrict their interest to particular kinds of fields or assume a priori the logic holding together a particular field, but rather treat as problematic the process through which actors come to understand the boundaries of collective projects.

Defining social movements as collective efforts to create new fields or to transform existing fields theoretically justifies the study of the full range of social change projects. This approach allows us to analyze efforts to change the rules of the game, whether that game is literally being played on the playground or has to do with the trade of currencies. What defines the study of social movements is the interest in collective challenges to the rules of the game—action that is not simply reproducing the rules of a given arena.[43] PP/RM privileged collective action challenging the state.[44] A cultural-institutional approach to movements also studies collective action challenging the rules governing other arenas. Contentious politics occurs in all arenas. These processes are of interest to both social movement and organizational scholars.

Not all movements aspire to (or achieve) the degree of institutionalization necessary to qualify as a field. Many social movements disband once they achieve (or fail to achieve) changes in the rules structuring the wider field in which they are embedded. Sometimes the creation of a movement field is an unintentional consequence of social movement activity. In other cases, such as the case of the women's movement in the United States from the 1940s through the 1960s, creating a field is necessary to ensure movement survival.[45] Creating a new field often requires changing the rules of the larger field in which it is embedded. Some movements attempt to change the rules in a localized arena (e.g., campus governance) while other movements engage in much more ambitious field formation projects (e.g., the formation of the European Union).[46] Efforts to transform these arenas may emerge, succeed, and disappear; emerge, fail, and disappear; or emerge and become ongoing institutionalized projects that are, in turn, challenged. Fields form, change, and dissolve, sometimes as a result of social movement efforts, sometimes as a result of other processes.

Organizing social movement analysis around the concept of field makes processes of institutionalization and deinstitutionalization visible. Field theory, based as it is on institutional analysis, is highly sensitive to the degree to which various arenas and practices are institutionalized. Characterizing phenomena according to their degree of institutionalization invokes an analytical dimension underdeveloped within social movement theory. This absence is puzzling, given that the study of social movements is about understanding how and why people endeavor to change established institutions and why they are (or are not) successful.

Historically, the analytical power of social movement scholarship has been impoverished by simplistic assumptions about the degree of institutionalization of both social movements and the fields they have targeted for change. For example, it is frequently assumed that the targeted field is institutionalized while the movement is not. In fact, the degree to which targeted fields are institutionalized is highly variable. There is perhaps even more variance in the level of institutionalization of challengers. Contemporary social movement scholars have had a hard time making sense of cases where challengers are highly institutionalized. By defining the study of movements as the study of noninstitutionalized action, institutionalized movements such as the labor movement have been seen as not really fully legitimate objects of study for social movement scholars. Understanding such phenomena requires moving beyond assigning organizational sociologists the task of understanding stability and social movement theorists the task of understanding change.[47] Social conflict often produces, and is in fact a necessary precursor to, the establishment of order, in the form of new fields. To understand stability we need to understand change, and vice versa. Thus, in addition to broadening the arenas of social life considered appropriate terrain for investigation by social movement scholars, a field approach also dismantles a tacit understanding that movement scholars limit their investigations to action outside the bounds of mainstream political institutions.

Field theory also enables scholars to make more careful distinctions when describing and explaining change processes. Scholars committed to the perspective that high-risk political behavior challenging state institutions is uniquely central to fundamental societal change might argue that a field approach unravels decades of scholarship establishing the specific determinants of such behavior. However, a field approach need not treat all change efforts as equally salient or interesting. Institutionalists see society as composed of a multiplicity of fields, of varying levels of institutionalization, organized around varying logics. These fields are both overlapping and nested. Powerful fields exist in all arenas of social action, including political, economic, educational, medical, cultural, and scientific arenas. The state is, of course, uniquely important because it establishes the rules that govern all the other fields of society. Understanding fields as nested in this way allows distinctions to be made between important and trivial social change efforts. Efforts to transform fields that are deeply structuring of society, if successful, will be more consequential than efforts to transform other fields.

The Transformation of the Gay Field

When applied to the gay movement, this cultural-institutional approach to social movements enables a description of the transformation of the movement impossible within a PP/RM framework. Without the privileging of politics oriented to the state, it was possible to see that for actors the primary cognitive divide was between "gay" and "straight" worlds, not between that which was "movement" and "nonmovement" within the gay world. The project was one of creating and expanding gay social and political space, not simply one of sustaining a gay political movement or pursuing political grievances. This movement included gay rights organizations, but it also included lesbian quilters, the freedom day parades, and lesbian/gay newspapers. It was simultaneously cultural, political, and organizational. Indeed, the melding of cultural and political is precisely what was novel and challenging about this particular social movement.

With the sensitivity to institutionalization processes of a field approach, I was able to see that a gay identity movement crystallized in the early 1970s. Institutionalization is neither "movement" nor "outcome"; thus in the PP/RM perspective it vanishes from view in the void between concepts. Many of the signals of the consolidation of something new (e.g., the sudden appearance of annual parades and resource guides) fall outside of the social movement gaze, because they are not explicitly *political* in nature. Organizational proliferation does not register as being particularly salient to PP/RM scholars, unless this proliferation is of social movement organizations. By attending only to the most explicitly political of organizations, the shift over time appears simply as a shift from a movement seeking liberation to a movement seeking rights. While the move to a focus on rights was part of the shift that occurred in the early 1970s, it was only a part. The shift to a rights agenda was intimately connected with the consolidation of an identity-building project. What happened in the early 1970s was no less than the fundamental reconstruction of the set of cultural rules producing sexual identities.

In fact, this perspective allowed me to see fundamental shifts in the core *political logics* guiding the movement. Political logics are background sets of assumptions about how society works, the goals of political action, and appropriate strategies to pursue desired ends. The concept of "political logic" is similar to both Roger Friedland and Robert R. Alford's "institutional logic" and David Snow and Robert Benford's "master frames."[48] Master frames, like more simple collective action frames, provide shared understandings of the world that define problems, assign causes, and legitimate and motivate collective action. Master frames operate as the cultural backdrop of movements; they "color and constrain [the frames] of any number of movement organizations."[49] Referring to "political logics" instead of "master frames" highlights the taken-for-granted, constitutive character of these theories about the nature of the world and the kind of action needed to improve it. New political logics cannot simply be created at will through the strategic framing efforts of activists, but only emerge under specific conditions of heightened cultural creativity. Social movement organizations are shaped by, but not reducible to, underlying political logics.[50] Change in movement organizations is driven by change in political logics.

This perspective allowed fine-grained analytical distinctions. It brought into focus both continuities between the contemporary gay movement and its pre–New Left forebears and differences between the gay movement and kindred movements. While NSM theorists see a class of "new social movements," a cultural-institutional perspective sees the development of a new political logic, which expanded the repertoire of political and cultural tools available to activists in the post-1970 era. While it is possible that changes in the fundamental nature of society have occurred, it is not necessary for them to have occurred to explain the production of this new political logic. This logic was available to all post-1960s movements, accounting for observed similarities among these movements. But it was incorporated differently in each movement.

The cultural-institutional approach shaped data collection and analysis. Institutionalists use a variety of sources to gain insight into how people cognitively organize their worlds. They pay particular attention to organizations, both the kinds of organizations formed and the relationships among those organizations. Thus, institutional sociology guided me toward an examination of the organizational infrastructure of the lesbian/gay community. The central task was to describe, as systematically as possible, the development and transformation of the project of extending gay social space and defining, to the extent that it was possible, the boundaries as activists and community members defined them. I constructed a systematic data set of all the lesbian/gay organizations in San Francisco during the years 1964–1994 to provide a bird's-eye view of the organizational life of the community.[51]

I analyzed this exhaustive organizational data set both qualitatively and quantitatively. I noted changes in the numbers of organizations, the changing cultural content of organizations, and changes in the distribution of various kinds of organizations over time. I also collected and analyzed primary historical documents. Documents such as resource guides and newspapers provided crucial documentation of the way people understood their activities at particular moments in time. Successful institutionalization projects often produce a collective amnesia about their recent origins and possible alternatives.[52] It is therefore crucial to be skeptical of accounts constructed well after the events in question. Focusing on one case allowed me to produce a thorough and systematic analysis of the development of the arena over time. Extending the time frame backward captured the early phases of field formation.

Describing the Lesbian/Gay Field

Lesbian/gay organizations in San Francisco proliferated over time. Activists founded the first nonprofit homosexual organizations in the 1950s. Organizations accumulated slowly in the 1950s and 1960s, accelerated in the 1970s, exploded in the 1980s, and declined slightly in the late 1980s and early 1990s (see figure 1.1).[53] However, this simple quantitative story does not capture the complexity of changes over time. Close analysis revealed dramatic change in the types of organizations created at different moments in the development of the field.

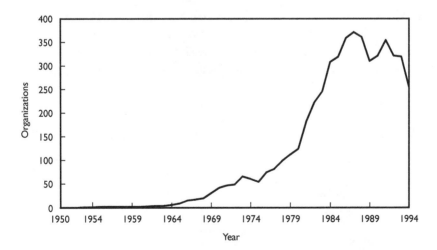

Figure 1.1 Lesbian/Gay Nonprofit Organizations in San Francisco, 1950–94

Public homosexual organizations founded before 1969 were shaped by an *interest group political logic* (see table 1.1).[54] Activists at the time referred to their organizations as "homophile organizations." Between 1969 and 1971 new organizations saw themselves as participating in the gay liberation movement. Gay liberation organizations were torn between a *redistributive political logic* and an *identity political logic.* Beginning around 1970, new organizations began to clearly reflect an *identity political logic.*

Figure 1.2 shows the changing representation of these organizations over time. In the 1950s and 1960s, homophile organizations were the only public homosexual organizations. The tiny numbers and beleaguered state of organizing suggest that the field at this time was emerging, rather than fully formed. In the years 1970 and 1971, homophile, gay liberation, and gay identity organizations were all founded, with no one kind achieving numerical dominance, suggesting instability and competition among political logics. In 1971 and 1972 gay identity organizations began to outnumber homophile and gay liberation organizations. Gay identity organizations dominated after 1972, while other kinds of organizations fell by the wayside. The proliferation of gay identity organizations beginning in the early 1970s reflected a crystallization of the field around an identity political logic.

To understand the meaning of this transformation, it is necessary to understand the political logics shaping the gay movement and how these three logics were reflected in the various kinds of gay organizations. Table 1.2 summarizes these distinct political logics.

Interest group politics assumes that American society is composed of intersecting constituencies, each of which has a fair opportunity to influence policy according to its interests.[55] Problems arise but are corrected through reform when a group builds a unified voice and a voting bloc and is thus able to effect policy change. Discrimination against groups is targeted through ad-

Table 1.1 Homophile, Gay Liberation, Gay Identity, and Other Lesbian/Gay Organizations Founded in San Francisco, by Time Period

Year	Homophile	Gay Liberation	Gay Identity	Other*	Total
1953–68	15 (71)	0 (0)	0 (0)	6 (29)	21
1969–71	2 (6)	12 (33)	12 (33)	10 (28)	36
1972–94	0 (0)	11 (1)	859 (95)	31 (4)	901
Total	17 (2)	23 (2)	871 (91)	47 (5)	958

Note: Percentages are in parentheses.

* "Other" organizations include motorcycle clubs (29), queer organizations (13), and organizations that did not fall into any of the categories (5).

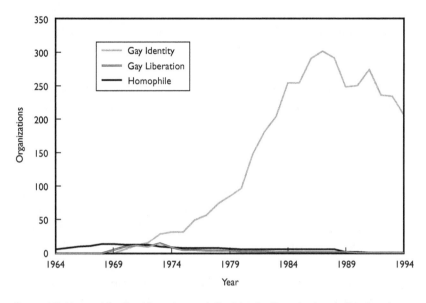

Figure 1.2 Homophile, Gay Liberation, and Gay Identity Organizations in San Francisco, 1964–94

Table 1.2 Interest Group, Redistributive, and Identity Political Logics

	Interest Group	Redistributive	Identity
Problem	discrimination	structural inequality	alienation
Goal	reform; rights	societal transformation	authenticity, broadened range of expression
Strategy	lobbying, influencing elections	mass movement (demonstrations, boycotts, strikes)	prefigurative politics
Organizations	few, large, professional, bureaucratic	ephemeral social movement organizations	many, small, informal, diverse, egalitarian
Identity seen as	means to end	means to end	end in itself

vocating for rights. Change should and can be effectively achieved by using the channels made available in a democratic society, including lobbying and influencing electoral outcomes. With a focus on influencing elite groups, interest group organizations frequently locate in the nation's capital and direct attention toward building a national movement. Interest group organizations tend to be formally structured and bureaucratic. Their legitimacy increases with the size and unity of their constituency, so interest group politics tends to produce large single-issue organizations, each of which attempts to monopolize a particular cause (e.g., the American Association of Retired Persons [AARP] and the National Rifle Association [NRA]). Multiple organizations representing the same constituency tend to see each other as competitors.

Typically, when we think about social movements, we think about politics organized around a logic of redistribution. Based on a Marxist analysis of society, a redistributive model sees structural inequality, particularly economic inequality, as the underlying problem that social movements must address. From an interest group perspective, society is seen as basically just, although in need of reform. Within a redistributive model, society is seen as exploitative. The goal of political change is to transform the structure of society in ways that lessen material injustice. Elite groups are seen as controlling economic and political rules, with the implication that meaningful change must usually be initiated through noninstitutionalized channels. Thus, movements based on a redistributive politics typically engage in marches, rallies, demonstrations, boycotts, and strikes. Social movement organizations tend to be less formally structured, less bureaucratic, and more ephemeral than interest group organizations. While unity within the interest group model is conveyed by the size and strength of large single-issue organizations, solidarity within mass movements tends to be measured by the size, frequency, and complexity of the events movements can sustain. Participation is organized around ideology or structural position, not around identity. The difference between mobilizing participants based on structural position rather than identity is subtle but important. Those mobilized around structural position are organized through criticizing the system for relegating them to a particular category, while organizing in behalf of identity is about affirming and solidifying the category.

Identity politics rejects both the notion that society is basically just but in need of reform and the idea that society is exploitative and in need of structural overhaul. In the identity model, the fundamental problem with society is alienation.[56] People are estranged from society and from themselves. They lack sources of meaning and are blocked from expressing themselves in an authentic manner. The goal of political change is thus to reduce alienation by making society more connected, meaningful, and authentic. This quest for authenticity may involve the creation and affirmation of collective identities. In his investigation of the New Left, Doug Rossinow argues that "individuals define their politics along lines of race, gender, ethnicity, and sexual identity, in part to make themselves feel rooted, real, solid."[57] The affirmation of previously marginalized or stigmatized identities is seen as creating spaces for people to express themselves. Within this framework, according to Kauffman, "identity itself—its elaboration, expression, or affirmation—is and should be a fundamental focus of political work."[58] While interest group politics suggests lobbying for legislative change and redistributive politics implies mass demonstration, identity politics suggests that creating and expressing alternative selves and alternative communities is the way to achieve change. Change happens from the bottom up, through the creation of the desired society in miniature. Wini Breines referred to this feature of the New Left as "prefigurative politics"; movement communities are supposed to "prefigure" the ideal society.[59] The transformation of individuals is central, as it is believed that, as Pamela Allen puts it, "a human politics will not grow from people who fear honest human relationships but through ones who are willing to share of their total selves."[60]

Differences in the logics guiding the movement were reflected in differences among the organizations constituting the movement at each point in time (see table 1.3). The logic organizing the field shaped the goals, strategies, size, formality, display of identity, and degree of psychological focus of the organizations produced. In addition, political logic also shaped relationships among organizations, the total numbers of organizations produced, and the likelihood of organizations being similar to or different from each other.

Homophile Organizations and Interest Group Politics

That homophile activists attempted to engage in interest group politics is evident in how they framed their goals and the characteristics of the organizations they built (see table 1.3). Homophile organizations endorsed the notion that reform would come through the gradual change of existing institutions. Working from the interest group notion that change comes from the top, they were particularly interested in the education of elite heterosexual groups, such as psychologists and lawmakers. The names and the goals of these organizations suggest that homophile organizations were not centrally concerned with building a public identity, but instead with seeking rights and improving public opinion (e.g., Society for Individual Rights). Homophile organizations rarely included sexual identity terminology in their names. The most well-known of homophile organizations founded in the 1950s and 1960s (such as the Mattachine Society and the Daughters of Bilitis) used names that had special meaning to insiders but did not suggest the sexual identity of the organization to outsiders. If a reference to sexual identity did appear in an organizational name, as it did in one or two instances, it was "homophile" or "homosexual." While homophile activists saw the psychological

Table 1.3 Political Logics and Gay Organizations

	Homophile	Gay Liberation	Gay Identity
Political logic	interest group	redistributive, identity	identity (with interest group subordinated)
Goals	homosexual rights	gay liberation as part of societal transformation, visibility and pride	visibility, pride, public gay identity, gay rights
Strategy	influence elite groups, lobbying, electoral politics	alliance with other oppressed groups around social justice agenda, coming out	coming out, zap, identity display; also lobbying, electoral politics
Explicit identity in name	no	yes	yes
Psychological focus	no	yes	yes
Number of organizations	few	few	many
Relationships between organizations	competitive	competitive	more cooperative—articulated structure
Size and formality of organizations	large and bureaucratic	ephemeral social movement organizations	variable, ranging from small and informal to large and bureaucratic
Diversity	limiting of diversity	generative of diversity	generative of diversity

costs of the oppression of homosexuals every day, they did not conceive of the problem or the solution in psychological terms. The homogeneous and competitive nature of homophile organizations also expressed an interest group logic, as each new organization attempted to present itself as the one organization that could best represent the interests of all homosexuals.[61]

The Political Logics of Gay Liberation

Gay liberation was torn between redistributive and identity political logics in its brief life. The most radical strain of gay liberation, which I refer to as gay power, was committed to a redistributive politics. These gay liberationists advocated the overthrow of capitalism, believing that change would come through a total transformation of society (see table 1.3). They supported black power, women's liberation, and other nongay causes. In turn, they demanded the support of others in the New Left. These organizations were the first to use the term "gay" in their names. The terms "homophile" and "homosexual" vanished practically overnight from the names and mission statements of organizations. They endorsed a mass movement style of political activism, participating in marches, rallies, and demonstrations. However, this belief that the fate of gay liberation rested on the fate of a variety of other social justice causes coexisted uneasily with a new kind of identity politics developing within the New Left and gay liberation. Gay pride and coming out rested upon the notion that the fate of homosexuals rested not on a societywide revolution, but on the development of a proud and public new gay identity and world.

Gay Identity Organizations and the Logic of Identity Politics

The prevalence of an identity logic in the post-1970 gay movement is revealed in the emergence of organizations whose central goal was the elaboration or display of identity; the use of explicit sexual identity in organization names; the proliferation of support groups and of small, informal organizations loosely connected to each other in an articulated fashion; and the functional and identity diversification of those organizations (see table 1.3).

Centered on the innovation of "coming out," gay identity organizations highlighted identity building, pride, and visibility. Many of the organizations formed after 1969 defined their missions around the elaboration, protection, and cultivation of gay identity. Such organizations included libraries, archives, and history projects; newspapers, resource guides, and other periodicals; and committees that put on parades, street fairs, and film festivals. GLAAD (Gay and Lesbian Alliance against Defamation, 1989–) and GLHS (Gay and Lesbian Historical Society of Northern California [now known as the Gay, Lesbian, Bisexual, Transgender Historical Society of Northern California], 1985–) were typical organizations of this kind.[62] Thus GLHS described itself as an "independent, nonprofit, educational organization whose purpose was to collect and preserve historically significant materials that document the lives of lesbians, gay men, bisexuals, and transsexuals." A lesbian/gay archive premises that a group identity exists, that it has a history, and that the history is worth saving.

While homophile organizations supported their members, lesbian/gay organizations explicitly defining themselves as "rap groups," "consciousness raising groups," or "support groups" were not formed before 1970. More than two hundred such groups were founded in San Francisco between 1970 and 1994. These new support groups were premised on the notion that individual psychological health was a key movement objective, on its own terms, and not something that would simply be an inevitable consequence of structural changes in society.

The notion that the goal of change was to broaden the range of lesbian and gay self-expression opened the door to organizational diversification in terms of *function* and *identity*. New organizations began to define themselves in terms of the specific tasks or functions they intended to accomplish, rather than as general multipurpose organizations. This functional elaboration happened so rapidly, on so many dimensions simultaneously, that it was difficult to discern patterns. Cultural, hobby, political, professional, relational, religious, sexual, social, and service organizations all proliferated wildly. Table 1.4 lists typical organizations of each of these types.

The names of these organizations followed a pattern. The template for gay identity organizations was gay plus one other function or identity. The explicit use of "gay," "lesbian," or other sexual identity label signaled that gay visibility was positive and that building gay identity was a desired end goal. The second dimension of the organization, which ranged from the banal (e.g., gay postal workers) to the transgressive (e.g., lesbians into S/M) indicated the distinct contribution the organization made to the project of elaborating gay identity. The vast majority of this diversification was banal. While there were some organizations like the Safe Sex Leather Sluts, most organizations more closely resembled Federal Lesbians and Gays (FLAG), an organization of lesbian/gay federal employees (1984–94) or the San Francisco Hiking Club, an organization of lesbian/gay hikers (1984–). Banal functional diversification suggested that gay identity was, like a traditional ethnic identity, not just about sex, but also about work, family, worship, hobbies, and service.[63] Once the process of functional diversification began, it created its own momentum. The creation of Dignity (1973–), an organization of lesbian/gay Catholics, suggested the necessity of a gay religious organization for every religious denomination. By 1994, sixty-three lesbian/gay religious organizations had been formed in San Francisco, including organizations of Catholics, Episcopalians, Jews, Lutherans, Quakers, and Mormons.

Table 1.4 Diversification of Gay Identity Organizations

Functional Area	Representative Organization
Cultural	Bay Area Gay and Lesbian Bands
Hobby	San Francisco Tsunami Gay/Lesbian Swim Club
Political	Libertarians for Gay and Lesbian Concerns
Profession	Lesbians in Law (LIL), Hastings College of Law
Relational	Lesbians Planning to Parent
Religious	Presbyterians for Lesbian and Gay Concerns (PLGC)
Sex	Safe Sex Leather Sluts
Social	Men's Associated Exchange (MAX)
Service: general population	Gay Medical and Dental Referral Service
Service: vulnerable population	Alanon for Black Gay and Lesbian Adult Children of Alcoholics

The proliferation and diversification of gay organizations after 1970 did not reflect interest group politics, which would have produced fewer and larger organizations. Nor did this proliferation and diversification reflect redistributive politics, as few of the new organizations focused on the political or economic transformation of society. The proliferation and diversification of gay organizations made sense within a political logic that defined expanding the gay world as the central goal of politics. The gay movement understood the broadening of freedom of expression to extend to variation internal to gay identity, even if exposing this diversity reduced the plausibility that there existed sufficient shared experience to even define an identity. Other identity movements have understood the goal of authentic expression more narrowly, in terms of winning recognition of an identity representing itself as internally homogeneous.

Gay rights organizations were among the most successful gay organizations formed after 1970. The presence of these interest group organizations in the post-1970 era is consistent with my claim that the movement was fundamentally structured around an identity logic. Gay rights organizations could be and were treated as simply organizations expressing one of many legitimate ways to be gay. In addition, a gay rights agenda was, to a large extent, built into gay identity, defining the somewhat minimum set of characteristics people interested in same-gender sexuality could be said to share.

In summary, what this discussion of the transformation of the lesbian/gay movement in San Francisco shows is that the gay identity movement crystallized in the early 1970s. Before this moment the project of expanding homosexual social space did not have the stable, organized properties of a field. In the 1950s and 1960s, it attempted to organize around an interest group logic. The encounter between the homophile movement and the New Left produced a vibrant gay liberation movement torn between redistributive and identity political logics. In the early 1970s, the gay movement coalesced around an identity political logic, but in such a way that the pursuit of interest group politics was defined as complementary. The movement constructed an identity that allowed for the expression of an unusual degree of internal diversity. It was at this moment that the gay arena acquired the character of a mature, organized field.

Overview of the Argument

With the task of describing the phenomenon under explanation accomplished, the rest of the book explains how the field crystallized as a gay identity movement in the early 1970s and the consequences of this crystallization for later events. The first half of the book focuses on the question of origins. The second half of the book examines the consequences of field formation.

Explaining Field Formation

The gay identity movement was forged by a historically and culturally specific set of events. Chapters 2 through 5 analyze the four crucial junctures producing field crystallization in the early 1970s: homophile politics before 1969, the cultural innovations of the New Left, the sudden decline of the New Left in the early 1970s, and the efforts of activists to ensure the survival of a gay movement. Each of these developments was necessary, but only together do they explain field formation. Each of these crucial junctures produces a puzzle. How was it that homophile organizations reached the state of development that they did before 1969? How was it that the New Left so dramatically transformed the gay movement? Why did the gay movement survive when other branches of the New Left fell into disarray? What explains field crystallization right at this juncture?

Chapter 2 asks how San Francisco acquired its first nonprofit homosexual organizations in the 1950s. What kinds of processes might be typical of the preliminary, subterranean stages of forming a new field? The chapter shows that nonprofit homosexual organizations built upon long-term historical processes. What made these organizations novel was that they moved homosexual life from a private to a public organizational existence. Homophile activists made this leap by drawing on an existing interest group model of organizing. This suggests that new fields may evolve through the extension of existing organizational models to new groups. The chapter shows that this early stage was characterized by low returns to high inputs of organizational energy, by a complex relationship with an evolving political environment, and deep conflict about issues of identity, goals, and strategy.

In 1969, the gradual expansion of homosexual social space came to an abrupt end with the sudden appearance of the gay liberation movement. Chapter 3 asks where the gay liberation movement came from and how it was able to accomplish so much so quickly. How was it able to change the gay world so thoroughly? How was this explosive growth possible? Explaining the growth of gay liberation depends upon explaining the emergence of the political strategy of "coming out." In contrast to much scholarship on the gay movement, I emphasize that coming out built upon groundwork established by the homophile movement, which had established the political need for a public homosexual identity. In addition, I argue that existing accounts uncritically accept the movement's claims about the origins and meaning of coming out. This narrative claims that the public display of identity became possible because gay liberation enabled gay people to overcome self-loathing in favor of self-love. In contrast, I argue that coming out was made possible by the logic of identity politics produced by the New Left, which increased the *salience* of issues of self-esteem. The conventional narrative implies that contemporary concern with authenticity and self-esteem are timeless and unchanging. This is not so. Homophiles did not advocate public revelation of sexual identity because they did not yet have access to a political model that defined it as personally and politically meaningful. By increasing the salience of self-esteem and the desire for authenticity, the politics of identity thus changed the very terms of the cultural calculus of costs and benefits of public exposure of sexual identity. Within this new frame of reference, public revelation appeared to be a highly politically effective and immensely personally fulfilling act, thus making the possible rejection by family, friends, and mainstream society seem worth it.

Gay liberation was torn between identity and redistributive politics. In this way, it was like the New Left of which it was a part. The New Left elaborated on American themes of authenticity in such a way that made the political logic of identity widely available. In a similar fashion, the New Left also diffused proposals for the radical economic and political restructuring of American society. Some movement activists, including gay liberationists, believed that inequalities on the basis of race, gender, class, and sexuality were deeply interconnected. Others did not. At the peak of gay liberation, in 1969, 1970, and 1971, the presence of these contradictory logics produced debilitating internal struggles.

Scholars and activists expected gay liberation, as part of the New Left, to share the fate of the larger movement. Chapter 4 argues that the existence of multiple logics within gay liberation was crucial to the gay movement's survival of New Left decline. The rapid decline of the New Left discredited radical social justice politics and undermined even much less radical redistributive politics. By abandoning the redistributive agenda and embracing the powerful identity politics strategy of coming out and the rhetoric of gay pride, the gay movement gained internal coherence and reduced internal conflict about goals and strategies. The presence of multiple political logics within gay liberation, while debilitating at the peak of the movement, provided gay activists with a fully formed alternative during the brief, crucial moment that determined the fate of the movement. Ironically, the sudden retraction of political opportunities on the national level increased the chances that the gay movement would survive. A more predictable political context enabled activists to arrive at more consensus about what would work and what would not.

The movement crystallized quite rapidly after the decline of the New Left. But this crystallization was not inevitable. While the decline of the New Left resolved potentially paralyzing internal conflict, gay activists still faced a highly diverse potential constituency and multiple ways of organizing collectively. While we tend to see gay pride and gay rights as complementary, activists in the early 1970s had difficulty reconciling these two quite different approaches. The identity politics of gay pride suggested a purely individualistic expressive politics, while the interest group politics of gay rights suggested a homogenizing group-oriented approach. Chapter 5 addresses the puzzle of how gay activists were able to create a coherent movement. How did a gay identity movement become institutionalized at this moment? This coalescence was possible because the logic of identity politics provided a way for activists to organize around building a positive gay identity, while avoiding divisive ideological homogenization. Activists used the notion that social change was the result of each person "doing their own thing" to justify the inclusion of gay rights politics and the commercial sexual subculture under the movement umbrella. Activists asserted that diversity was strength, not weakness. Individuality, or difference, was paradoxically defined as a point of commonality. Rhetorically organized around the slogan "unity through diversity" and concretely manifested in community events such as the annual lesbian/gay freedom day parades, this new model encouraged individuals to form organizations, each expressing a unique version of gay identity.

It was not inevitable that activists would highlight identity politics instead of interest group politics, nor was it inevitable that they would figure out how an identity logic could justify a vision of a unified but diverse movement. But the cultural materials available to activists made this interpretation likely. The crystallization of this movement thus owed a little to the social skill of activists and a lot to the larger forces that provided them with a rich array of cultural materials and a unique window of opportunity.

Implications of Field Formation

Chapters 6 through 9 explore the implications of the crystallization of the gay movement in the early 1970s. After consolidation in the early 1970s, the gay identity project grew rapidly. Chapter 6 documents the explosive growth of the gay identity movement in San Francisco in the 1970s. This chapter argues that the rapidity of growth was possible because it built on consolidation of the gay identity movement in the early 1970s. The consolidation of the gay identity movement enabled it to both exploit and create political opportunities. The rights, pride, and commercial aspects of the movement reinforced each other in a highly generative fashion.

While the gay movement claimed to be diverse, not all who tried to participate found it to be so. Chapter 7 addresses the discrepancy between the movement claims of diversity and the exclusion experienced by white lesbians, gay men of color, and lesbians of color. This chapter argues that the movement bound an ideologically diverse array of middle-class white men. Thus, the field was indeed exclusive. And because the exclusions were embedded in the fundamental logic of the field, they were difficult to challenge. That the field excluded some people is not surprising. In addition to generating possibility, field formation also limits possibility. Some things become thinkable while others become less thinkable. The logic of gay identity made it increasingly difficult for people to interpret same-gender sexual practices and relationships, indeed all sexual practices and relationships, using any other classification system. Field formation sets up the rules of the game in ways that benefit some more than others. This understanding of the meaning of same-gender sexual relationships emerged from urban, white, middle-class American men and mapped best onto their experiences. Within the United States, women, people of color, rural, working-class, and poorer people found themselves marginalized or invisible within this ordering of the sexual landscape.

Chapter 8 discusses the way the gay identity movement provided both resources for response to the AIDS epidemic and also created blind spots that made it more difficult to effectively respond to it. Fields establish the meaning system through which events are understood. Initially, interpreting AIDS through the lens of gay identity blinded policy makers, scientists, and the gay community to basic epidemiological principles; the disease did not respect social identity boundaries. Ultimately though, the level of social and political organization within the gay identity movement proved to be a powerful resource for political response to the epidemic. The story of the gay response to the AIDS epidemic is about how a community responded to attacks on multiple levels: on the very lives and bodies of those who claimed membership and on its sexual practices, its organizations, and the assumptions around which it was organized. This gay response contributed to the production of a new, competing field of AIDS organizations.

The gay identity movement, as it was forged in the early 1970s, had contradictions embedded within it, producing both recurrent conflicts over core principles of the field and the potential for field transformation.[64] The contradiction between the claim of diversity and the racial and gender homogeneity of the field described in chapter 7 was one of these contradictions. Chapter 9 explores how contradictions internal to the field manifested themselves in struggles in the late 1980s and 1990s. Queer politics, fueled by a critique of the exclusivity of the field, attempted to dethrone gay identity as the core principle around which the field was organized. This challenge was defused through neutralization and incorporation. In contrast, it is unclear whether a second challenge to the logic of identity politics will be similarly defused. In the late 1990s, the size and power of a few interest group organizations increased dramatically, producing the possibility that interest group politics may replace identity politics as the dominant logic of the movement. The gay identity movement may have, ironically, planted the seeds of its own demise, both by creating the public collective identity needed for interest group politics to be effective and by encouraging interest group organizations to grow and become more successful. But now that these organizations have grown so large, it is unclear whether their increasing dominance in the movement can be checked.

This book tells the tale of the transformation of an underground subculture into a culturally vibrant, politically ambitious, organizationally complex gay identity movement.[65] While cultural understandings of same-gender sexuality are inevitable, these meanings are culturally and historically specific. The particular understandings that have come to dominate in the United States were forged out of the nexus of homophile politics, the New Left and its decline, and efforts of activists to ensure the survival of gay organizing. This new consensus was shaped by exposure to an identity political logic made widely available by the New Left. An intense focus on individual expression and personal authenticity fueled the growth of a huge collective action project and provided the tools to prevent its fragmentation. That individualism organized and structured collective action is, on the face of it, counterintuitive. But in this case the collective agreement about the centrality of individual freedom of expression generated an ever-expanding array of organizations and identities.

PART ONE

Forging a Gay Identity Movement

TWO

Beginnings: Homosexual Politics and Organizations, 1950–1968

> *Homophile politics in San Francisco remained within the limits of reformism during the 1960s and actively involved only a small fraction of the city's lesbian and gay male population. . . . Yet the movement had achieved a level of visibility unmatched in other cities, so that by the late 1960s mass-circulation magazines were referring to San Francisco as the gay capital of the United States.*
>
> John D'Emilio, "Gay Politics, Gay Community:
> San Francisco's Experience"

Those who write about the New Left often assume that it gave birth to gay liberation.[1] However, public organizing in the United States on behalf of rights for homosexuals predated gay liberation by almost two decades. That homosexual politics was well developed prior to the New Left was crucial to the emergence of gay liberation and to the later crystallization of a gay identity movement.[2] This earlier movement, which referred to itself as a "homophile" movement, established the legality of homosexual organization and a precedent of interest group politics on behalf of homosexual rights.

The homosexual community in 1968, on the eve of the gay liberation movement, was much better organized than it had been fifteen years earlier. Organizations pursuing rights for homosexuals did not exist before the 1950s in the United States. In fact, homosexuals as a public group on whose behalf one could pursue rights did not exist. While individuals thought of themselves as homosexual and congregated with others who were interested in same-gender sex, they did so privately, in social forums, with little thought of making claims as a legitimate social collectivity.

This changed in the 1950s. Activists began to propagate the view that homosexuals were a minority group, like other minority groups. They formed public nonprofit educational organizations to advance the rights of homosexuals as a group. While this initiative was small, localized in major urban centers, and little known to the general public, it was an important change, as it marked the birth of a public homosexual identity in the United States. This was a first step toward the creation of a gay identity movement.

A public homosexual identity developed during a highly repressive period in American history. How did the project of creating a public homosexual identity come into being at such an inauspicious moment? How did the obstacles faced by the early activists shape this developing field?

Drawing on the work of historians, particularly that of John D'Emilio, and primary documents from the homophile period, this chapter explains how public homosexual organizations and identity emerged in the 1950s.[3] I show the obstacles activists faced as they attempted to create organizations and how interactions with the evolving political environment shaped the character of this field.

Homosexuals, starting from a group consciousness that had developed by the 1950s, extended the existing interest group model to their situation, producing a new kind of organization—a public organization devoted to the pursuit of homosexual rights. The way they arrived at this new idea shows how the formation of new fields relies on borrowing and recombining existing cultural and organizational models, in this case by applying an existing cultural model to a new group.[4] This kind of borrowing may characterize the origins of many kinds of new fields. Elisabeth Clemens, in her book on the rise of interest group politics in the United States, suggests that social movements tend to "remake and rearrange organizational forms, thereby changing the rules about who may use them and to what ends."[5]

The homosexual movement remained small throughout the 1950s and 1960s for a number of reasons. First, homophile activists found that they had to confront and change an environment that withheld the legal use of basic organizational techniques. Second, they found it difficult to effectively pursue interest group politics without an established public collective identity. Homosexual ambivalence about identity building and the lack of effective identity-building tools within interest group politics further impeded movement development. And finally, even when homophiles successfully employed interest group politics, the logic of interest group politics produced only a few organizations, all of which competed with each other.

Despite the obstacles facing this subterranean field formation project, activists succeeded at creating two new organizations by the late 1950s. Barriers to the growth of the homosexual movement began to crumble in the 1960s. Ironically, attempts by authorities to forestall further growth jumpstarted field formation in the early 1960s. By the mid-1960s San Francisco was swept up in the political movements of that decade. These movements began to influence the homophile movement in the late 1960s. Homophile activists were particularly intrigued with the New Left concern with authenticity and individual psychological growth. Homophile activists began to view privacy about sexual identity as inauthentic and psychologically unhealthy. However, they failed to take the next, most definitive step, that is, the defining of public revelation of sexual identity as a personally and politically liberating act.

Borrowing Models and Going Public: The First Homophile Organizations, Early 1950s

The 1950s were a difficult time for progressive organizing in the United States. Widespread anticommunism and the campaigns of Senator Joe McCarthy produced fear, suspicion, and isolationism among left social movements.[6] Anticommunists assumed that homosexuals were particularly vulnerable to betraying their country. They attempted to eliminate homosexuals from positions in the civil service.[7] The repressive context did not change the fact that by the 1950s large-scale historical processes had created a homosexual group consciousness centered on bars, motorcycle clubs, and private social groups.[8] And movements such as the women's, labor, and civil rights movements existed. Individuals with experience in the homosexual subculture began to wonder if it would be possible for homosexuals to develop the same kind of public political existence that other groups, such as women and African Americans, had. Thus, the first public homosexual organizations grew out of the notion that homosexuals could and should be able to pursue rights in the same fashion as other minority groups in the United States. This new outward focus transformed a private group-building process into a public social movement.

Homosexual bars, restaurants, cafes, bathhouses, and motorcycle clubs served as predecessors to the public homosexual nonprofit organizations upon which I focus; I located 107 commercial organizations founded before 1969. Homosexual bars and bathhouses operated in San Francisco as early as the 1930s.[9] Motorcycle clubs, a lesser-known form of homosexual socializing, emerged in the 1950s. According to Gayle Rubin,

[Motorcycle clubs] provided a social life outside the bars, and would sponsor "runs"—weekend camping trips to rural areas where gay men could relax and socialize with more freedom than was then possible in the bars. . . . The first gay motorcycle club in the United States was the Satyrs, founded in Los Angeles in 1954. Two clubs vie for the honor of having been first in San Francisco. The Warlocks appear to be the oldest club and the California Motor Club (CMC) appears to have been the first to incorporate.[10]

The California Motor Club was founded around 1960.[11] At least five homosexual motorcycle clubs existed in San Francisco as early as 1966.[12] Motorcycle clubs were (and are) informal, acquiring members through friendship networks. Like the bars, motorcycle clubs provided space for homosexuals to gather and socialize, but they did not attempt to make a profit. Instead, they engaged in fund-raising and donated money to charitable organizations. Motorcycle clubs developed close associations with some homosexual bars.

Until the 1950s, bars and other subculture organizations were "the only place in town" for homosexuals to gather and socialize.[13] Even after the formation of nonprofit homosexual organizations, bars remained the most accessible place for homosexuals to gather. In *Boots of Leather, Slippers of Gold: The History of a Lesbian Community,* Elizabeth Lapovsky Kennedy and Madeline D. Davis document lesbian bar culture from the mid-1930s to the early 1960s in Buffalo, New York. They argue that:

> By finding ways to socialize together, individuals ended the crushing isolation of lesbian oppression and created the possibility for group consciousness and activity. In addition, by forming community in a public setting outside of the protected and restricted boundaries of their own living rooms, lesbians also began the struggle for public recognition and acceptance.[14]

In San Francisco as well, gay bars and other subcultural institutions were important for developing a group consciousness and the beginnings of a more public identity. Bars were certainly the most public aspect of submerged, private communities. While the creation of a public identity was not the primary goal of bars, as commercial endeavors they were subject to the laws governing businesses. This brought them to the attention of the police, alcoholic beverage–regulating agencies, and the city government.[15]

This encounter with the state was important in establishing the legality of the public association of homosexuals. Despite constitutional protections of the right to association, before the 1950s the gathering of homosexuals in bars was treated as grounds for arrest, regardless of the presence of illegal activities.[16] The California Alcoholic Beverage Control (ABC) Department tried to close San Francisco's Black Cat Cafe in 1949 on the grounds that it was used as a "meeting place" for "persons of known homosexual tendencies."[17] The owner of the Black Cat, Sol Stoumen, with the financial support of his employees and patrons, challenged this decision.[18] In 1951, the California Supreme Court clarified that it was unconstitutional to revoke the liquor license of a bar solely because of the character of its clientele.[19] While this decision affirmed the legality of homosexual association, it was undermined by a statute passed by the state legislature in 1955 that "allowed the ABC to revoke the liquor license of a premise that served as a 'resort for sexual perverts.' "[20]

While homosexual association was purely social and of uncertain legality, the public organization of other groups was far more developed. By the 1950s, a substantial number and variety of interest group organizations devoted to civil rights and antidiscrimination existed, such as the National Association for the Advancement of Colored People, the National Woman's Party, and the American Civil Liberties Union.

These organizations reflected a particular set of assumptions about the nature of society and how to achieve change. Clemens defined interest group politics as "political organization mobilized around specific issues or policy demands and sustained not only by financial resources . . . but by extrapartisan voting blocs."[21] Interest group organizations tend to be single issue. For example, the National Woman's Party, one of the primary carriers of the women's movement in the 1950s, was "a small, exclusive single-issue group . . . [that] brought together individuals and groups interested in the ERA and other issues of concern to women [and] issued information on the status of the ERA."[22] In typical interest group fashion, the Woman's Party lobbied Congress and organized letter-writing campaigns in support of the ERA.[23] Assuming that social improvement can and should be achieved in a top-down legislative fashion, interest group organizations engage in lobbying and attempts to influence electoral outcomes through constructing voting blocs. A small, intensely committed core of leaders and activists, sometimes professional, represents the interests of the larger constituency. Interest group organizations tend to be hierarchical, centralized, and bureaucratic. Interests can be most powerfully represented to policy makers by presenting large numbers unified around a particular agenda. Interest group politics therefore produces the idea that it is ideal to create one main organization to represent each issue. This, in turn, creates competition among interest group organizations. Interest group politics builds upon an already existing identity. Awareness of group membership is assumed. The building of identity and group culture is not generally a central goal of interest group politics.

The interest group model was the most legitimate organizational model available, but it was not the only one. The Communist Party, in contrast, employed a secretive, cell-like, hierarchical structure.[24] The cell structure protected the identities of members of the organization, as members of various cells were connected to each other only through leaders.

As homosexual group consciousness developed, individuals began considering the possibility that forms of organization used by other groups might work for homosexuals. The founding of the first American homosexual organization, the Mattachine Society, illustrates this.[25] In the early 1930s, founder Harry Hay was immersed in homosexual friendship circles in San Francisco. Later he became involved with the Communist Party. Leaders of the party counseled him to repress his homosexuality, which he did for many years. In 1948, after joking with a group of homosexual men about mobilizing behind the Henry Wallace presidential campaign as "Bachelors for Wallace," Hay began considering the possibility of creating a homosexual political organization. Gradually he became committed to turning the organizational skills he had developed in the context of Communist Party organizing to the task of organizing homosexuals.

Fear of repression and their Communist Party backgrounds led Hay and others to use a secretive, cell-like structure when founding the Mattachine Society in Los Angeles in 1950. This structure worked to protect the club and its members from exposure, but it reinforced the notion that participation in such an organization was of dubious legality.[26]

Recognizing that this structure did not convey the message that homosexuals were a legitimate minority deserving of rights, the founders transformed it into a public organization as soon as they felt bold enough to do so. In the summer of 1952 they decided to incorporate as a nonprofit educational organization. Homophile activist Marvin Cutler boasted in 1956 that Mattachine was "incorporated under the strict requirements of California law, to insure impeccable propriety and civic non-partisanship at all times."[27] Incorporation, according to D'Emilio, "offered a simple answer to the many anxious newcomers about whether participation in a homosexual organization was illegal."[28]

San Francisco's first homophile organization was founded in February 1953 as a chapter of Los Angeles's Mattachine Society.[29] Gerry Brissette, a lab technician at the University of California at Berkeley, brought the idea of the Mattachine Society north. Like Mattachine's Los Angeles founders, he had prior political experience, in his case as a pacifist. In his original letter to the Mattachine Society, he "spoke of his dissatisfaction with the gay subculture," suggesting his belief that other forms of association should be available to homosexuals.[30]

San Francisco's second homophile organization, the Daughters of Bilitis, founded by Del Martin, Phyllis Lyon, and others in 1955 was founded without prior knowledge of the Mattachine Society.[31] Martin and Lyon formed the Daughters of Bilitis as a social club,[32] with the intent of providing an alternative to the bars. The Daughters of Bilitis also pursued incorporation soon after founding the organization as a way of sending a message to "those who doubted its legality or permanency."[33] The Daughters of Bilitis "became a full-fledged, non-profit corporation under the laws of the State of California in January, 1957."[34]

Organizational sociologists are well aware of the universality of organizational imitation, referring to it as "mimetic isomorphism."[35] Imitation of mainstream organizations was particularly self-conscious in this case. Homophile activists saw the creation of conventional organizations as evidence of their seriousness and legitimacy. D'Emilio describes the formal character of the conventions held by homophile organizations in the late 1950s:

> In mimicking the rituals of mainstream voluntary associations, those in attendance gave themselves comforting proof of their own legitimacy. Respectably dressed in their best attire, delegates sat through keynote speeches, award banquets for distinguished service, elections of new officers, and debates over constitutional revisions. The organizations rented hotel space, placed ads in local newspapers, listed the events with convention bureaus, catered meals, and printed programs available to onlookers—assertions of the right to associate in public which the movement perceived as setting precedents.[36]

Even late in the 1960s, when the homophile movement might have shifted its reference to the exciting new movements of the New Left, they still looked to mainstream voluntary organizations as models. In a 1967 letter to the *Vector,* Robert Walker insisted that:

> what [the Society for Individual Rights] desperately needs is leadership which has some practical knowledge of the functioning of membership organizations. . . . Any person who has served a few years as an officer or board member of ACLU, Junior Chamber of Commerce, Kiwanis, Rotary, Optimist, an individual church, a country club, NAACP, Young Republicans or Democrats, etc., is by reason of this

experience able to separate those problems which are organizational in nature from those problems which are homophile in nature.[37]

This passage suggests that until late in the 1960s homophile activists believed their cause advanced by use of conventional organizational forms. While critical of SIR, Walker was not critical of existing approaches to voluntary organization or of their usefulness to homosexuals.

Barriers to Public Homosexual Organizing, 1950–1968

The emergence of the desire to form homosexual interest group organizations was just the first step. Homophile activists encountered formidable barriers to the formation and success of their organizations. Basic organizational tools routinely available to other groups, such as the freedom to meet and to disseminate organizational information publicly, were not legal for homosexuals.[38] Thus, homophile activists worked to establish the right of homosexuals to associate without arrest, to list their organizations in a separate category within the telephone directory, and to distribute flyers in public places.[39] In addition, interest group politics presumes the prior existence of a group whose interests could be defined and represented in the public sphere. Lacking a defined public group identity, homosexuals found interest group politics to be of limited utility at this stage. And while forming public, nonprofit organizations contributed to the creation of a public homosexual identity, the logic of interest group politics did not provide the organizational technology necessary to create homosexual identity on a large scale. Complicating efforts further was the ambivalence of homosexuals themselves, even activists, about establishing a public homosexual presence. The idea that homosexuals should have a public identity displayed by public organizations was new and highly controversial. Even when they did successfully manage to create homosexual organizations, the effort to unify homosexuals within one organization provoked competition. Such conflict occupied much homophile energy.

Limited Access to Organizational Tools

Homophile activists encountered a variety of restrictions on the use of basic organizational tools. They feared that they would be arrested simply for gathering. They had difficulty securing office and meeting spaces. Obscenity laws restricted the printing and distribution of materials. They found it hard to publicize their ideas and the existence of their organizations through mainstream channels such as listings in the telephone directory and the public distribution of organizational materials.

To distinguish between what authorities would not permit them to do and what they simply feared they could not do, homophile activists had to courageously test the waters. For example, in the very early years of the Mattachine Society in Los Angeles, members were not sure if it was legal to associate as homosexuals in any venue for any purpose. Marvin Cutler, in a 1956 volume documenting homosexual organizations and publications, explained that during the earliest meetings, "they locked the door, pulled down the shades, chose a chairman and leaned forward to talk in modulated tones. They did not know then that such forums are not illegal."[40] When the police did not disrupt the meetings, they realized they could associate in this manner without risk of arrest.[41]

Frequently, however, authorities rejected their attempts to employ basic organizational tools. When this happened, homophile activists responded by challenging the legality of such actions. In 1966, homosexual organizations planned to operate a booth at the state fair in Sacramento to "acquaint the general public with the true nature of homosexuality through distribution of literature which would focus on the myths and stereotypes that surround the subject."[42] Before the fair, state officials cancelled the booth due to the "controversiality of the subject matter"[43] (see figure 2.1). Homophile organizations responded by filing a petition in the Sacramento superior court. They argued that the exhibit should be permitted because "a cancellation constitutes a denial of 'equal protection of the law' under the U.S. and California Constitutions."[44] Filing the petition did not persuade authorities to allow homophile activists to operate a booth. Homophile activists responded by distributing protest flyers at the fair, which earned them highly positive coverage in the mainstream press. In a delighted assessment of the event, a homophile activist noted that the "government agency found itself in the role of villain and the homophile in the role of minority downtrodden by bureaucracy."[45]

In 1968, homophile organizations attempted to obtain a separate category heading in the yellow pages of the San Francisco phone directory, under the designation "Homophile Organizations."[46] The Pacific Telephone Company denied the request. Homophile activists managed to get their case heard before the Public Utilities Commission, where they argued:

> We are here today because the phone company has failed to recognize the growing importance and acceptability and seriousness of purpose of the homophile movement. We are here today because the phone company took this request for a listing as a humorous and frivolous item and a publicity gimmick. . . . The homosexual must have full

vector

VOLUME II - NO. 10   **SEPTEMBER 1966**

Published monthly by the Society for Individual Rights, 83 Sixth Street, San Francisco, California

STATE FAIR BOOTH CANCELLED

LEGAL PANEL CITES NEED

TO LITIGATE HOMOSEXUAL REFORMS

The homophile in the next few years must look to the judiciary, and not to the Legislature, for relief from police oppression and reforms in the law. This was the consensus of a panel of lawyers--two of them San Francisco Assemblymen --who discussed the subject of "Homosexuality and the Law" at the SIR Community Center on August 23, 1966, in a seminar which was part of the week-long National Planning Conference of Homophile Organizations. The seminar was moderated by the Reverend Clay Colwell, President of the Council on Religion and the Homosexual.

Mr. Stefan M. Mason, Editor-in-Chief of the U.C.L.A. Law Review, and one of the authors of the recent law-school study of homosexuality and law-enforcement in Los Angeles County (reviewed in the last issue of VECTOR), summarized the recommendations made by the student group. According to Mr. Mason, proscription of sex acts solely on the grounds of "morality" is not a proper function of the penal law; instead, felony statutes which now prohibit specific acts should be deleted and replaced by a single misdemeanor statute covering only offensive behavior which occurs in public. The study also proposed reforms in the legal definition of entrapment which would require the police decoy to conform his behavior to that of a "normal" man. Litigation in areas where harrassment occurs was also suggested, since such police activity violates the constitutional guarantee of equal protection of the law. But merely to put these suggestions on paper, Mr. Mason said, is not enough. Reforms will be achieved only if the Community is willing to go into court and litigate.

Mr. Ephraim Margolin, attorney and lecturer on law at the University of California, stated that the problems faced by the homosexual are also those of the poor and other minority groups, who find themselves arrested simply because the police do not approve of them. He stressed that legislative action should be considered very cautiously in order to avoid the danger of achieving "martyrdom, but not results."

Mr. Douglas Corbin, Senior Attorney for the San Francisco Public Defender's office, commented that many attorneys are hesitant to go to trial because of the severe penalties faced on conviction, and therefore will advise their client to "cop out" to a lesser misdemeanor offense. If present felony acts committed in a secluded public place in the dead of night were misdemeanors, attorneys would be more apt to try the cases. By thus taking the "tribulations out of trials," he said, "justice would be meted out to a large segment of the
(cont'd on page 9)

The homosexual information booth at the State Fair in Sacramento was abruptly cancelled by State officials last month because of the alleged "controversiality of its subject matter." The purpose of the booth, to have been operated by ARC with an assist from SIR members, was to acquaint the general public with the true nature of homosexuality through distribution of literature which would focus on the myths and stereotypes that surround the subject. The booth also would have illustrated the theme that "One out of every ten people in the Nation is homosexual."

According to the Reverend Clay Colwell, President of the Council on Religion and the Homosexual, application for the booth was made in May through ARC, the Sacramento counterpart of SIR. After the purpose of the booth had been fully explained to State Fair officials, a contract was signed, a fee of $15 was paid, and a location assigned for the booth. Then, in August, officials requested samples of the literature to be distributed, and these materials were delivered in Sacramento on the 18th. The next day the booth was cancelled as being too controversial. The Reverend Colwell pointed out, however, that space was also allotted for the planned parenthood league and various "peace" groups which were not cancelled.

San Francisco attorneys, Evander C. Smith and Herb Donaldson, have filed a petition for a writ of mandate in
(cont'd on page 9)

Figure 2.1 The Society for Individual Rights newsletter, the *Vector*, announces the cancellation of the planned homophile booth at the 1966 California state fair. *Vector*, September 1966. Courtesy GLBT Historical Society of Northern California.

and ready access to every method and avenue of communication. The telephone must be in truth a public utility which can be fully utilized by the homosexual and those interested in his cause in the same manner and to the same degree as it is made available to and utilized by the heterosexual.[47]

That homophile activists doggedly pursued the issue of a separate listing in the telephone book indicates how serious they were about establishing access to mainstream organizational resources.

The Quandary of Identitylessness

Interest group politics is most successful when an organization can claim to represent the interests of a large, unified, powerful constituency. While interest group politics provided homosexuals with a template for how to organize, their constituency was not large, unified, or visible enough to produce interest group organizations able to impact policy. While Mattachine wanted to engage in "political action to erase from our law books the discriminatory and oppressive legislation presently directed against the homosexual minority," it actually spent most of its energies trying "to provide a consensus of principle around which all of our people can rally and from which they can derive a feeling of 'belonging.' "[48] Homophiles could not simply represent an established constituency; they needed to first create one. Both the Mattachine Society and the Society for Individual Rights devoted themselves to unifying homosexuals and creating a community characterized by "dignity" and "self-respect."[49] They made more progress toward unifying the group than they did toward changing public policy. The creation of a public organization contributes to identity building by asserting the public existence of a group and making it possible for interested individuals to find it. The activities, publications, and events of these organizations certainly built homosexual identity. But interest group politics was limited as a way of creating a new public identity. It did not provide reason for massive numbers of homosexuals to become visible to the mainstream of society—which was what was ultimately needed to create homosexuals as a large, visible constituency that could produce truly powerful interest group organizations.

The building of a public homosexual identity was further complicated by homosexual ambivalence. In the 1950s and 1960s, homosexuals were conflicted about the creation of public identity. On one side, those who espoused a minority group position were entirely supportive of the creation of public identity and organizations. In the middle were assimilationists, who wanted to improve the status of homosexuals through public organizing, but to do so without creating homosexuals as an identifiable minority group. And on the other side, there were those I call "pleasure seekers," who felt that the well-being of homosexuals would be ensured by avoiding public exposure and quietly building and protecting spaces for homosexual socializing.

The minority group position was present from the origins of the homophile movement and represented throughout the 1950s and 1960s. Harry Hay and the other founders of the Mattachine Society defined the purpose of the society as "to unify isolated homosexuals, educate homosexuals to see themselves as an oppressed minority, and lead them in a struggle for their own emancipation."[50] Hay argued that homosexuals were victimized by a "language and culture that does not admit the existence of the Homosexual Minority" and that homosexuals remained "largely unaware" that they in fact constituted "a social minority imprisoned within a dominant culture."[51]

Other homophile activists rejected the idea that homosexuals were or should be made into a minority group. By the time a chapter of the Mattachine Society was founded in San Francisco in 1953, Harry Hay and his cohort had been cast out of the leadership of the Los Angeles chapter. Assimilationists argued, "We know we are the same, no different than anyone else. Our difference is an unimportant one to heterosexual society, *unless we make it important.*"[52] These leaders believed that "never in our existence as individuals or as a group should we admit to being a minority. For to admit being a minority we request of other human beings that we so desire to be persecuted."[53]

Given the level of racial discrimination in the United States in the 1950s, hesitation about defining oneself as a visible minority group is understandable. Organizations advocating for racial justice themselves held assimilationist positions. However, an assimilationist politics of race had an entirely different meaning than an assimilationist politics of sexuality, given the different historical experiences of African Americans and homosexuals. For African Americans, advocating integration meant rejecting forced social, political, and economic segregation. But homosexuals were not segregated. They had no public group identity and were not identifiable as individuals. Thus, the homophile assimilationist position was problematic, as it was unclear what such a politics could accomplish. Their problem was too little visibility, not too much.

Supporters of both the minority group and assimilationist positions saw the primary goal of homosexual organization to be increasing the respect that homosexuals received from mainstream society. I refer to both of these positions as "legitimacy seeking." They believed that the quality of the indi-

vidual lives of homosexuals depended on changing the attitudes of heterosexuals and explicitly framed their efforts in terms of acquiring "legitimacy"
or "respectability." They differed, however, on the necessity of homosexual
visibility in acquiring this respect. Minority group advocates believed that developing a public presence was necessary. They believed that homosexual invisibility reinforced the notion that homosexuality was shameful. In contrast, assimilationists felt that advocating for the rights of individuals to
privately engage in homosexual sexual practices could be done without increasing the visibility of individuals or the group. Minority group advocates
wanted to create visible organizations with formal legal status. The assimilationist position coexisted uneasily with organization building, given the tendency of organization building to concretize group boundaries.

Pleasure seekers believed that the quality of the individual lives of homosexuals depended on the richness and security of the territory protected for
socializing. To this end, the organizational activities of pleasure seekers were
directed inward. While interested in building group solidarity, they were not
interested in building the broader legitimacy of the group or in developing a
public sexual identity recognized by outsiders.

While legitimacy seekers craved the status that incorporated nonprofit
organizations could provide, the environment and their own ambivalence
led them to worry about the risks of public exposure. This organizational
tension between privacy and exposure parallels the ways individuals "passed"
as heterosexual, revealing or concealing sexual identity according to the situation. Revelation of sexual identity at the organizational level is different
from doing so in face-to-face interaction. Clues can be more quickly revealed
or hidden in face-to-face interaction, depending on the reaction of the audience. An incorporated organization, by contrast, is solid, permanent, and
public. The names of their organizations reflected this tension between secrecy and disclosure. They selected organizational names that subtly conveyed the homosexual content of the organization to those in the know. For
example, "Mattachine" refers to "the fools and jesters of legend who spoke
the truth in the face of stern authority."[54] The name "Daughters of Bilitis"
was proposed by one of the founding members who had happened upon a
book of prose poems about Sapphic love by Pierre Louÿs called *Chansons de Bilitis* (1894). The founders believed that while insiders would know the reference, outsiders would assume that Daughters of Bilitis was "like any other
women's lodge."[55]

Another way legitimacy seekers tried to reduce the risks associated with
visibility was to separate the reputations of members from the reputation of

the organization. At times in its history, the Mattachine Society of San Francisco billed itself as an organization "interested in the problems of homosexuality" but denied that it was a homosexual organization.[56] In 1959, the Mattachine Society filed a slander suit against a candidate for mayor of San Francisco, Russell Wolden, accusing him of saying that Mattachine was composed of "organized homosexuals."[57]

In order to substantiate the claim that their organizations served homosexuals but were not composed of homosexuals, legitimacy seekers found they had to be extremely careful about organizing or promoting social activities, even those that were not explicitly sexual. Involvement in homosexual socializing suggested that the organizations were composed *of* homosexuals and were not simply "interested in problems of homosexuality." If all the organization's members were homosexual, this sabotaged the claim that the cause of homosexual rights was one of abstract social justice and instead suggested that the organization was purely self-interested. And given that homosexual behavior was illegal, sponsoring social functions could jeopardize the legality of these visible organizations. While they sponsored some social activities, legitimacy-seeking organizations tended to conceal the social nature of these events.[58]

Legitimacy-seeking organizations thus did not serve the needs of pleasure seekers. Pleasure seekers felt threatened by the public nature of these organizations. They felt that the agenda of legitimacy seekers attracted unwelcome attention. They saw few benefits and many risks from the additional exposure that inevitably accompanied the legitimacy-seeking project. Legitimacy seeking "attracted attention to behavior that was safest when it went unnoticed."[59] They preferred organizational names that dropped no hints about sexual identity. Differences on this issue led to organizational splits, even within the more public organizations. For example, the Daughters of Bilitis split when it became evident to some members that the founders intended for the organization to develop into a political and educational organization. Those interested in a purely social group left to form Nova.[60]

Just as pleasure seekers found the existence of more public organizations threatening, legitimacy seekers were threatened by the vitality of the organized subculture. Legitimacy seekers were well aware that many of the sexual pastimes of homosexuals were not acceptable to mainstream, heterosexual society (e.g., multiple sexual partners, the use of pornography, sex in public places, cross-dressing and other forms of gender role deviation, sex with minors, sadomasochism and other forms of fetishism).[61] Because they endeavored to persuade mainstream society that most homosexuals did not engage in these practices, legitimacy seekers were frustrated by the efforts of pleasure seekers to build and protect spaces that encouraged these styles and practices, and in the case of bars, made them visible to mainstream society.[62] The negative attitude of homophile activists toward bars is captured in this passage from *The Ladder,* a publication of Daughters of Bilitis:

> Bars have their place, yes, but only the people with real strength can fight their way out of the example they see there that reeks of defiance, disillusionment, and despair. The defiance, disillusionment and despair, we all know, lie there under the mask of "gaiety" which [patrons] of the bars put on![63]

The segregating of political-educational and social functions into different organizations came at a cost. By refusing to incorporate social activities, public nonprofit organizations made themselves irrelevant to those whose major concern was finding ways to socialize with other homosexuals. Locating sexual partners, life partners, and sympathetic friends was difficult in this era, and homosexuals looked to the few specifically homosexual venues for these social connections. While many homosexuals were not wholly satisfied with the sexualized environment of bars, they still found the social climate more appealing than the seriousness of the homophile organizations.[64]

While the bars did not make building a public identity a part of their agenda, they were visible simply because of their status as commercial enterprises. But this visibility placed bars in a highly vulnerable position vis-à-vis mainstream society. Homosexual life before the 1960s was defined by waves of police crackdowns on bars, by the arrests and exposure of individuals who frequented bars, and by the fear of arrest and exposure.[65] Bars and other commercial enterprises were limited in their abilities to protect their clientele.[66] The location of bars at this vulnerable nexus of the social and the political ultimately produced an opportunity for integrating the political-educational and social-sexual aspects of the homosexual community.[67]

Interest Group Politics and Organizational Competition

Within interest group politics, a group is seen to be powerful if its interests can be coherently presented by one organization speaking with a single voice. Thus, ideological conflict and schisms within and among organizations are common as organizations compete for the position of being the one that legitimately represents an issue. Homophile reliance on interest group politics thus escalated competition among homophile organizations.

When participants in the earliest homophile organizations first became aware of similar groups, they viewed them as competitors to be eliminated. Activists believed that homosexuals would be best served by creating one central organization. They urged their diverse constituency to get along within the confines of a single organization.

This commitment to building unity by building one central homophile organization blinded activists to the possibilities of a division of labor among homophile organizations. Even in the face of men's and women's very different needs and experiences, activists in the central male-dominated homophile organizations were ambivalent about women's insistence on organizing separately in the Daughters of Bilitis. Martin and Lyon, the founders of DOB, reveal this ambivalence:

> Representatives and leaders of [Mattachine and ONE, a Los Angeles–based homophile organization] were extremely cooperative when we finally did meet them. Though their groups were open to both men and women, they had never been able to attract Lesbians in large number, and they offered encouragement and hope that we could manage to organize the women to swell the ranks of the homophile movement. Despite their show of generosity and help, for which we are forever grateful, there has always been the private (and sometimes not so private) resentment against the separatist and segregationist policies of DOB, which restricted its membership to women only.[68]

The central, primarily male, homophile organizations did not regard multiple homophile organizations as evidence of movement strength. While viewing DOB's separatism as potentially divisive, male homophiles were forced to accept DOB because their primarily male organizations were not attracting many women to the homophile cause.

This commitment to building unity through building one central homophile organization generated even more resistance to a division of labor among multiple male homophile organizations. The resistance manifested itself in competition for the position of being *the* organization that would represent homosexuals. When a new homophile organization formed, it tended to form in the same niche as already existing organizations; such organizations tried to *replace* the extant organizations.

When the Society for Individual Rights was formed, its intention was to supersede both the League for Civil Education (discussed below) and the Mattachine Society. It was successful. LCE disbanded in 1967. Hal Call, the central figure of the Mattachine Society, admitted in a recent autobiographical interview that Mattachine "went downhill from the time the Society for

Individual Rights came into being in 1964."[69] SIR cofounder Bill Beardemphl bragged about SIR's successful deposing of Mattachine as the central homophile organization and suggested that had Mattachine been doing the job well, its turf would have been much more difficult to take over:

> In six short months, we have become the largest local group ever to exist as an active homophile organization in the United States. This is shocking and somewhat surprising to those of us who helped formulate S.I.R. and its policies, because the "professional homosexuals" in the homophile field had created a false concept of a job accomplished and criticized us by saying we were only doing that which already had been done.[70]

Organizational competition eased somewhat in the late 1960s, as the political environment improved. Homophile activists gradually acknowledged that the existence of multiple organizations was inevitable and perhaps even desirable. They also began to see that organizations could coexist and that more could be accomplished if the organizations could cooperate. They began to combine the project of building a unified homosexual identity with the project of unifying existing homosexual organizations.

In a 1965 letter to the Society for Individual Rights from the newly formed Council on Religion and the Homosexual, the founders reassured existing organizations that CRH saw its work as complementary to that of SIR, not as a challenge:

> The Council [on Religion and the Homosexual] . . . recognizes the important work of existing homophile organizations and does not intend to replace or superimpose itself on these groups. Rather it intends to supplement the work of these groups where such action seems appropriate and to establish dialog (mutual communication) with many influential segments of San Francisco leadership.[71]

The fact that this reassurance was offered suggests that the idea of a division of labor among homophile groups was indeed new.

In the late 1960s, cooperation among homophile organizations was difficult to achieve. Activists such as Bill Beardemphl expressed frustration about the perpetual conflict that impeded organizational cooperation:

> Our work is to create a Community feeling that will bring a "Homophile Movement" into being. Every homosexual must commit himself to the overriding necessity that we be UNITED. . . . Personality con-

flicts, ideological differences or "bitch fights" must not deter us from
our goal of mutual cooperation.[72]

San Francisco homophile organizations made valiant, if sometimes unsuccessful, efforts to work together and congratulated themselves on successful
collaboration.[73] The Council on Religion and the Homosexual, the Society
for Individual Rights, the Daughters of Bilitis, the Mattachine Society, Strait
and Associates,[74] and the Tavern Guild collaborated on one of the first public
homosexual demonstrations in San Francisco. The 1966 protest at the federal
building plaza on Armed Forces Day protested exclusion of homosexuals
from the draft. Later in that year, the same group of organizations cooper-
ated on protesting the cancellation of the homophile booth at the state fair
(described earlier in this chapter). In speaking about the successful state fair
collaboration, the president of ARC, a Sacramento homophile organization,
asserted that successful organizational cooperation was evidence of unity.
"The unity achieved by the six participating organizations," he wrote, "was
another step toward a broader unity based on realization of sameness of purpose—the fight for equal rights—which cuts across all differences such as
gender, organization structures, distance, or sexual orientation."[75]

As the power and size of the homophile movement increased in San
Francisco during the late 1960s, it did so primarily through the growth of the
Society for Individual Rights. As homophile activists succeeded in employing
the interest group model, the result was one highly successful organization
and a few smaller organizations. The interest group model did not generate
large numbers or a great diversity of organizations.

While some saw homophile success as flowing from the ability of homophile organizations to emulate mainstream organizational forms, by the end
of the 1960s some activists were beginning to express frustration with the limitations of these hierarchical and bureaucratic forms. In a frustrated critique
of his own and other homophile organizations, Society for Individual Rights'
Beardemphl worried in 1968 that "organizationally, if a group is always concerned about rules, points of order, titles, by-laws, credentials, etc., there is
no time to be concerned about, or organize and put into operation social action programs."[76] In 1972, sociologist Laud Humphreys also noted that homophile organizing had been paralyzed by the overuse of mainstream organizational forms:

> Closely defined goals and selective admission may be functional for
> Rotary International or the Masons; the very forms that help provide
> legitimacy for most voluntary associations, however, may throttle

change organizations and render them ineffectual. Roberts' Rules of Order, credentials committees, formal committee structures in general, and constitutions contribute legitimacy to organizations only because legitimate groups employ them.[77]

Humphreys recognized that the quest for legitimacy made the adoption of such rules appealing, but questioned whether the adoption of such rules was in the best interest of the homosexual movement.

The Homophile Movement in a Changing Environment, 1959–1968

Despite the barriers described above, homophile activists had achieved a modest level of success in building and maintaining organizations by the end of the 1950s. This success provoked a wave of repression in the late 1950s, which, ironically, sped up processes of field formation and redirected it in fortuitous ways. And then, by the mid-1960s, the political movements of the era began to influence both the homophile movement and the local political environment.

In October 1959, San Francisco mayoral candidate Russell Wolden tried to discredit incumbent mayor George Christopher by accusing him of allowing "the Mattachine Society to [make] San Francisco 'the national headquarters of organized homosexuals in the United States' " in a front-page article entitled "Sex Deviates Make San Francisco Headquarters," published in the San Francisco *Progress.*[78]

Initially, the tactic backfired. Wolden was condemned for "stooping to such tactics," which "insulted" and "stigmatized" the city.[79] Christopher won the election. The unsolicited publicity immediately helped Mattachine and the Daughters of Bilitis. This attack, meant to undermine homophile organizations, furthered the homophile mission of creating a public sexual identity. As D'Emilio observes, "The affair generated more publicity for the movement than it had received in all its previous years. With such a barrage of headlines and editorials, it is doubtful that many gay men and women in San Francisco remained ignorant of the movement's existence."[80] Repression thus furthered homophile goals by acknowledging their emergent identity and defining the organizations as worthy of attack.

While it was the visibility of Mattachine that stimulated the initial attack, homosexual bars were more vulnerable. Mattachine and Daughters of Bilitis had carefully protected their legality. Once elected, Mayor Christopher announced a " 'vigorous new campaign' against gay bars in San Francisco."[81] In October 1961 the Alcoholic Beverage Control Department revoked the liquor licenses of twelve gay bars.[82] The concerns of the pleasure seekers were justified. The visibility of the homophile organizations brought repression down on the bars.

The attack forced the bars into a defensive position. While bar proprietors and patrons preferred to remain quietly apolitical, they had to defend themselves or be eliminated. Bars did not set out to build a public identity, but city politics, the police, and the Alcoholic Beverage Control Department defined homosexual social space as a political battleground.[83] Olzak and West have observed that repression "both enhances and suppresses ethnic organizations," depending on the level of repression:

> Relatively mild levels of repression (or a shift toward lower levels of repression) open new opportunities for challengers to act collectively to demand their rights and make claims against the state. In this "political process" view, small amounts of repression may be necessary to motivate activity and overcome apathy. But intense repression causes collective action to diminish or even disappear.[84]

In this case, repression of homosexual organizing was strong enough to stimulate a response, but not enough to quash the impulse to organize.

The defense of homosexual bars took several forms. Activists continued challenging the legality of police actions against bars in court.[85] In April 1961, Guy Strait formed the League for Civil Education, the first homophile organization to distribute its publications in the bars. The Tavern Guild was founded in 1962 specifically to protect homosexual bars and bar patrons from arbitrary law enforcement. John D'Emilio, historian of the homophile movement, describes the activities of the Tavern Guild as follows:

> Through fund-raising social events and regular dues, the guild retained a lawyer and bail bondsman for anyone arrested in or near a gay bar and coordinated the efforts of owners to fight the capricious procedures of the [Alcoholic Beverage Control Department]. At election time the bars became the scene of voter registration drives. The Tavern Guild financed the printing and distributed copies of the "Pocket Lawyer," a wallet-sized legal guide on what to do in case of harassment or arrest. The very existence of the guild was a statement that gay bars were a legitimate form of business enterprise that deserved freedom from arbitrary harassment.[86]

The attack on homosexual bars temporarily reduced their numbers. The famous Black Cat tavern closed in 1963.[87] But the defense of the bars, particularly the successful challenge to laws regulating them, created the conditions for a resurgence. Organizing for defense bound the bars into a field, centered on the Tavern Guild. After reaching a low point in 1963, when there were fewer than twenty, the number of homosexual bars increased to fifty-seven by 1968.[88] Thus were pleasure seekers politicized.

The legitimacy seekers also began to support more social activities. The Society for Individual Rights (SIR), founded in September 1964, placed the provision of social activities for homosexuals at the heart of its agenda. The founders recognized that homosexuals were more likely to get involved in a political-educational organization if the organization met their social needs. This formula worked well. SIR rapidly became the largest homosexual organization in the country.[89]

With this new focus on social events, all of the community's homophile organizations collaborated to sponsor a fund-raiser to launch the newly formed Council on Religion and the Homosexual. The New Year's ball of 1965 proved a turning point for San Francisco's homosexual community. This was another instance when repression backfired. The police turned out for the ball with squad cars and paddy wagons.[90] They photographed guests as they entered the ball. When they attempted to enter the event without a search warrant, lawyers for the Council on Religion and the Homosexual tried to stop them. Three lawyers and a woman taking tickets were arrested.[91] However, in this instance the harassment took place in front of respected heterosexual clergy, who were horrified. Homophile activist and ball attendee Del Martin observed that "this is a type of police activity that homosexuals know well, but heretofore the police had never played their hand before Mr. Average Citizen."[92] This display of public discrimination further legitimated homophile organizations and raised concerns among a sympathetic heterosexual audience.

Therefore, while it appeared successful in the short term, repression actually sparked further political organizing within the homosexual community, helped to build a public identity, and integrated the political and the social aspects of the project. The acceleration of homosexual organization can be seen in figure 2.2, which shows that the number of homophile organizations increased more rapidly in the late 1960s. The attacks on the bars illustrated that when the more politicized parts of the community distanced themselves from the bars, they left the bars vulnerable. Recognizing this set

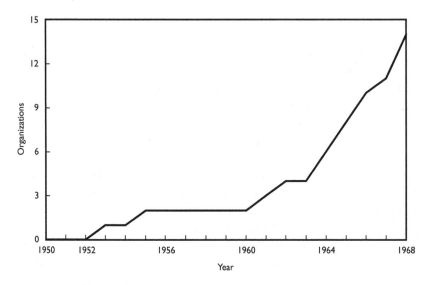

Figure 2.2 Homophile Organizations in San Francisco, 1950–68

the stage for the emergence of new organizations, such as the Society for Individual Rights, which included both political-educational and social-sexual
activities within one organization.

The nature of repression of homosexuals contributed to the unique
integration of the social and the conventionally political that would dif-
ferentiate this movement from kindred movements. The social and cultural life of the group was experienced by mainstream society as extremely
threatening. Thus, defending spaces for sociality became central to gay politics.

The outraged response of sympathetic heterosexuals to the police harassment of the New Year's ball of 1965 was indicative of a general decline in
public support for such harassment in the political climate of the 1960s.
Given the magnitude of the political and cultural movements coursing
through San Francisco and the whole United States at this time, this should
not be surprising. These were the years of the Free Speech Movement, the
Black Panthers, the antiwar movement, and the counterculture.

The homophile movement was not blind to the new movements and
the ideas they introduced. Homophile activists made comparisons and borrowed ideas, but remained distinct from the main currents of the New Left.
Homophile activists were particularly interested in the rapid changes in African American politics. As black movements rejected integrationist politics in

favor of more separatist agendas, homophile tensions between assimilationist and minority group positions resolved in favor of a minority group position.[93] Homophile activist Franklin Kameny, in a July 1964 speech to the New York Mattachine Society, drew parallels between the situation of homosexuals and blacks. "In all of these minority groups, we are interested in obtaining rights for our respective minorities *as* Negroes, *as* Jews, and *as* homosexuals. Why we are Negroes, Jews, or homosexuals is totally irrelevant, and whether we can be changed to whites, Christians, or heterosexuals is equally irrelevant."[94] But this shift to a minority group position was gradual and not universal. Some individuals still adopted an assimilationist position in the later 1960s. For example, in 1966 Shirley Willer, president of Daughters of Bilitis, denied the usefulness of defining homosexuals as a "unique minority": "Demonstrations which define the homosexual as a unique minority defeat the very cause for which the homosexual strives—TO BE CONSIDERED AN INTEGRAL PART OF SOCIETY."[95] Exposure to the New Left, particularly to its radical race politics, swept away lingering homophile ambivalence about identity formation by the end of the 1960s.

In the black community, the turn to a more separatist politics was connected with a new focus on the psychological well-being of black individuals. L. A. Kauffman explained, "Black Power's primary thrust was to place the redefinition and affirmation of the black self at the core of its politics."[96] Homophile activists were intrigued with the implications of this focus on individual psychology. In June 1968, homophile activist Franklin Kameny described his reaction to Stokely Carmichael's position and what he thought this meant for homosexuals:

> We must instill in the homosexual community a sense of the worth of the individual homosexual. A sense of high self-esteem. We must counteract the inferiority which ALL society inculcates into him in regard to his homosexuality. . . . The other day, on television, I saw Stokely Carmichael before a group of Negroes chanting: "Black is Beautiful." To a Negro, living in a society in which "white," "snow," "purity," and "good" are all equated together, and "black," "evil," "darkness," "dirt," and "ugliness" are all equated together, Carmichael's tactic, is understandable—and necessary, and desirable. Within our somewhat different framework, we need the same kind of thing.[97]

Activist Craig Rodwell noted that black politics influenced both his thinking and homophile politics in general. He said that "in adopting the slogan 'Gay is Good,' the NACHO took a cue from our black brothers' slogan, 'Black is

Beautiful.' "[98] (NACHO was North American Conference of Homophile Organizations, an organization active in the late 1960s whose goal was to build a coalition of all the major national homophile organizations.)

This new concern with the psychological well-being of individual homosexuals provoked a reassessment of the costs and benefits of privacy about sexual identity. During the homophile period, a few individuals had had to be publicly identified as homosexual to represent the organizations and to demonstrate to heterosexual society the positive qualities of homosexual people. These individuals were defined as courageous martyrs, sacrificing their reputations to the cause.

The emphasis on self-esteem and pride, however, suggested the possibility that public revelation of sexual identity might have personal psychological rewards. Homophile activists began to worry about the psychological toll of privacy. Homophiles began to define it as "lying" and to claim that it contributed to internalized self-hatred, as this 1966 *Vector* article reveals:

> We lie so that we may live. Whether it is to our boss, or the draft board, or the civil service, we rarely can afford to divulge the simple truth of our homosexuality. But this is merely the beginning. Lying begets lying: we have to cover up for so many of our activities and doings that we find ourselves in a mire of untruths. . . . (The rare homosexual who volunteers the fact that he is gay learns fast enough the toll straight society can exact for telling the truth.)[99]

Concealing sexual identity came to be seen as a barrier to the development of the self-acceptance and dignity that homophile activists saw blacks acquiring. The definition of privacy as lying was immediately followed in this 1966 article by a reminder of the high stakes of public revelation; this was typical of the ambivalence of the late homophile period.

Cecil Williams, the minister of Glide Church, a straight man deeply influenced by the civil rights movement, was one of the first to urge homosexuals to go public. In November 1968 he proclaimed, "It is time that Homosexuals begin to understand themselves more, begin to accept themselves more, and say to the world (including their parents): 'I'm a homosexual, and proud of it.' "[100] His appeal for homosexuals to publicly reveal their identity was a rarity for the period before 1969. Generally, activists stopped *just* short of advocating public revelation. Concealment was viewed as lying and a source of low self-esteem, but disclosure was viewed as too risky. A statement by Don Collins, made in 1969 right as gay liberation was emerging, captures the fundamental ambivalence and contradictions that plagued the homophile movement: "It is not necessary to carry a banner proclaiming one's sexual orientation. . . . However, there is no reason to subvert one's life style or create elaborate facades attempting to disguise an individual life style."[101] Of course, carrying banners proclaiming sexual identity was *precisely* what gay liberationists would define as absolutely imperative.

Right up until gay liberation exploded onto the scene, even the most optimistic of homophile activists could not begin to imagine how radically the movement would be transformed. Larry Littlejohn, writing in the *Vector* in November 1968, optimistically asserted that:

> I do not expect that this month all homosexuals in America will drop their masks and stop hiding their homosexuality. But gradually more and more people will say first to themselves and then publicly: I am homosexual. I am proud of my homosexuality. And eventually the time will come when there will no longer be a homosexual "problem." When I say "gradually" and "eventually" I do not mean after hundreds of years. I expect that before my life is over I will see this change.[102]

When he wrote, there were still only fourteen homophile organizations in San Francisco, and the terms "coming out" and "gay," which we take for granted today, had not fully acquired their contemporary meanings. No one could have predicted that, within a year, the homophile movement would be swept up into the New Left. Chapter 3 turns to an analysis of the encounter between the homophile movement and the New Left. I show how the remarkable creativity of the New Left made it possible for activists to come out, a step that even the most radical homophile activists just could not bring themselves to take.

THREE

Innovation: Gay Liberation and the Origins of Coming Out, 1969–1970

Gay liberation, on the surface, is a struggle for homosexuals for dignity and respect—a struggle for civil rights. Of course, we want to "come out" (that is, to end our hiding), to forbid such terms as "faggot," "dyke," and "queer," to hold down jobs without having to play straight, and to change or abolish those laws which restrict or denigrate us.

But the movement for a new definition of sexuality does not, and cannot, end there. . . . The revolutionary goals of gay liberation, including the elimination of capitalism, imperialism and racism, are premised on the termination of the system of male supremacy.

Allen Young, "Out of the Closets, into the Streets" (1971)

By 1968, homophile activists had accomplished much of the cultural work involved in defining what would become a gay collective identity. The homophile movement had even edged up to the public revelation of sexual identity but could not take that final step. As we saw in the last chapter, the political logic employed by the homophile movement, the interest group model, could never have produced the kind of gay movement that developed. That model, with its formally structured, centralized, bureaucratic organizations, was suited for lobbying, policy reform, and litigation in the pursuit of group rights. But it was not well suited to the project of building and displaying collective identity. While homophile activists were beginning to be influenced by the New Left in the late 1960s, it would require full immersion and exposure to the logic of identity politics to produce the dynamic gay liberation movement.

In 1969, after almost twenty years of steady organizing by a relatively stable group of activists, the landscape of homosexual organizing changed dramatically and permanently. Gay liberation burst onto the scene. It accomplished more in two years than the homophile movement had in the previous twenty, as measured by organizational growth, visibility, and political action. How was this possible? Where did gay liberation come from and how was it able to accomplish so much so quickly?

Gay liberation was born out of the encounter between the homophile movement and the New Left.[1] Gay liberation built on the foundation laid by the homophile movement, which provided the notion that same-gender sexuality could be the basis for a minority group identity. The homophile movement also built the organizations and publications that made this idea an emerging reality. The New Left transformed homosexual organization through exposure to an identity political logic. Based on the assumption that alienation is the fundamental problem with society and achieving authenticity the ultimate goal of progressive social change, the logic of identity politics transformed the meaning of secrecy about sexual identity. Homophile activists viewed privacy as necessary and self-protective. In the context of the New Left, privacy came to be understood as dishonest and psychologically unhealthy. Combined with the belief that social change was accomplished from the bottom up through the aggregation of individual acts, instead of through top-down policy change, this emphasis on authenticity produced the definitive contribution of gay liberation: the political strategy of "coming out."

The identity political logic provided the framework that defined public revelation of sexuality as both an important political act and a crucial step to psychological health. Exposure to the logic of identity politics thus solved the major problem confronting the homophile movement in 1968—how to create a public collective identity powerful enough to effectively engage in interest group politics. By making public revelation of sexuality deeply meaningful at the individual level, the identity political logic persuaded masses of people to "come out."

The development of a gay identity politics within the New Left did not lead smoothly to the gay identity movement of the 1970s. While exposing homosexual organizing to identity politics, the New Left also brought it into contact with a particularly radical form of redistributive politics. The gay power strand of gay liberation took the position that sexual liberation was only a part of a larger movement seeking economic, racial, and gender justice. This multi-issue campaign of radical social change was utterly at odds with the reform-minded, single-issue, interest group politics of the homophile movement, producing conflict between homophile and gay liberation politics, as well as paralyzing conflict within gay liberation itself.

The argument presented here challenges conventional understandings of how the New Left influenced gay politics. All accounts, including this one, agree that the New Left was critical to the emergence of gay liberation and to the movement that later developed. However, most sociologists who have written on gay liberation have not attended to evidence indicating that gay liberation developed out of the interaction between an already existent movement and the New Left, preferring to treat gay liberation as one of several outgrowths of the New Left. In contrast, historians of sexuality have been aware of the contributions of the homophile movement, but have viewed the contribution of the New Left primarily in terms of providing a political context that made possible the normative reevaluation of gay identity. In this view, coming out was made possible by casting off shame and developing pride. This account neglects the historical novelty of intense concern with the psychological issues of "shame" and "pride." Before exposure to an identity political logic, psychological aspects of homosexual life were not foremost among the concerns of homophile activists. By intensifying concern with the psychological aspects of oppression, the identity logic simultaneously constructed and vanquished shame. Finally, most scholars assume that the role of the New Left in the gay movement was entirely facilitative. I rebut this view by showing that the role the New Left played in the gay movement was mixed. By providing the gay movement with multiple new ways to think about organizing around sexuality, the New Left both provoked the dynamic growth of the movement and created new and potentially paralyzing internal conflict.

The New Left and Identity Politics

The 1960s were a time of great cultural change in the United States. Moments of such dramatic cultural change are rare. Most of the time society is constituted by an interlocking network of fields, each organized by taken-for-granted rules. The institutionalized character of individual arenas and the collective weight of related fields reinforcing one another limit both what it is possible to think and what it is possible to do. Actors usually have a good idea of what kind of action is possible and what kind of action is not possible. These perceived limits shape what people can even imagine wanting. The more stable the interlocking set of fields, the more limited is cultural creativity. The events of the 1960s threw multiple fields into crisis simultaneously. The generalized nature of the cultural crisis, which called into question the rules of multiple arenas, produced a context highly generative of new ideas. Crisis tends to cause intense interaction, as actors try to further destabilize existing fields, to develop new ways to organize society, or to reassert existing sets of rules. Moments when people interact intensely foster creativity. In situations of crisis, the environment becomes difficult to read, making it impossible to accurately assess the limits of the possible. When people question the established limits of the possible, the horizon of the possible itself changes. Thus, situations of high environmental uncertainty can produce great cultural creativity. In such contexts, actors may borrow cultural elements from unexpected places and combine them in new ways.

This moment of crisis produced and disseminated ways of thinking about how to pursue change quite distinct from, and challenging to, the interest group model that dominated earlier. While the quest for personal authenticity has been a recurring preoccupation of American culture, an intensification of this quest in the postwar period fueled the rise of the New Left and gave rise to a new logic of political action.[2] People, particularly young people, became deeply concerned with achieving personal fulfillment and increasingly critical of a society that they saw as alienating. New Left documents suggest the centrality of this search for authenticity. The Port Huron Statement, a foundational document of the New Left, proposed that the "goal of man and society should be . . . finding a meaning in life that is personally authentic."[3]

Young people identified the bureaucratic organization of society as stifling to individuals. This theme was central to the Free Speech Movement at Berkeley in the fall of 1964. Students saw the university as "a faceless and inhumane bureaucracy."[4] Activists generalized this critique of large bureaucratic organizations to all organizations, even their own. Breines explains that "the fear that bureaucracy and centralized organization took on lives of their own and subverted original goals was responsible for the movement's wariness of even its own political organization."[5]

This critique of bureaucracy led to a search for alternative ways of organizing for social change. Activists struggled to create ways of doing politics where the desired society, characterized by equal, democratic, authentic relationships, was present in the process of pursuing change. Breines refers to this form of politics as "prefigurative politics."[6] By this she means that social relationships within the movement prefigured, or served as a model for, the society envisioned. Creating the conditions for individuals to express themselves, to become empowered, and to form authentic connections was both a means to an end and an end in itself. Activists felt that movement participation should be personally fulfilling and therapeutic, not simply altruistic. They envisioned a model of social change in which there was a synergistic relationship between meeting the needs of individuals and the pursuit of collective goals.

The New Left experimented with several ways of pursuing change that allowed individuals to express themselves. They believed that large-scale structural changes could, in some cases, be achieved through the spontaneous expression of shared sentiment. In this case, "a political movement is created by thousands of individuals who say 'no' to the structures and politics of the dominant society."[7] Instead of achieving goals through building a representative organization, each individual acts directly. This vision seemed plausible at the peak of the New Left. At this unique moment, collective action sometimes seemed to happen with relatively little intentional organization. Wini Breines describes how this was possible in her discussion of the Free Speech Movement:

> No central political organization was responsible for popular mobilization. People participated because the issues struck a chord, because many students believed in FSM's principles, and because they were generally both dissatisfied and hopeful.[8]

This way of pursuing change, however, works only when individual sentiment is spontaneously moving in the same direction. Even at the peak of the New Left, activists recognized that organization was usually necessary to achieve collective ends. The New Left tried to create social movement organizations that protected individual expression while making it possible to pursue large-scale structural changes. These "structureless" organizations were designed to be participatory and democratic. They "[had] a different moderator for each meeting instead of officers; organiz[ed] ad hoc groups instead of formal committees; bas[ed] decisions on consensus reached through discussion rather than on the vote of the majority; and permit[ted] access to all comers rather than establishing requirements for admittance and membership."[9] Activists found structureless organizations dissatisfying because they did not provide channels through which members could arrive at binding decisions needed to plan political action. Attempts to decide among incompatible perspectives frequently led to organizational paralysis and personal hostility.

Consciousness-raising groups, which originated in the women's and gay liberation movements, also came out of the search for ways of achieving change that valued the individual. Pamela Allen described the purposes of "small groups" within women's liberation in her pamphlet *Free Space,* written about Sudsofloppen, one of the earliest women's liberation consciousness-raising groups formed in San Francisco:

> The small group is especially suited to freeing women to affirm their view of reality and to learn to think independently of male supremacist values. It is a space where women can come to understand not only the ways this society works to keep women oppressed but also ways to overcome that oppression psychologically and socially. It is Free Space.[10]

These groups were based on the premise that knowledge comes from experience, not from outside experts. Knowledge did not come from raw experience, but from a collective process of reinterpretation. Spaces free from the presence of oppressors were necessary for this process to happen. In these small committed groups, talk was the primary activity. Sharing the whole self in a trusting environment was seen as key to both personal change and more general social change.[11] Consciousness-raising groups endeavored to both affirm the identities of their members and to analyze the situation of women. The twin convictions that personal problems arise out of the political organization of society and that private interaction and individual lifestyle choices have political import were captured in the women's liberation slogan, "the personal is political."[12]

These ideas presented a radical challenge to the premises of interest group politics. Interest group politics presumes that change occurs when organizations successfully change policy through representing a group that claims to be united and relatively homogeneous. Identity politics suggests that change occurs when individuals express their opinions or identities or when organizations create a context in which individual expression can occur. Meaningful change happens not only through top-down policy change, but also from the bottom up, through the creation of supportive conditions for individual self-expression.

Identity Politics and the Origins of Coming Out

The encounter between the established homophile movement and the ideas of the New Left produced gay liberation. Specifically, this encounter produced the new and successful strategy of coming out. Coming out was not simply a way of describing the public revelation of sexual identity; it was also an organizational and political strategy built upon the logic of identity politics. The preoccupation with authenticity and the belief in the political effectiveness of individual action transformed homophile ambivalence about identity into the proud, public assertion of gay identity. Consciousness-raising groups provided vehicles to assist in the individual and collective process of coming out. Homophiles, to the extent they endorsed the building of minority group identity, saw it as a means to an end, as necessary for the successful elimination of discriminatory policy. Gay liberationists, with authenticity the touchstone, saw the creation and visible display of gay identity as an end in and of itself.

The view that the encounter between the homophile movement and the New Left produced gay liberation leads to an understanding of the origins of the movement at odds with the conventional account. The conventional account identifies New York's Stonewall uprising of June 1969 as the trigger for a national gay liberation movement. The Stonewall story has become a "repeated and cherished" movement myth; it is neither an accurate description nor a compelling explanation of the origins of gay liberation.[13] Stonewall did not spark gay liberation in San Francisco, which had been under way for at least two months, perhaps considerably longer. The events surrounding the Stonewall Inn raid were barely acknowledged in San Francisco's homosexual press in 1969.

The interactions between homophile organizations and the New Left that produced gay liberation occurred simultaneously in several urban areas in the late 1960s. Chapter 2 traced the beginnings of the encounter between the homophile movement and the New Left in San Francisco and the resulting increase in concern among homophile activists about psychological issues of self-esteem and authenticity. Historians are accumulating evidence of other forms of New Left influence on homosexual organizations pre-Stonewall. Susan Stryker dates the origins of gay liberation in San Francisco to 1966, both because of an event that paralleled the Stonewall Inn riots and because of the existence of an organization called Vanguard. In August 1966, street queens who frequented Compton's Cafeteria in San Francisco's Tenderloin "broke out the windows, began throwing dishes and trays at the police, and burned down a nearby newsstand" in response to police harassment.[14] Founded in 1966, Vanguard engaged in outreach to gay youth of the Tenderloin. Its statement of purpose reads:

> Vanguard is an organization for the youth of the Tenderloin attempting to get for its citizens a sense of dignity and responsibility too long denied. We of Vanguard find our civil liberties imperiled by a hostile social order in which all difference from the usual in behavior is attacked. We find our rights as human beings scorned and ridiculed. We are forced to accept an unwarranted guilt which is more the product of "society's" hypocrisy than scientific fact. We have fi-

nally realized that we can only change these processes through the strength we develop through our own efforts. Vanguard is determined to change these conditions through organization and action.[15]

Stryker argues that this organization of young gay hustlers marks the beginnings of gay liberation in San Francisco for three reasons. Vanguard's style and militancy bore a distinctive New Left stamp; it defined itself in opposition to established homophile organizations; and it used the term "gay."[16] The existence of Vanguard casts serious doubt on the Stonewall origins story and supports the view that gay liberation grew out of the interaction of the homophile movement and the New Left. However, Vanguard's impact on the homosexual movement as a whole was limited. Vanguard did not challenge, at least not successfully, the claims of the established homophile movement to speak in the interests of homosexuals in general and received little coverage in San Francisco's dominant homosexual newspaper, the *Vector*, in the late 1960s. It is also unclear whether Vanguard advocated the public revelation of sexual identity as a strategy for political change.

Leo Laurence, a young Bay Area homosexual, returned from the 1968 Democratic convention in Chicago with ambitions to radicalize homosexual organizing in San Francisco. Laurence did not immediately form a new organization to pursue this goal. Instead, he attempted to use the established Society for Individual Rights to influence the tenor of homosexual organizing. He began his campaign by publishing a piece in the *Vector* in January 1969 entitled "My Boss Knows: Gay-Is-Good at Work, Too!" He asserted pride in an open gay identity: "At work, they now know that I'm a homosexual, and frankly, I feel more like a man than ever before because of it."[17] Laurence had clearly departed from homophile waffling about public revelation. To increase his influence over the content of SIR's publication, Laurence ran for and won the position of *Vector* editor in early 1969. He edited the March and April issues of the *Vector* that year, but was removed from the position before he could edit the May issue.[18] While Laurence was on thin ice due to his general radicalism and his stance about public revelation, what incensed SIR's officers was a piece in the April *Vector* entitled "Gay Revolution." Laurence claimed that

> timid leaders with enormous ego-trips, middle-class bigotry and racism, and too many middle-aged uptight conservatives are hurting almost every major homosexual organization on the West Coast and probably throughout the nation. . . . Most of them are their own worst enemy, afraid to become militant, afraid to put personal conviction behind their hypocritical mouthings that Gay-Is-Good.[19]

In this piece, Laurence used his position as *Vector* editor to attack the organization publishing the magazine! This attack began what would quickly escalate into a full-scale battle between young "gayrevs" and the homophile establishment.

In March 1969 the *Berkeley Barb* published a photo displaying a bare-chested Gale Whittington embraced by his lover, Leo Laurence, accompanied by a story about their relationship[20] (figure 3.1). The photograph and article got Whittington fired from his position as a file clerk with States Steamship Lines.[21] Unsuccessful at radicalizing SIR, and with a grievance to protest, Laurence and Whittington formed the Committee for Homosexual Freedom. On April 9, 1969, the Committee for Homosexual Freedom, "made up of hippie-radical young gays, some of them also SIR members," began picketing the States Steamship Lines' headquarters.[22]

Gayrevs continued to challenge homophile organizations. On October 15, 1969, the Committee for Homosexual Freedom "liberated" a Society for Individual Rights meeting on the grounds that on the day of the Vietnam War Moratorium, SIR should have focused on antiwar activities.[23] Explaining the need to liberate SIR to the *San Francisco Free Press,* a gayrev stated:

> The Society for Individual Rights, also known as the Society for Idle Rap, is a goodgrey organization dedicated to total integration within the establishment and to the proposition that, with a little help from a haircut and a suit and tie, all men can look equal. Passing for straight is SIR's ideal, and "Really, You don't look it" the highest compliment it can receive. . . . SIR is the gay establishment, and as such an obstacle to the Gay Liberation Movement's construction of an alternative that truly serves and liberates its people.[24]

A photograph of a gay liberationist burning his SIR card accompanied the *San Francisco Free Press* article describing the liberation of the SIR meeting (see figure 3.2). This act and its photographic documentation reveal both the theatrical style of gay liberation and its antipathy toward its predecessor. Gayrevs continued attacking the "gay establishment" in the *Berkeley Barb* and the *San Francisco Free Press* throughout 1969.

The Committee for Homosexual Freedom departed from the homophile movement in three key ways, all evident in Laurence's comments quoted above: in the willingness to go public with sexual identity, in a generational divide characterized by antagonism toward the homophile movement, and in a commitment to New Left politics. These younger activists had direct experience in the civil rights movement, the student movement, the

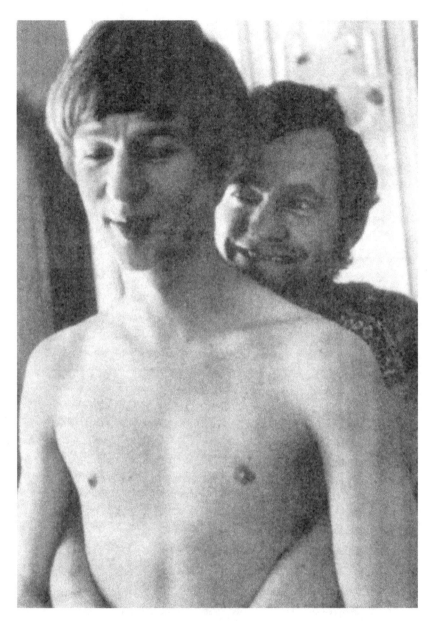

Figure 3.1 In March 1969 the *Berkeley Barb* published this photograph of Gale Whittington and Leo Laurence. The photo and the accompanying article provoked the firing of Whittington (left) from his job at the States Steamship Company in San Francisco; the Committee for Homosexual Freedom was formed to protest the firing. *Berkeley Barb*, March 1969.

Figure 3.2 In October 1969, gay liberationist Pat Brown burned his Society for Individual Rights membership card. *San Francisco Free Press*, November 1, 1969.

women's movement, or the counterculture. While the homophile movement had observed the 1960s from a distance, carefully selecting which ideas
to incorporate and which to reject, this new cohort saw itself as part of the
New Left.[25]

Gay lib was intensely aware of the homophile movement, defining its de-
struction as one of its goals. The relationship between the two approaches
had a familial quality to it. The youthful gayrevs accused homophile activists
of being middle-aged, while the homophile activists retaliated with accusations of immaturity.[26] Gayrevs relied on homophile politics as a starting
point, both ideologically and organizationally. Without being consciously
aware of it, gayrevs took for granted the key idea of the homophile movement—that same-gender sexual attraction was sufficiently salient as a dimension of human experience to form a base for a minority group identity.
They were unaware that it was homophile activism that had made this
course of action seem so obvious and inevitable. Gay liberation activists
also wanted to control the organizations the homophile movement had so
laboriously created. These organizations, with their access to an organized
homosexual constituency, were an invaluable resource that gay liberationists wanted to appropriate.

As is evident above, gay liberationists experienced their willingness to go
public as distinguishing them from homophile activists. Scholars have typically defined coming out as the *essential* difference between the homophile
movement and gay liberation.[27] The willingness to go public *was* a sharp and
important rupture. That the homophile movement had no expression to refer to the revelation of homosexual identity to heterosexuals suggests the
magnitude of this shift. Before gay liberation, coming out referred to the
revelation of homosexuality to in-group members. George Chauncey, in his
exhaustively researched book on the New York gay world before World War
II, documented that

> like much of campy gay terminology, "coming out" was an arch play
> on the language of women's culture—in this case the expression
> used to refer to the ritual of a debutante's being formally introduced
> to, or "coming out" into, the society of her cultural peers. . . . A gay
> man's coming out originally referred to his being formally presented
> to the largest collective manifestation of prewar gay society, the enor-
> mous drag balls that were patterned on the debutante and masquer-
> ade balls of the dominant culture and were regularly held in New
> York, Chicago, New Orleans, Baltimore, and other cities.[28]

"Coming out" was used this way in San Francisco as late as the June 1970 issue of the *Vector:*

> Have you come out yet? I mean, have you ever been formally pre-
> sented? Well, here is your chance to be introduced socially in the
> grand manner befitting a Hillsborough debutante. . . . This is the gay
> community's counterpart to the debutante balls in which young
> maidens are formally introduced to society for the first time.[29]

Before 1970, the expression "coming out" was also used in the homosexual community to refer to one's first same-gender sexual experience.[30] Gay
liberation activists *deliberately* changed the meaning of the term, remaking
what was once a private act into a public one. The self-consciousness involved in the transformation of the meaning of this expression is indicated in
an interview with gay liberation activists on the Dick Cavett show on November 27, 1971:

> We've a phrase called "coming out"—gay people, when they first re-
> alize that they're gay, have a process of coming out, that is, com-
> ing out sexually. We've extended that to the political field. We feel
> that we *have* to come out politically, as a community which is aware
> that it is oppressed and which is a political power bloc feared by the
> government. Until the government is afraid of us—afraid of our
> power—we will never have our rights.[31]

By mid-1969 gay liberationists in both New York and San Francisco used
"coming out" in this new way.[32] The usage of the term pioneered by gay liberation has become so commonly accepted that it seems like it was always part
of American vocabulary.

Despite the importance of this break, scholars have written surprisingly
little about what it was about this moment that made the crucial shift, unthinkable even a few years before, suddenly possible. Accounts are usually descriptive—gay liberation created coming out and it was important—rather
than analytical. Given the importance of coming out to contemporary gay
politics, it is important to develop a deeper analysis of how and why this new
strategy emerged when it did. Why did the homophile position on public exposure suddenly seem so timid and hypocritical? How was such an abrupt
change on the issue of public exposure possible? What was it about participation in the New Left that led this new cohort of activists to view the issue with
such different eyes?

The answer lies in the way the New Left changed the cultural context in which individuals assessed the costs and benefits of public exposure. Coming out emerged when individuals (like Leo Laurence) had exposure to *both* the New Left and the established homophile movement. The heightened concern with personal authenticity characteristic of the New Left made privacy about sexual identity seem obviously unhealthy and dishonest, and exposure of sexual identity clearly therapeutic. Unaware that the very meaning of sexual privacy had been transformed, the new cohort of activists simply assumed they were more committed and courageous than earlier ones.

Gay liberation activists spoke about public revelation in a markedly different way than had homophile activists. In language typical of the era, gay lib activist Gale Whittington explained the price of concealing sexual identity: "Liberation will come when total honesty is no longer repressed. Anything less than total honesty is slavery."[33] That he equated secrecy with "slavery" reveals the high value placed on personal authenticity. Activist Lois Hart described her personal experience in the first issue of *Come Out!*:

> There is no question that you will feel more whole and happier when you can be who you are all of the time. This is no easy thing, I know. It took me until age 32 to finally give in to myself and though it felt at the time that I was losing everything (the good opinion and sanction of this society from my family right on up to any career dreams I have had), I have in truth gained the whole world. I feel at a loss to convey to you right now what that means. I can just say that I have never felt better in my life. I know now in retrospect that I only began to be really alive when I was able to take that step.[34]

In similar fashion, another gay liberation leader explained, "There came a point when I just stopped running. I wasn't going to flee from my tormenters anymore. I turned and faced them—stood my ground—and told them to go fuck themselves! Man, that was like breathing for the first time!"[35] Individuals who had come out and experienced it in a positive way began to offer up their stories. Coming out stories, which have become a genre of fiction and biography, have the twin goals of further healing the author by providing a forum for coming out and persuading others to follow in their footsteps by providing evidence of the psychological rewards of doing so.[36]

Flowing from the preoccupation with authenticity among New Leftists was a deep concern about the psychological dimensions of oppression. In 1972, gay liberationist Martha Shelley argued that poor self-esteem resulting from secrecy was worse than the repression that exposure sometimes provoked:

> Understand this—that the worst part of being a homosexual is hav-
> ing to keep it *secret.* Not the occasional murders by police or teenage
> queer-beaters, not the loss of jobs or expulsion from schools or dis-
> honorable discharge—but the daily knowledge that what you are is
> so awful that it cannot be revealed.[37]

In the homophile calculus, threats of arrest, violence, and loss of employment had been seen as far more serious than the psychological consequences
of secrecy. By intensifying the emphasis on authenticity and psychological
welfare, the identity logic suddenly reversed the calculus. The costs of concealing identity suddenly seem much greater than the possible costs of revealing it. This shift happened much too rapidly to be accounted for by
changes in the actual risks associated with public revelation.

If secrecy was the problem, the solution was visibility. Thus, visibility became a primary goal of gay liberation. The New Left valorized individual political resistance and conceived of individual political action as effective. In
this context, coming out was not simply something one should do for psychological health but was conceived of as a highly effective political act. Every
person who came out improved life for all other gay people. Remaining
"closeted" then logically indicated not only poor mental health but also a
cowardly betrayal of one's gay brothers and sisters. This perspective is evident
in this passage from Carl Wittman's "Gay Manifesto": "To pretend to be
straight sexually, or to pretend to be straight socially, is probably the most
harmful pattern of behavior in the ghetto. If we are liberated we are open
with our sexuality. Closet queenery must end. Come out."[38]

Coming out was, by definition, an act of self-assertion and pride. Being
forced to be secretive caused psychological damage. Coming out repaired this
damage and produced pride. Gay activists borrowed the language of pride
from the New Left. Black power, in particular, provided a model of the affirmation of cultural values at odds with the mainstream. San Francisco activist Charles Thorp encouraged homosexuals to imitate blacks in the assertion of pride in identity:

> The Negroes are saying "I'm Black and I'm proud" and saying it loud.
> Also they say "Black is Beautiful" and it is beauty! Well, what are our
> people saying? Inside I know I'm saying, "I'm a Homosexual and I'm
> Proud." And for me "Male is Beautiful." What is the rest of the com-
> munity saying?[39]

Gay liberationists urged people to identify as "gay" rather than as "homosexual." Charles Thorp, in his keynote speech for the National Gay Liber-

ation Front student conference held in San Francisco in August 1970, justified the change of labels:

> So let me say a little about "Gay" as opposed to "Homosexual." They are opposites. . . . Those who say they like the word Homosexual better than Gay say in essence they accept our sick-psychiatrist friends' definition of us. They also miss out on the difference between the words. Homosexual is a straight concept of us as sexual. Therefore, we are in a sexual category and become a sexual minority and are dealt with in this way legally, socially, economically, and culturally . . . rather than an ethnic group, a people! But the word Gay has come to mean (by street usage) a life style in which we are not just sex machines; when something goes wrong it is not blamed on our sexuality alone. We are whole entities.[40]

Gay liberationists saw "gay" as positive, self-defined, and nonapologetic. The term "homosexual" was seen as negative and externally defined.[41] This paralleled the rejection of "negro" in favor of "black" in the black movement. Thorp's insistence that gay identity refers to "an ethnic group, a people" shows that the notion of homosexuals as a "minority group," developed and debated within the homophile movement, was core to the creation of gay identity.

Women's liberation and gay liberation developed new organizational forms ideally suited to furthering the goals of building and displaying gay identity. Undoing the damage inflicted by mainstream society could not always be accomplished alone, by an individual, simply by proclaiming one's identity. Support groups provided a forum for gay people to gather to work through the shame and fear that had prevented them from being able to come out. These groups helped individuals construct gay identities and provided recognition and affirmation of those identities. In 1970, one man described the need for consciousness-raising groups in this way:

> I need to be together with other Gay men. We have not been together—we've not had enough self-respect for that. Isolated sex and then look for another partner. Enough of that, that's where we've been. Let's go somewhere else. Let's go somewhere where we value each other as more than a hunk of meat. We need to recognize one another wherever we are, start talking to each other. . . . We need consciousness-raising groups and communes. Our Gay souls have nearly been stomped to death in that desert called America. If we are to bloom, we can only do it together.[42]

This passage reveals the belief that simply being with other gay men, away from the values of mainstream society, was therapeutic. The emphasis on self-respect and recognition again reveals the focus on individual psychological welfare.

Gay liberationists saw identity as the goal—not as something that was easily known, but rather as something developed and elaborated through a process of collective discovery. As the Gay Liberation Front declared:

> [Consciousness-raising] provides a format in which this potential can develop and operate. We use it to discover our identity as gay men, to recognize our oppression in a straight society, and to seek a collective solution to mutual problems. We as gays must redefine ourselves in our own terms, from our own heads and experience because no political philosophy designed by white heterosexual men can be adequate for us.[43]

This passage reveals a belief in the value of homogeneous spaces and a rejection of expert knowledge in favor of knowledge produced through collective analysis of experience. These organizations required participants to bring the entirety of their selves to the organization, with the expectation that the organization would respond by recognizing and affirming all aspects of the self.

Consciousness-raising groups, which evolved into contemporary support groups, were based on fundamentally different premises than interest group organizations. Interest group organizations represent a group of individuals and see themselves as effective insofar as they change policy or public opinion. Support groups do not attempt to represent the interests of a group, but rather to provide a forum for *individuals* to express themselves. As such, they are effective insofar as they help individuals in the process of discovery, affirmation, and expression of identity.

Belief in the therapeutic value of homogeneous groups leads logically to *identity credentialing*. Identity credentialing is the practice of requiring a particular identity for membership in an organization. Identity credentialing in gay liberation groups is in direct contrast to the practice of homophile groups, which actively sought out heterosexual members. At the 1969 Eastern Regional Conference of Homophile Organizations (ERCHO) Gay Liberation Front members expressed outrage that Madolin Cervantes, the heterosexual treasurer of the Mattachine Society of New York, was being permitted to participate.[44] Complaints about heterosexual participation were unthinkable before the emergence of gay liberation and the logic of identity politics.

The New York gay liberation group Homosexuals Intransigent! not only required gay identity for membership, but also "that its members, in order to gain the right to vote in club decisions, acknowledge their homosexuality to any questioner at any time."[45] At the 1970 North American Conference of Homophile Organizations (NACHO) conference in San Francisco, gay liberation activists turned the homophile convention upside down by rejecting the elaborate system homophiles used to determine who was allowed to attend and vote at the convention. This bureaucratic system apportioned votes to delegates from around the country empowered to represent particular organizations. In contrast, a young gay activist asserted that no member of the "oppressed class" should be excluded from decision making on movement matters. The young gay liberationist argued,

> Look, that man out there won't let you in because you're gay. You don't qualify for his job, his church, his bar, or even the use of his streets—because you suck cock! Then don't tell me I can't vote because I didn't pay your dues or meet your fuckin' standards. Being human gives me the right to vote. My credentials are being gay![46]

As at the earlier ERCHO conference, the participation of heterosexuals was again called into question. In this case, according to Humphreys, "one heterosexual woman, long active in the homophile movement, was called a 'fag hag' and told to 'shut up.' There was extended discussion about whether straights should be allowed to participate in the meetings."[47]

Coming out proved to be a brilliant strategy for the creation of an ever-expanding gay minority group. Initially, gay liberation offered a culturally resonant combination of promises (of psychological health), appeals (to responsibility to others), and threats (of being stigmatized as a closet queen) that were more compelling to gay liberationists than the quite real risk of loss of friends, family, and employment. But the need for these promises, appeals, and threats rapidly diminished. As more people came out, the benefits of joining a vibrant community increased and the risk of repression decreased. By creating a critical mass of out gay people, gay liberation created a self-generating process. John D'Emilio describes the generative, escalating effects of visibility: "Visible lesbians and gay men, moreover, served as magnets that drew others to us. Coming out quickly captured the imagination of tens of thousands, perhaps hundreds of thousands of lesbians and gay men. A mass movement was born almost overnight."[48] While many people came out simply because of a desire to belong to a community, those who developed public gay identities made themselves vulnerable to further political recruitment. As D'Emilio explains:

Coming out also became the key strategy for building a mass movement. When gay women and men came out, we crossed a critical di-
viding line. We relinquished our invisibility, made ourselves vulnerable to attack, and became personally invested in the success of the
movement in a way that mere adherence to a political line could
never accomplish.[49]

In his history of gay liberation, Toby Marotta indicated that activists were
quite aware that "homosexuals who were 'out' would be most inclined to
support gay political organizations and to become conscientious members of
a gay political bloc."[50] Coming out was thus a political strategy that created
issues around which to protest. By bringing discrimination to the surface, gay
activists could actually provoke repression, thus putting the pace and timing
of protest activity in their hands. No longer did they have to wait for straight
institutions to act, and then to react in a defensive way.

In addition to coming out and consciousness-raising groups, gay liberation also pioneered the "zap." Zaps were carefully staged, often highly theatrical, political confrontations. They "combined consciousness-raising tactics
with politicizing and pressuring tactics."[51] Zaps were particularly useful in
targeting the media, which were seen as crucial players in shaping gay identity but difficult to attack politically. The goals were to vividly reveal the antigay attitudes of individual politicians or corporations and to insert a positive
gay perspective into public view. While policy change was desirable, visibility
was the primary goal. For example, in response to antigay remarks made on
the Dick Cavett show, activists demanded equal time on the show. Activists
forced the issue by threatening to disrupt taping of the program. When it became evident that Gay Activists Alliance activists would do just that, Cavett
agreed to let two GAA members appear on the show.[52]

Another example of an early zap was organized by the GAA in New York
in response to an offensive September 1970 *Harper's* article by Joseph Epstein.[53]
The goal of the GAA members organizing the zap was "to make an impres-
sion not only on *Harper's* but on the whole literary establishment, and to win
the support of homosexuals, liberals, and others sensitive about freedom of
the press."[54] After *Harper's* refused to publish a rebuttal to Epstein, the GAA
organized a sit-in at *Harper's* on October 27. The activists set up a table serving
coffee and doughnuts in the reception area, leafleted every desk, and introduced themselves to *Harper's* employees saying, "Good morning, I'm a homosexual. We're here to protest the Epstein article. Would you like some coffee?"[55] The zap as a political strategy was made thinkable by an identity

political logic—it required activists to be able to see broadening of the range of cultural expression as a political goal.

Gay liberation created a new arsenal of political strategies—the zap, coming out, and conscious-raising groups. These new ways of doing politics became thinkable when the pursuit of authenticity became defined as a fundamental task of progressive social change.

Conflict between the New Left and the Homophile Movement, 1969–1970

The New Left also involved an economic critique of capitalism. Many New Left activists believed class, race, and gender oppression were connected and that a revolutionary movement of all oppressed people could transform the system. As part of the New Left, gay liberationists applied this politics of redistribution to the oppression of homosexuals. That the New Left introduced homosexual activists to multiple, contradictory ways to think about political change was a result of the tremendous cultural vibrancy of the times. But while this feeling of infinite possibility was conducive to cultural creativity, it also made it difficult for activists to choose among the options. Without a clear way of assessing the limits of the possible, people disagreed about how to proceed. The presence of multiple, contradictory logics within gay liberation, illustrated in the epigraph of this chapter, produced conflict between homophile and gay liberation politics, as well as paralyzing conflict within gay liberation itself. The multi-issue redistributive aspect of gay liberation was at odds with the reform-minded single-issue interest group politics of the homophile movement. Thus, while coming out was the defining contribution of gay liberation, it was not the point of greatest conflict between the homophile movement and gay liberation.

As we saw in chapter 2, the homophile movement was a doggedly single-issue movement. It concerned itself with the pursuit of homosexual rights. While ambivalent about the issue of public revelation, the homophile movement had no doubt about who it was working for—those individuals interested in same-gender sexual relations. The strategy of coming out, which encouraged people to publicly claim a gay identity, was consistent with the homophile vision of the relevant constituency.

But the radical gay power aspect of gay liberation rejected single-issue politics. Gayrevs viewed the oppression of homosexuals as only one of the many forms of oppression that would be overcome with the toppling of "this rotten, dirty, vile, fucked-up capitalist conspiracy."[56] They believed that socialist revolution would be achieved if all the oppressed worked in concert. Allen Young wrote, "Gay liberation . . . has a perspective for revolution based on the unity of all oppressed people—that is, there can be no freedom for gays in a society which enslaves others through male supremacy, racism and economic exploitation."[57] Gayrev activists supported other New Left causes, sometimes viewing the concerns of other groups as of higher priority than gay issues.[58] They believed that mobilizing against homophobia within the New Left was an important first step. Activist Bernard Lewis proclaimed in the New York Gay Liberation Front's publication *Come Out!* "that only in getting our rightful place in the movement and demanding an end to our oppression can we ever really make changes for homosexuals."[59] The term "gayrev" itself suggested the split loyalties of gay liberationists—they were both "gay" and "revolutionary."

Homophile activists were horrified by the prospect of throwing the energies of the gay movement behind other causes. From the fall of 1969 through the spring of 1970, the *Vector* was riddled with angry attacks on gay liberation and careful attempts by homophiles to distinguish their position from that of gay liberation.[60] Homophiles argued that commitment to other causes was misguided. They feared that homosexual concerns would be lost, that other movements would not return the support, and that a commitment to multiple issues would split homosexuals. They saw homosexuals as a very diverse group and felt that they could not be expected to agree on issues other than homosexual rights. In January 1970, the *Vector* reiterated SIR's commitment to an exclusive focus on homosexual issues:

> There is a developing determined and very vocal viewpoint that the homosexual movement must be "radicalized." This position holds that the best way to accomplish the goals of the homophile movement (respect from society and equal treatment and opportunities under the law) is to align the homophile movement with the New Left or with the Radical Movement. This position holds that homosexuals as homosexuals and homosexual organizations as representatives of the homosexual community should take stands on issues such as abortion, capital punishment, draft resistance, Vietnam, the Grape Boycott, student strikes, and so called "militant" political activity. This position is in dramatic opposition to what is the traditional position of S.I.R. namely that S.I.R. is a one issue organization limiting itself to a concern for the welfare and rights of the homosexual as a homosexual.[61]

The tendency of some gay liberationists to take a position on every issue of the day was mocked in a September 30, 1970, cartoon in the *Advocate* (figure 3.3).

The conflict about relations with other movements was related to conflict over strategy. The homophile movement firmly believed that homosexual rights could be achieved through interest group politics. It believed in American political institutions and was firmly committed to working within those institutions to extend to homosexuals the rights granted to other groups within a liberal democracy. In contrast, gayrevs saw working within mainstream institutions as futile and contaminating[62] and were even sometimes willing to condone violent means to achieving political ends.[63] While gay liberationists did not usually participate in violent efforts to destabilize

Figure 3.3 "Aren't you guys jumping on the wrong bandwagon?" Cartoon by Buckshot, *Advocate*, September 30, 1970.

the government, they were often dismissive of homophile efforts to reform existing institutions.

The inflammatory rhetoric of gayrevs provoked bouts of virulent anticommunism from homophiles, such as in a letter by Perry George in the *Vector*: "I believe that this Gay Bolshivik [*sic*] Baby must be crushed in the cradle [*sic*]. . . . We must completely denounce the sillyness [*sic*] of the homosexuals' place in a community revolution and get down to serious work."[64] Homophile activists devoted a great deal of space in the *Vector* in late 1969 and 1970 to denounce the use of violence to advance the agenda of homosexuals. They found the gay power conviction that socialist revolution would eliminate discrimination against homosexuals to be ludicrous. They pointed to existing communist countries, which were venerated by the New Left, as evidence that the institutions of American society allowed for more civil liberties than communist societies:

> These "Gayrevs" will hold up such sterling examples of social equality as Castro's Cuba or Maoist China and say this is what homosexuals must work for. These people are either too young, too stupid, or most likely a combination of both and are unaware of history. The facts art [*sic*] clear that no country under Communist rule can boast of furthering the position of the homosexual since that government forms [*sic*] inception.[65]

Gay liberation was not simply an extension of the homophile vision; it rejected fundamental homophile premises. It challenged homophile notions of both who should be the beneficiaries of a movement (just homosexuals or all oppressed people) and how the movement should proceed (through interest group politics, identity politics, or revolution).

The Victory of Gay Liberation?

Initially it appeared that gay liberation had vanquished the homophile movement. In 1970, the *Advocate* reported on "the battle that ended the homophile movement." Since 1966, the major homophile organizations of the country had been meeting annually in various cities around the country as the North American Conference of Homophile Organizations (NACHO).[66] San Francisco hosted the final annual NACHO convention in August 1970. Following hard on the heels of the first National Student Gay Liberation Conference, this conference was an irresistible target for gayrevs. Rob Cole, a reporter for the *Advocate,* described the clash as follows:[67]

Gay Liberation and the homophile movement met head-on at the 1970 convention of the North American Conference of Homophile Organizations at the Society for Individual Rights Center here August 25–28.

The result was a bruised, battered, and radically altered NACHO, a little better understanding of the radical young by some of the older homophile leaders, a great deal of ill will, and a series of resolutions supporting the Black Panthers, Women's Liberation, and "all oppressed people," and calling for an immediate American withdrawal from Vietnam.

An invasion by Gay Lib demonstrators near the end of the convention brought a threat to call the police. The demonstrators withdrew at that point but wound up in virtual control of the convention anyway.[68]

After the conference, Rev. Jim Rankin published a eulogy for the homophile movement in Berkeley's *Gay Sunshine* magazine:

This was the battle that ended the homophile movement. It began twenty or more years ago, it produced men and women of great stature, it had its martyrs, it made possible to a large degree everything that a new movement is going to do. It was a noble thing. We respect it. We love those who were a part of it. They were brave and strong when it was difficult. We fear having to match their stature in our own situations. But it is now time to move on, and the ground rules and basic assumptions of that movement are no longer acceptable or effective.[69]

Rankin was one of the few who, at the time, recognized the debt of gay liberation to the homophile movement. His observation that the "ground rules and basic assumptions" had changed was remarkably insightful.

The organizational record confirms that 1968 was the last year that all the public homosexual organizations founded considered themselves homophile (see figure 1.2). Gay liberation organizations accounted for virtually all of the public homosexual organizations formed in 1969 (see table 3.1). Gay liberation organizations, such as the Committee for Homosexual Freedom, San Francisco Gay Free Press, the Gay Liberation Front (of which there were at least two incarnations), the Institute for Homosexual Freedom, Free Particle, and San Francisco Gay Women's Liberation, were ephemeral, short-lived, and hard to document. In sharp contrast to the tight rein homophile organizations had over the activities and events of the homophile movement, gay

Table 3.1 Homophile, Gay Liberation, and Gay Identity Organizations Founded in San Francisco, 1968–71

Year	Homophile	Gay Liberation	Gay Identity	Total
1968	3 (100)	0 (0)	0 (0)	3
1969	0 (0)	5 (100)	0 (0)	5
1970	0 (0)	5 (45)	6 (55)	11
1971	2 (20)	2 (20)	6 (60)	10

Note: Percentages are in parentheses.

liberation events and energies were only loosely associated with organizational carriers.

In summary, gay liberation was born out of the encounter between an established homophile movement and the New Left. In 1970, gay liberation was energized by a powerful new politics of visibility, but it was also committed to participation in the broader New Left alliance. The homophile vision of a narrow, single-issue movement in pursuit of rights also remained viable. Allen Young, in the 1971 passage used as the epigraph of this chapter, endorsed interest group, identity, and redistributive political logics in a single passage, when he defined gay liberation as being about civil rights, coming out, and revolution. These three distinct logics manifested themselves not only within single organizations, but also within individuals. This highly unstable combination would cohere for less than a year. By the end of 1971 radical gay liberation would be in decline, along with the rest of the New Left. Chapter 4 explains how gay organizing survived this sudden retraction in political opportunities.

FOUR

Opportunity: Gay Liberation and the Decline of the New Left, 1969–1973

Out of the decay of the New Left came the modern feminist and gay liberation movements.

Barry D. Adam, *The Rise of a Gay and Lesbian Movement* (1987)

Gay liberation in 1969 and 1970 had an effervescent quality. Ideas spread rapidly, capturing imaginations all over the country. Gay liberation organizations sprung up everywhere. Activists on both coasts documented their expansive vision of human possibility, producing collections of movement writings that still quicken the pulse. Members of the Bay Area's Gay Liberation Theatre claimed that for some the movement was "a way of life, for others life itself."[1] Radical gay liberationists saw revolution as imminent, participated in antiwar demonstrations, and aligned themselves against racism and sexism.[2] But this moment of effervescence was brief. By the end of 1971 it was over. Gay liberation organizations had disappeared, as had the term "gayrev." But the gay movement was far from dead. Activists began creating gay organizations of every imaginable kind.

Given the rapid decline of the New Left in 1970–1971, the decline of gay liberation is not surprising. Gay liberation saw itself as part of the New Left. Indeed, the New Left provided the context in which gay liberation made sense. In 1971, with the New Left in decline, it would have been reasonable to predict that the gay movement would self-destruct through factionalization or that it would hold on to an improbable political vision and produce a small, marginalized movement. Indeed, some observers at the time expected the decline of the New Left to end gay organizing. Sociologist Laud Humphreys, observing at close range, was prepared to pronounce the end of gay organizing in 1971.[3]

How gay organizing survived the decline of the New Left has not been adequately explained. From the perspective of the present, the dynamism of the gay movement in the 1970s appears so natural as to seem inevitable. Scholars and activists have forgotten that at the time the fate of the movement was not certain. To the extent that the survival of the movement has been explained, it has been treated as an inevitable moderation of political ambitions in a political climate growing more conservative. When the decline of the New Left destroyed the plausibility of the idea that the United States was on the brink of revolution, gay activists assessed the new environment and moderated their political ambitions. Gay pride and gay rights survived because they were viable in the new, more conservative, context. This explanation, however, does not account for why the gay movement was able to successfully moderate its ambitions while other parts of the New Left imploded.

The task of this chapter then is to explain how the gay movement survived the decline of the New Left. The answer to this puzzle lies with the contradictions internal to gay liberation discussed in the previous chapter. The rapid decline of the New Left eliminated the credibility of a redistributive political logic without undermining the viability of interest group and identity politics. The presence of multiple logics meant that viable alternatives to the revolutionary gay power strand of the gay liberation movement existed before and during the decline of the New Left. In fact, the rapidity of the ideological pruning energized the gay movement by reducing internal conflict. The first section of the chapter documents the rapidity of the decline of the New Left, while the second delves more deeply into the multiple political logics of gay liberation. The third section shows how, before the New Left crumbled, conflict among gay pride, gay power, and gay rights threatened to paralyze gay liberation. The fourth section explains why gay activists rapidly abandoned gay power (redistributive politics) in favor of gay rights (interest group politics) and gay pride (identity politics) strategies.

Instead of assuming that a change in opportunities naturally produces a successful adjustment in movement frames, this argument challenges conventional wisdom by suggesting that a movement's ability to respond to a changing environment depends not only on the *nature* of the change in opportunities, but also on the *way* the change occurs. I suggest that actors may interpret changes in opportunities differently, depending on whether the change in opportunities happens rapidly or slowly. The ability of movements to develop frames suitable to new circumstances cannot be simply assumed. While the expansion of political opportunities may encourage cultural creativity, retraction in opportunities may dampen it. Had a viable alternative to gay power not already existed within gay liberation, there was no guarantee it would have been generated in this moment of political crisis. The decline of the New Left might have led activists to cling to a gay power agenda. Thus, the creation of particularly appealing new political strategies within the New Left may have placed the gay movement in a better position to respond to a changing political environment than other parts of the New Left.

The Rapid Decline of the New Left

At the height of the 1960s, many movement activists believed the United States was on the verge of radical social change.[4] This optimism faded quickly as the 1960s came to a close. Scholars point to the 1968 election of Richard Nixon as a political turning point. Debra Minkoff writes, "The 1968 election of Richard Nixon signaled a turn away from the supportive political agendas associated with the Kennedy-Johnson [years], and as antiwar and student movements escalated, a period of intensive political retrenchment began."[5] By the early 1970s, it was clear that revolutionary change was not at all likely.

The Students for a Democratic Society (SDS) "burned up and out in a spectacular fashion" in 1969 and 1970.[6] Alice Echols notes that "the conventional sixties' story line," developed by white male leaders who have written on the New Left,[7] tends to equate the disintegration of SDS with the end of "radicalism," finalized by the February 1970 Greenwich Village townhouse explosion.[8] The Kent State University killings in May 1970 have also been seen as an important turning point.[9]

Feminists Wini Breines and Alice Echols deemphasize SDS in their accounts of the radicalism of the times and claim that male leaders exaggerated the importance of its demise.[10] Breines writes:

> What is overlooked in accounts that focus on the fate of SDS as an organization is the mass movement after 1968, regional and local activity not dependent upon a national organization, students organizing and grass-roots activists (including women and people of color), the counterculture, and the significance of the birth of other movements such as the women's liberation and gay movements.[11]

Echols argues, "If one's narrative is conceptualized around the idea that radicalism was simply played out by the decade's end, then there really is only token narrative space available for women's liberation (or for the Chicano, Native American, or gay and lesbian movements)."[12] Breines and Echols have a point. Radicalism did survive beyond 1970, but the demise of SDS in 1970 marked a fundamental shift in the nature of activism and the optimism associated with it. Activism shifted away from an effort to bring about a socialist transformation of society and from Marxist-influenced, class-oriented, redistributive politics.

While opportunities for some forms of political action contracted in the late 1960s and early 1970s, other opportunities began to expand. Debra Minkoff shows in her work on women's and racial-ethnic organizations that while it became more difficult to form and maintain protest organizations, the environment improved for more moderate service and policy advocacy organizations.[13] She argues that "the increasing efforts at 'law and order' during the Nixon administration and into 1980s did not so much repress collective action as channel it into more institutionally acceptable organizational activity."[14] Minkoff, drawing on the work of Jenkins[15] and Walker,[16] points to the improved "funding opportunities" for "interest groups and a broader range of policy advocacy organizations" in the 1970s.[17] Foundations increased their level of support for nonprofit organizing. "Congressional reforms that began in the early 1960s gradually decentralized authority, creating broader opportunities for nonprofit advocacy."[18] In 1969 and 1976 the tax deductibility of contributions to nonprofit organizations involved in political advocacy were liberalized.[19] McCarthy, Britt, and Wolfson describe the emergence of a "tangle of incentives" pushing movements toward nonprofit organizational forms.[20]

While more radical socialist ideologies lost their luster, the pursuit of ethnic group equality and civil rights remained viable. Together, the Civil Rights Act of 1964, the Voting Rights Act of 1965, and the Equal Employment Opportunity Act of 1972 enhanced the political utility of an ethnic self-characterization. An ethnic framing of gay identity and an orientation toward gay civil rights fits nicely with the structure of American politics.[21] Steven Epstein notes, "This 'ethnic' self-characterization by gays and lesbians has a clear political utility, for it has permitted a form of group organizing that is particularly suited to the American experience, with its history of civil-rights struggles and ethnic-based, interest-group competition."[22]

In addition, the cultural permissiveness introduced in the 1960s survived well into the 1970s. A revolution in the sexual mores of heterosexual Americans, particularly the young, was ongoing. The broader cultural focus on authenticity, therapy, self-actualization, and "doing your own thing" supported an acceptance of gay identity and lifestyle as one possible result of a search for a "true self."

The Competing Political Logics of Gay Liberation, 1969–1970

In 1969 and 1970 gay liberation was composed of three analytically distinct currents.[23] Gay power sought the overthrow of capitalism and the creation of a liberated society in which sexual identity categories would no longer be necessary. Gay power activists, who saw themselves as gay revolutionaries, fought for sexual liberation for all, not just rights for gay-identified people. This strain of gay liberation, organized around a redistributive political logic, was deeply indebted to the socialist ideas of the New Left. A second strain, which I refer to as gay pride, sought to achieve gay visibility and build a positive gay identity. The third current, inherited from the homophile movement, believed that the situation of gays could be improved through single-issue interest group politics seeking gay rights.

Gay power and gay pride disagreed on basic political premises. Gay power activists considered themselves revolutionaries first, gays second. They saw themselves as a vanguard, as part of a movement that would improve society for everyone, not just for a particular group. Everyone would benefit from sexual liberation and from race, class, and gender justice. In contrast, gay pride activists identified themselves primarily as gay and worked to improve life for gay people. Gay pride activists, while critical of capitalism, were never convinced that revolution was the answer. Indeed, they were often skeptical about how homosexuals would fare under socialism.[24] They believed in the reform of the current system and advocated working within mainstream institutions. Gay pride activists criticized gay power's attention to issues other than those of concern for homosexuals. They questioned whether other radicals would reciprocate and take up homosexual issues. Gay pride activists rejected violent means in favor of working within the political system and engaging in zaps.

While all gay liberationists endorsed coming out and the building of gay identity, gay power and gay pride disagreed about the role of coming out in the movement and the reasons for building gay identity. Gay pride endeavored to build gay culture and community through forming support groups and other kinds of gay organizations. In contrast, gay power activists did not see the affirmation of gay identity as the end goal of sexual politics. Gay power saw the creation of gay identity as merely a step toward the goal of getting rid of sexual identity categories altogether.[25] Gayrevs believed that "everyone is gay, everyone is straight," and that gay liberation should lead to "a far greater acceptance of human sexuality and with that . . . a decrease in the stigma attached to unorthodox sex and a corresponding increase in overt bisexuality."[26] Consequently, in their view "gay, in its most far-reaching sense, means not homosexual, but sexually free."[27] Dennis Altman describes the difference in the positions as follows: "The liberal sees homosexuals as a minority to be assisted into a full place in society. The radical sees homosexuality as a component of all people including her- or himself."[28] Gay power activists thought all revolutionaries should come out as gay, thus contributing to the blurring of sexual identity categories. Gay power suggests a strategic notion of identity—one based on political loyalty rather than on the discovery and revelation of deeply rooted sexual desires.

Gay power and gay pride also disagreed on gender politics and their attitudes toward the commercial subculture. As part of the cross-fertilization of ideas that occurred at this vibrant moment in American history, gay power activists were influenced by feminism. Gay power saw the situation of gay men in terms of gender-based oppression. They applied the feminist critique of male sexual objectification of women to the sexual objectification of men by other men. These gay radicals envisioned the reconstruction of male sexual desire in a way that was less objectifying. In their view, gay bars and the sexual subculture had a negative impact on gay men's sexuality. Their goal was to create new kinds of spaces for gay people to connect. These spaces would help gay men develop healthy friendships and relationships. They insisted that the movement "demand the complete negation of the use of gay bars, tearooms, trucks, baths, streets, and other traditional cruising institutions. They are exploitative institutions designed to keep gay men in the roles given to them by a male heterosexual system."[29] Gay power activists also criticized bars on the grounds that they were part of the capitalist system and, even worse, tended to profit organized crime rather than the gay community or individual gay capitalists. In contrast, gay pride activists recognized that the subculture had some less than positive features, but they were hesitant to criticize it, as they saw those who participated in it as their core constituents.

Paralyzing Conflict between Political Logics, 1969

These political logics did not coexist easily within gay liberation. Conflict among these approaches threatened to paralyze the movement. Late in 1969 the New Left was starting to unravel, but its fate was not yet clear. The uncertainty produced wildly conflicting assessments of political possibilities. Some still felt that revolutionary change was possible, while others had lost faith. Activists fought as much about their different visions of what was politically possible as about what was politically desirable. Conflicts between gay power and gay pride played themselves out in painful and divisive ways through the fall of 1969.

Whether gay liberation should support the Black Panthers proved to be a watershed issue on both coasts. In November of 1969, the Gay Liberation

Front (GLF) in New York agonized over this issue. Marotta describes the situation:

> When Bob Kohler proposed that the GLF contribute money to a bail fund for imprisoned Panther leaders, Robinson and Owles argued that the needs of homosexuals and their groups should take priority over the needs of other minorities and theirs. After GLF's general assembly spent three consecutive meetings trying to arrive at a consensus on the matter of Panther donations, [Robinson and Owles] insisted that a vote be taken so that important matters would no longer be delayed.[30]

During the first vote, the suggestion to support the Panthers was defeated. The following Sunday, a Panther sympathizer asked for a recount. The late arrival of a contingent of gay power women turned the vote in favor of the Panthers.[31] This bitter meeting produced a "hemorrhage" from the GLF.[32] Those who fled GLF formed a new organization, the Gay Activists Alliance, in December 1969. Kay Tobin explains that the founding document of the Gay Activists Alliance "was very carefully worked over because we were trying to build in all the safeguards, so that we wouldn't be co-opted and wouldn't fall apart—or fall into something different."[33] The founders of GAA wanted to prevent their efforts "from being impeded by those interested primarily in ideological debate, non-gay causes, or revolution."[34] Gay pride principles were stated in the preamble of the founding document, which, according to Marotta, "made the clearest statement yet of reformist gay liberationist ideals."[35] The splitting of the Gay Activists Alliance from the Gay Liberation Front meant that, as of late 1969 in New York, gay power and gay pride perspectives had distinct organizational homes.

Gay liberation on the west coast also faced the Black Panther issue. Gay liberationists participated in the November 15, 1969, March for Peace (see figure 4.1). According to the Right Reverend Michael Irkin this event revealed:

> a clear division in the ranks of the Homosexual Liberation Movement as represented by the Committee for Homosexual Freedom, the Gay Liberation Theatre, the Gay Liberation Front, and some other groups. [This] became clear to all during the rally at the Polo Grounds when, during the speech of David Hilliard of the Black Panther Party, dissension broke out when some of our members, among them the author of this article and some others under our banner, joined with other

Figure 4.1 GLF participated in the November 15, 1969, March for Peace under the banner "Homosexuals against the war." *San Francisco Free Press,* December 7, 1969. Courtesy GLBT Historical Society of Northern California.

pacifists in shouting down David Hilliard's speech with cries of "Peace, Now!" while others showed their support of his statements with clenched-fist salutes and cries of enthusiasm.[36]

Irkin, from a gay pride position, was critical of the Black Panther Party, while the gay power activists were enthusiastic supporters. Irkin felt that "under the pretense of speaking for peace, [Hilliard had] called for violence. . . . We cannot see that violence, in any man's hand, is any less violence."[37] In response, Irkin clarified the ideological differences internal to gay liberation:

> [The Committee for Homosexual Freedom] at present has among its members many who have not come to any particular socio-economic or political philosophy. While the majority of our members . . . call themselves socialists, I know personally of at least a few members who believe that capitalism should continue in some modified form.[38]

The Panther issue did not produce an organizational split in San Francisco. Activists did not need a new organization to represent the gay pride position. Instead, the still vital Society for Individual Rights evolved in the direction of a gay pride position.

Gay pride activists wanted to build gay versions of cultural and political organizations typical of traditional ethnic communities.[39] Taken to extremes, this perspective suggested gay nationalism. Don Jackson presented his vision at the Berkeley gay liberation conference of December 28, 1969:

> I have a recurring daydream. I imagine a place where gay people can be free. A place where there is no job discrimination, police harassment or prejudice. . . . A place where a gay government can build the base for a flourishing gay counter-culture and city. . . . It would mean gay territory. It would mean a gay government, a gay civil service, a county welfare department which made public assistance payments to the refugees from persecution and prejudice.[40]

California's Alpine County, population 165, was selected for takeover. The Alpine County takeover ultimately failed, due both to practical difficulties (e.g., midwinter temperatures often reached twenty degrees below zero) and lack of support. But some gays purchased property and moved to Alpine.[41] Gay power vociferously objected to the Alpine County takeover, viewing it as giving up on the revolution. The Red Butterfly cell of New York GLF articulated gay power antagonism to the plan: "Gay nationalism will not be the answer to ending the oppression of gay people. It only satisfies the part of our oppression that deals with working in the present system. Gay nationalism's goals are to be oppressed like every other minority in Amerikkka today."[42] Separatism contradicted gay power's vision of a society in which sexual hierarchies, like those of race, class, and gender, were obsolete. Gay power was reticent to create gay-only organizations, particularly permanent ones.

Gay pride and gay power battled over issues of loyalty: which was more compelling, an alliance with the left or an alliance based on shared sexuality? The continued existence and growing vitality of the sexual subculture brought home the reality that many gays were not politically radical. Gay power, with its primary allegiance to the New Left, rejected the gay subculture. Activist Gale Whittington referred to gay bars as "walk-in closets."[43] Marcus Overseth further elaborated this view of the subculture:

> The barscene is a game. It is a great circus managed by straight and gay capitalists out to make a buck. So they pack them in from all over the country. The barscene in San Francisco is at once a refuge and a nirvana for Plasticgays from every crossroads hamlet in Amerika. Used to playing the game of the bars, Ghetto-gays soon lose all perspective of reality. They are so busy playing hunter or game that they

can perceive no other reality, including the deeper reality of their own existence as gay people.[44]

Gay power activists felt that they had little in common with "gay capitalists," "Plasticgays," and "Ghetto-gays." On the other hand, gay pride activists, whose primary loyalties were based on shared sexual identity, found it

> impossible . . . to escape a crucial fact: aside from the meetings of gay organizations, these bars are the only places where large numbers of gay people get together. . . . As congregating places for gay people, the gay bars are the focal points of conflict between our new spirit of liberation and the forces which would keep us in our place. In other words, they are community institutions, as the community is now constituted.[45]

Consequently, gay pride activists thought that it was important to "preserve the bars as temporary gay turf where there is at least minimal freedom for gay people," while simultaneously attempting to provide alternative meeting grounds, such as coffee houses and community centers.[46] Gay pride was not willing to reject the most organizationally developed sector of the gay world.

Gay power saw its reference group as the radical movement, but the Gay Activists Alliance, like SIR, self-consciously oriented itself to homosexuals. According to Marotta:

> The radicals who ran GLF . . . worked to establish GLF as a homosexual division in the radical vanguard. But the creators of the Gay Activists Alliance, aspiring to make their group the political representative of all homosexuals, structured it with an eye to winning the acceptance of those they considered the leaders of the local gay minority.[47]

Thus, at the end of 1969, the emergence of a gay identity movement was not inevitable. Conflict between gay pride and gay power positions might have destroyed the movement. But the rapidity of the demise of the New Left in 1970 and 1971 saved the gay movement from this destructive ideological conflict.

The Abandonment of Gay Power, 1970–1971

The gay power variant of gay liberation was born in 1969 and died by the end of 1971. According to Laud Humphreys:

By the end of 1971, gay liberation as a branch of the New Left alliance was in disarray. A number of centrist, single-issue groups had kept the Gay Liberation name, but without the alliances, goals, or methods of the original gayrevs. . . . Of radical gay liberation, little remained by 1972—a name, some meeting places, a few dedicated individuals, slogans, an impact on the cause that moved on without them.[48]

Terrence Kissack documented that GLF in New York was in trouble by the spring of 1971 and near collapse by the summer:

By the spring of 1971, the Gay Liberation Front had become increasingly attenuated. Fewer and fewer people attended meetings or participated in Front actions. The Gay Activists Alliance's tangible successes drew away many of the men. There had been a steady decline in the number of women participating in the Front since the formation of Radicalesbians in the spring of 1970. . . . By the summer of 1971, most of the Front's institutions had collapsed.[49]

In San Francisco, gay liberation organizations and periodicals declined sharply in the early 1970s (see figure 4.2).[50] Like gay liberation generally, gay liberation organizations were torn between gay power and gay pride approaches. In spite of the continued viability of gay pride, gay liberation organizations did not survive the abandonment of gay power. Organizations and periodicals (which were sometimes linked) were most active in 1970 and 1971, the peak years of the movement. Publishing activity declined sharply in 1972 (from twelve serials published in 1971 to four in 1972), while the number of organizations did not drop off until 1974 (when the number falls to nine from a peak of fifteen in 1973).

Gay power, with its call for a socialist revolution and its insistence that homosexual freedom could not be achieved without freedom for workers, women, and blacks, could not exist outside of a vibrant New Left. John D'Emilio explains that

one reason [for the demise] is that the soil that fertilized GLF, the radicalism of the 1960s, was drying up rapidly. The belief that a revolution was imminent and that gays and lesbians should get on board was fast losing whatever momentary plausibility it had. By the early 1970s, the nation was entering a long period of political conservatism and economic retrenchment. With every new proclamation of revolutionary intentions, radicals compromised their credibility.[51]

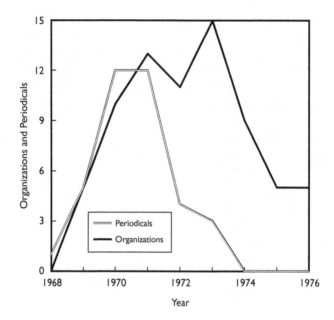

Figure 4.2 Gay Liberation Organizations and Periodicals in San Francisco, 1968–76

It was just no longer possible to believe that a movement addressing race, gender, class, and sexual inequalities was on the verge of overthrowing a corrupt capitalist system.

Mobilized gay activists did not simply give up organizing. Instead, they turned to gay pride and gay rights agendas, which did not depend on the viability of the New Left. The existence of these fully formed alternatives within gay liberation made this possible. Still, gay activists might have held more tightly to the multiracial, multi-issue approach of gay power. Other parts of the New Left, like women's and African American movements certainly did. The particular nature of gay liberation and its relationship with the New Left provided activists with compelling reasons to jump ship.

The most compelling reason to abandon gay power was that it was not the most innovative, exciting, and successful aspect of gay politics in 1970. Turning to gay pride did not feel like a retreat to an old style of politics, but felt ripe with fresh possibilities. The movement strategy of coming out had taken on a life of its own—people were coming out all over the country. In New York, the GAA staged highly successful cultural zaps. The GAA, tailored to the " 'hip' homosexual mainstream," [52] was "activist but nonviolent, imaginative, cool, and very successful." [53]

In San Francisco, the Society for Individual Rights was aware of the successes of GAA in New York. In June 1971, SIR's publication, *Vector,* expressed
admiration for New York's Gay Activist Alliance, while criticizing New
York's GLF. The *Vector* editor indicated that SIR needed to adapt to stay vital:
"Gay liberation is on the move and if SIR does not stay aboard it will go the
way of the Mattachine Society."[54] SIR organizers observed what seemed to
work for GAA and imitated it.

SIR experienced immediate success with the gay pride formulation. In
June 1971 SIR organized a "work-in" at the San Francisco federal building.
This ingenious demonstration involved homosexuals (with signs on their la-
pels identifying themselves as such) volunteering their services to the government

> until they were "fired" by the Security Guards. For a time, Uncle Sam
> had homosexuals working for free in the IRS, Federal Employment
> Information Center, the US Printing Office Book Store, and homo-
> sexuals working as Indian Guides, and elevator operators. The Feder-
> als went into a "panic" when a homosexual tried to be a janitor, by
> pushing a broom across the lobby.[55]

This demonstration was organized to protest "what SIR's president, Bill
Plath, called 'an unjust government policy in refusing to employ homosexuals.' "[56] The fact that displaying gay identity was central to the strategy of this
protest distinguishes it from a homophile protest. On the other hand, seeking government employment was not a gay power goal.

Gay activists also found it relatively easy to abandon the vision of a movement of all oppressed people because the movement was less intertwined
with the New Left than other movements. Emerging late in the cycle of protest movements of the 1960s, gay activists had had the opportunity to see all
the pitfalls of revolutionary politics, without having experienced the series of
events that led other movements down that path. The series of painful conflicts between gay pride and gay power strands of gay liberation (described
above) had clarified the differences between the various positions and disen-
tangled the previously intertwined approaches. In addition, painful experiences of homophobia within the New Left had prevented the development of
loyalty to other branches of the movement. Jim Owles, one of the founders
of New York's GAA, experienced the New Left as "viciously antihomosexual":

> When [gay liberationists] did go out to other actions—let's say a sup-
> port rally for the Panthers or the Young Lords or the more radical

groups—they didn't go as a homosexual group, they went as kind of an auxiliary unit. To me, they were begging for the same kind of acceptance they had accused some of the older homosexuals of wanting. . . . *And they were still getting spit at.* The word *faggot* was still being used at them. They were relegated to "back" roles, and were told, "Don't come out in front! We don't want our groups to become known as homosexual things." That happened in other groups: in women's lib the lesbians are told, "Get in the back. We don't want women's lib to be identified as a lesbian movement." It was just one put-down, spit-in-the-face thing all the way. And I just couldn't do that.[57]

Owles was explicit that this treatment contributed to his desire to work in a single-issue organization.

Strong roots in pre–New Left homophile interest group politics also prevented the gay movement from ever fully committing to the New Left project. The role of prior homophile involvement in easing the turn away from gay power can be seen in a comparison of San Francisco and New York. The turn to gay pride occurred at the same time in both cities, but it was much more painful in New York than in San Francisco. The turn to gay pride was less contentious in San Francisco because the homophile movement had been more vibrant in the late 1960s in San Francisco.[58] At the end of the homophile period, the Society for Individual Rights in San Francisco had been the largest and most successful homosexual organization in the United States. The homophile movement in San Francisco provided a source of constant criticism of gay power by influential and committed homophile activists. The more restricted nature of homophile organizing in New York before 1969 allowed it to become more closely tied to the New Left than in San Francisco. In New York, the separation of gay pride from gay power happened through a painful splitting of the Gay Liberation Front. In San Francisco, the Society for Individual Rights evolved smoothly and gradually from a militant homophile organization toward the gay pride position, while more radical gay organizations quietly vanished.

Some activists think that race, class, and gender loyalties were the main reason why gay activists so easily let go of gay power. Indeed, the split of GLF in New York occurred around the issue of the Black Panthers, giving the conflict between gay pride and gay power a distinctively racial cast. Some GLF activists viewed the abandonment of gay power and the formation of GAA as an expression of the class, race, and gender privilege of middle-class white gay men. When interviewed in the 1990s for the documentary *Out Rage '69,* African American activist Bob Kohler talked about his feelings about the founding of the GAA as if the events had happened yesterday. He explained that, in his view the Gay Activists Alliance

> was formed as a class thing. It was formed because of class and because of race. . . . The dirty little secret of the gay movement is how and why the GAA was formed. . . . They wanted white power. And so they let the freaks, the artists, the poets, the drag queens, the street people, the street queens, the blacks, and the colored people keep the GLF. We're going to go form this thing that is going to change laws. That is a good idea. Change laws. But it was mainly reformist. The vision was broken. The vision went.[59]

It is tricky to acknowledge that the fact that gay liberation activists were predominantly middle-class white men did influence the alacrity with which gay power was abandoned without falling into essentialist reasoning. Gay white men's "interests" are not inherently hostile to a gay power position. Interests are constructed and reconstructed and do not emerge directly from identity, which is itself a historical and political accomplishment. Some white men were, and still are, advocates of a multiracial, multi-issue social justice politics.

It is the case, however, that the New Left was not particularly successful at persuading white gay men to conceive of their interests as being furthered by a movement that also addressed issues of race, class, and gender inequality. For example, in May 1969, the *Advocate* published the comments of radio commentator Randy Darden who asserted that "the greater part of the gay community has a financial interest in a stable, affluent society. We rely on the patronage of well-heeled, middle-class heteros for our stage shows, beauty parlors, fashion shows and other services" and that "the goals of most homosexuals are opposed to the goals of other minorities represented in the New Left."[60] Relatively few gay men had been convinced by the plea of feminist-influenced gay power to abandon bars and bathhouses. Criticisms of the subculture jeopardized the support of those men for whom "being openly gay meant being enthusiastic about . . . cruising, promiscuity, and sex in gay-identified institutions and places."[61] For this group, the central *point* of gay activism was to protect and extend the subculture. In contrast, lesbians, gay people of color, and working-class gays had become more invested in the vision of a movement that could address class, race, and gender issues along with issues of homosexuality. They held onto gay power longer, and, in some cases, never adopted a gay pride perspective.

Thus, activists had many compelling reasons to abandon the gay power vision. It was becoming untenable in a political context growing more conservative, and investment in it had been limited in the first place. The gay pride alternative was sexy and successful, and it meshed with the way many gay white men interpreted their interests. Despite the compelling nature of the reasons for this shift, disappointment about the abandonment of the radical gay liberation vision permeates the writing and discussion of gay liberation by the activist intellectuals who have contributed much of the existing documentation of this movement. Some, like Bob Kohler, explicitly blame middle-class white gay men for the failure of gay power. Jewelle Gomez believed that gay power showed an "early political sophistication that has been difficult to regain."[62] These notions suggest that the gay movement would have been *more* successful had it not been for the limited political vision of its gay white male leaders. In 1970–71, with the New Left in disarray, facing the intractable reality of fading political opportunities, gay activists made a pragmatic decision—they pursued the strategy that was already beginning to achieve success in an emerging political context. This pragmatic decision involved setting aside the issues specific to lesbians, gay people of color, and poor gays. The willingness and ease with which middle-class white male gay activists made this move certainly reflected their race, class, and gender blind spots. But it is unclear what would have happened if they had held onto a redistributive agenda, even a substantially moderated one. The example of other New Left movements that retained a politics more indebted to the economic and social justice vision of the New Left suggests that the movement may not have survived at all or might have survived in the most marginal form. The gay movement could not base its politics on forming strong alliances with other groups when those other movements were in disarray.

This chapter shows that the multiple logics of gay liberation, while problematic at the movement's peak, contributed to its resiliency as the New Left declined. When redistributive politics was discredited, identity and interest group politics were waiting in the wings. The decline of the New Left removed a source of conflict. The stabilization of the contours of the new political environment also helped minimize conflict, as activists moved toward greater consensus about what was politically possible. The elimination of gay power still did not ensure the growth of a gay identity movement. But it did present a historically unique opportunity for the crystallization of a new field. However, activists still had to figure out how to reconcile the competing logics of identity and interest group politics and how to bind together a constituency growing ever more diverse. In chapter 5, I show how the movement crystallized as it hit upon a way to hold the various dimensions of the political project together.

FIVE

The Crystallization of a Gay Identity Movement, 1971–1973

Between the hard conservatives and the intolerant radicals, young Gays are finding the middle ground productive. From coast to coast, they are building new organizations modeled after New York's highly successful and active Gay Activists Alliance. The formula: just enough structure and planning to have a sound foundation but not so much that action is impossible. Also, most new groups are limiting their activity to gay-oriented issues, rather than tackling all the world's ills at once. It seems to be a formula that can win the widespread support that the GLF's were never able to get.

The Advocate (Los Angeles gay newspaper),
editorial, September 29, 1971

Chapter 4 explained how gay organizing survived the decline of the New Left. This chapter provides the next piece of the puzzle by explaining how gay organizing then began to thrive. In chapter 4 I showed that the existence of contradictory political logics within gay liberation allowed the movement to survive a dramatic moment of ideological pruning. However, the survival of gay organizing did not guarantee its growth. Differences between gay rights, premised on an interest group logic, and gay pride, which drew on an identity logic, could have proved to be debilitating. Binding gay individuals and the various strands of gay politics into a coherent political project presented activists with a challenge.

A coherent political project did emerge, and rapidly. Activists settled on a way to organize that reconciled the seemingly contradictory parts of the project in the early 1970s. The movement coalesced around the simultaneous pursuit of gay rights, gay pride, and sexual expression. That something new was coming together was evident to close observers at the time, such as the *Advocate* editorialist quoted in this chapter's epigraph. Sociologist Laud Humphreys noted in 1970 that the "the old-line, civil-libertarian thesis and the gay liberationist antithesis began to produce a synthesis."[1]

How were the potentially contradictory aspects of gay politics recon-

ciled? In this chapter, I show that the identity logic provided the cultural resources needed to defuse the threat posed by conflicting visions of the goals
and strategies of gay organizing. By seeing meaningful social change as a
product of individual self-expression, an identity logic suggested that positive
change could occur even if differences were not resolved. Change would occur simply through broadening the range of authentic expression possible in
society. Differences thus seemed less threatening and could be celebrated instead of resolved. Not all movements drawing on an identity logic highlight
its individualistic side. Identity logic more typically gave rise to a concern
with the internal homogeneity of identity categories. That the gay movement managed to play with both meanings of the term "identity" (sameness
and individuality) provided a powerful and generative ambiguity. The vision
of a unified but diverse movement became real as activists developed practices and rituals that substantiated the rhetoric—most notably, the annual
lesbian/gay freedom day parade. The parade, through its very structure, conveys the message of unity through diversity.

Cultural and political approaches were thus defined as complementary—some groups could focus primarily on gay rights, while others expressed gay pride, without forcing a decision about which should be *the* goal.
Affirming gay cultural identity provided gay rights with the identity needed
to claim a place on the American political scene. In turn, gay rights created
space for the elaboration of gay identity. But even those who could not agree
with a gay rights agenda could be included (although in a marginal place in
the movement). Interest group politics was not the glue holding the project
together. The glue was provided by shared gay identity and the celebration of
its expression. The movement became an "identity movement."

This analysis of the timing and nature of the transformation of the gay
movement in the early 1970s differs in several key ways from how this transition is generally described in the social movements and sexuality literatures.
That a transition occurred in the 1970s is widely accepted.[2] While some, like
Laud Humphreys, agree with the dating of the transition in the very early
1970s, others, like Steven Seidman, date the transition to later in the decade.[3]
With the exception of Humphreys, most others see the transformation as
happening gradually. For example, Seidman claims that "gay liberation came
to an end by the mid-1970s."[4] These other scholars, in contrast to the approach taken here, do not see the transformation in terms of a sudden crystallization of a new field.

In addition, sexuality and social movement scholars have seen gay rights
and gay pride as seamlessly compatible. In virtually all of the scholarship on

the gay movement, the politics of pride, display, coming out, and community building are seen to fit naturally with an interest group/gay rights politics. Seidman talks of the turn to "community building and winning civil rights."[5] John D'Emilio links gay rights and identity politics: "Gay rights activists retained a central emphasis on coming out; they engaged in militant, angry protests; they adopted the language of pride and self-affirmation."[6] Mary Bernstein explains that the "lesbian and gay movement [had] been altered from a movement for cultural transformation through sexual liberation to one that seeks achievement of political rights through a narrow, ethnic-like interest-group politics."[7] Because scholars have seen the fit between rights and pride politics as natural and obvious, they have missed the political work involved in producing this fit.

Without analyzing precisely how the movement that took shape in the 1970s merged interest group and identity politics, it is difficult to understand how it produced and supported such a diverse array of organizations. Interest group politics is suited for pursuing group rights, but not for building and displaying identity. An identity logic made the building and displaying of identity through building organizations and hosting events like the annual freedom day parade meaningful and possible.

While gay movement experts take for granted the synergistic relationship between community development and the pursuit of rights, they have not articulated the theoretical implications of this fit. They have not pointed out that this relationship defies the categories of political process theories of movements. By straddling the boundaries of the cultural and the political, not to mention the commercial, the gay identity movement refuses to be contained within a narrow definition of a "social movement." As we will see in chapter 6, the multifaceted nature of this project fueled its growth. The power of this project lay not only in the strength of a narrow political rights movement but also in the generative nature of its identity politics. Understanding the nature of this project, and of the synergy among its various components, is crucial to understanding the success of the gay identity movement in the 1970s and beyond. The first section below provides evidence of field crystallization in the early 1970s. The second section discusses the challenge of arriving at this consensus and the nature of the field formed.

Crystallization of a Gay Identity Movement

The comments discussed above provide one indication of the crystallization of the gay identity movement in the early 1970s. These observations were substantiated by a variety of other indicators of field formation. It was when I noticed the synchronicity of these indicators that I began to organize this story around this crucial moment in the history of the gay field.

The creation of the freedom day parade provided one indication of field formation. If the event had occurred only once, or only sporadically, or had stayed geographically localized, or varied over time in structure and organization, I would not attribute so much salience to its birth. But freedom day parades happen in all major cities and some small towns in the United States each year, employing the language and structure settled on in the early 1970s. San Francisco's gay community has organized a freedom day parade every year since 1972. Each year the language of "pride," "celebration," "unity," and "diversity" appears in parade themes and mission statements. Freedom day parades involved political, social, and commercial organizations from the early years. The participation of all these kinds of organizations shows that the collective project was not conceived in a narrowly political way.

Taken alone, the founding of the parade would not necessarily signify the crystallization of a new field. But 1972 also marked the first time, after years of effort, that a national conference of homosexual organizations reached a consensus on a political platform.[8] In February, at "A National Coalition of Gay Organizations," jointly sponsored by New York's Gay Activists Alliance and Chicago's Gay Alliance, eighty-five organizations from eighteen states agreed on a gay rights platform in preparation for the 1972 elections.[9] Never before had a national conference of gay organizations been able to agree on a gay stance. Throughout the late 1960s multiple attempts had failed to produce such a consensus.[10]

In addition, as I discussed in chapters 1 and 4, the creation of the parade and the new political consensus coincided with the sudden appearance of entirely new kinds of gay organizations. These organizations included gay religious organizations (e.g., the Metropolitan Community Church, founded 1970), gay self-help organizations (e.g., Gay Alcoholics Anonymous, founded 1971), gay hobby organizations (e.g., San Francisco Front Runners, founded 1974), and gay parenting groups (e.g., Lesbian Mother Union, founded 1971). The use of bold sexual identity terminology in organization names illustrated their new devotion to pride and identity building. The sudden explosion of support groups, which were unheard of before 1970, created contexts in which individuals could discover and express their authentic selves. The proliferation of varieties of gay organizations, both in terms of function and identity, suggested the salience of the vision of a unified but diverse movement. Most gay organizations created after 1972 pro-

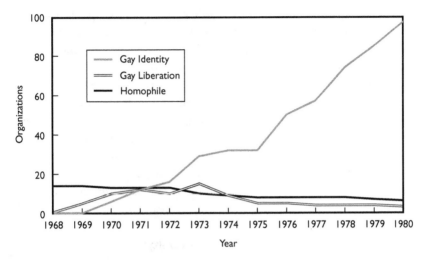

Figure 5.1 Homophile, Gay Liberation, and Gay Identity Organizations in San Francisco, 1968–80

claimed gay identity and the particular function or identity of the organization (e.g., Gay History Film Project, Slightly Older Lesbians). These new organizations were made imaginable, appealing, and obvious by the crystallization of a gay identity movement. While activists and community members may not have noted these new organizations until the mid to late 1970s, their distinctiveness was evident in the names and goals of organizations beginning in 1970. It is the proliferation and diversification of this particular kind of organization that accounts for the shape and size of the organizational infrastructure of the community to this day.

The changing density of various kinds of homosexual organizations provided yet another confirmation of the timing of the consolidation of the gay identity movement. Figure 5.1 shows the decline of homophile and gay liberation organizations and the emergence of the new kind of gay organizations, which I refer to as "gay identity organizations." Note that by 1972, gay identity organizations began to dominate. The existence of multiple kinds of organizations from 1969 to 1972 indicates the unsettled nature of the field and the contestation between multiple political logics that characterized those years. As the gay identity movement coalesced, gay identity organizations began to dominate. Homophile and gay liberation organizations declined.

The creation of resource guides in the early 1970s provided still another indicator of field crystallization. To build my organizational data set, I scoured archives, bookstores, libraries, and secondary sources for lists of lesbian/gay organizations. I found that while bar guides were published consistently throughout the 1960s, the first guides to list both nonprofit and commercial organizations were published in 1972. *Gayellow Pages,* the first national annual guide to both nonprofit and commercial organizations, was first published in 1973. Organizational researchers see the existence of resource guides as a good indicator of the existence of a field.[11] Guides provide evidence that participants are aware of being involved in a common enterprise. Guides also reveal the ways that participants conceived of their enterprise. That these guides listed nonprofit organizations, including both cultural and rights organizations, as well as commercial organizations, such as bars and bathhouses, showed that gay activists saw their project in terms of the expansion of all kinds of gay social space.

"Unity through Diversity"

How did this field finally lock in? What was the nature of this consensus? Answering these questions requires a deeper understanding of the challenges faced by activists as the New Left receded. I show that activists faced conflicting visions of the goals and strategies of gay organizing, but that the identity logic provided gay activists with a cultural framework that allowed for the finessing of the contradictions between these visions.

We have grown to accept the conflation of gay pride and gay rights as inevitable; it is difficult to imagine that they were not always natural bedfellows. However, they are based on fundamentally different notions about the nature of the oppression of homosexuals and how this oppression should be addressed. Gay pride, based on an identity logic, asserts that the goal of gay politics should be building a public, positive gay identity through coming out and identity display. Gay rights politics defines the goal of gay politics as battling discrimination through interest group politics. In 1970 and 1971, activists battled over the differences between these approaches. In his history of homosexual politics, Toby Marotta devoted a chapter of more than thirty dense pages to the conflict between "pride" and "rights" orientations in the Gay Activists Alliance in New York.[12] Gay pride advocates saw gay rights as missing the point, as they believed that fundamental change involved broadening the repertoire of acceptable cultural expression. Activist-analyst Peter Fisher, in a 1971 paper for a political science seminar, articulated this position:

> What use . . . was the passage of legislation that would enable homosexuals to be openly gay without fear of losing their jobs, if there was no way to be gay outside of the tawdry bar scene? What must be de-

veloped in order for political gains to be meaningful was a new life style, an integral gay counterculture which could draw uptight gays out of their closets of secrecy and shame into a new expressive and creative way of life. What was needed, in effect, was the initiation of a grand social experiment, the creation of a new society within the old.[13]

Fisher's vision of "the creation of a new society within the old" beautifully illustrates that gay pride politics was premised on the prefigurative politics of the identity logic. The resonance with the vision of Students for a Democratic Society (SDS) is striking. Greg Calvert, an officer of SDS, wrote in 1966: "While struggling to liberate the world, we would create the liberated world in our midst. While fighting to destroy the power that had created the loveless anti-community, we would ourselves create the community of love— *The Beloved Community*."[14] In contrast, those focused on gay rights, such as GAA's Marty Robinson, felt that those focused on cultural expression mistakenly believed they could "dance their way to revolution." Marotta explains that gay rights advocates felt that too much focus on the expressive "diverted energy and attention from important political enterprises."[15]

Complicating matters further was the fact that gay pride and gay rights were not the only models available for thinking about how homosexuals ought to act in pursuit of their interests. Many gay men were primarily interested in participating in gay social life. This understanding of gay interest was at odds with rights politics, which saw gay interests as dependent upon passing antidiscrimination legislation. This orientation toward partying was also at odds with the gay pride agenda; it was unconcerned with achieving social change through a politics of visibility. The pursuit of sex falls outside of every existing definition of political action. But it is collective action because the vitality of this sexual culture depended upon the health of commercial organizations. The pursuit of sex and sociality thus present a compelling alternative way of structuring the collective project. In Chapter 2 we saw that the history of this subcultural logic of organization extended back at least to the 1930s and presented homophile activists with a challenging alternative to their vision of a public interest group movement throughout the 1950s and 1960s.

This diversity of ways of envisioning a gay collective project was matched by individual-level diversity among gay men and lesbians. The success of gay liberation had intensified the internal diversity that had plagued homosexual organizing since its inception. Homosexuals came from all different kinds of backgrounds and were diverse in terms of ideology. Before gay liberation, this lack of shared socialization was overcome by the tight control homosexual subcultures maintained over the boundaries of their world and the processes of socialization into it.[16] With the sudden visibility of the gay movement in the early 1970s, the numbers of those identifying as gay grew fast. Many of these new converts lacked experience either in the New Left or in the gay sexual subculture. There were simply more people, from more different walks of life, willing and able to identify as gay. In addition, the movements of the 1960s left the whole society, including homosexuals, ideologically polarized.

Thus, at this crucial moment, three distinct visions about the nature and goals of gay collective action existed: gay rights, gay pride, and sexual pleasure seeking.[17] We saw above that these agendas became linked into one coherent project. The linking of these three agendas was not inevitable. As has been seen in other movements, cleavages can develop, weakening the movement as a whole. In the women's movement, the politics of cultural affirmation and the pursuit of rights developed into distinct, competing fields, referred to as "cultural feminism" and "liberal feminism." Each saw its analysis of women's oppression as correct and the analysis of the other as irrelevant or even harmful to the cause. The seductions of pure pleasure seeking might have eliminated all interest in gay rights or gay pride. Or interest group politics might have come to dominate, restricting the diversification of the community and slowing organizational proliferation.

The political logic of identity made it possible to reconcile pride, rights, and sexual expression. I show this through a close analysis of an important movement statement made by New York's Gay Activists Alliance leader Jim Owles, published in the April 1971 issue of the *Gay Activist*. In his 1972 analysis of homosexual liberation, Laud Humphreys identified this statement as one of "great significance."[18] Humphreys saw it as revealing "certain characteristics of the synthesis that has formed around one-issue organizations."[19]

Jim Owles recognized the tremendous growth of the gay movement and the resulting problem of the diversification of gay organizations. Other movement leaders were aware of the contradictions as well. Owles described the variety of approaches:

> There are gay organizations of all types. Some are politically oriented, some are socially oriented, some devote their energies to much-needed public education about homosexuals, and some are focusing on the problem of reconciling homosexuality and religion. Some groups have adopted specific ideological platforms, while others attempt to encompass gay people from all areas of the political spectrum.[20]

Owles only describes ideological diversity here—not race, class, or gender diversity. Race, class, and gender differences were not seen by white male leaders as serious obstacles to forming a coherent gay movement. Movement leaders were primarily concerned with trying to move beyond the ideological polarization of the 1960s and with garnering the support of middle-class white gay men who might have been alienated by the extremes of gay power.

After describing the diversity of gay organizations, Owles acknowledged that this diversity could potentially lead to destructive conflict. He moved quickly to emphasizing the possibilities for cooperation:

> Although there is a potential for disagreement among the many gay organizations with regard to ideology and priorities, this is greatly outweighed by the numerous areas of potential cooperation and mutual effort.[21]

Owles felt that responding to this diversity by attempting to create an ideologically homogeneous movement would be a mistake. He asserted that

> few of us are anxious to see a uniform and monolithic movement develop out of the foundations we have laid. We have seen other mass movements develop in this direction in the past, only to be torn apart by internal struggles over ideology and leadership, eventually to fail in achieving their goals.[22]

Owles saw efforts to develop ideological consensus to be dangerous, potentially leading to movement factionalization. His leeriness about homogenization was shaped by the value placed on individual expression within gay liberation and by the movement's late position in the cycle of protest.

After rejecting a "uniform and monolithic movement," Owles further discredited "uniformity" by pointing out that "one of society's favorite myths about gay people is that we are all alike." With this statement, Owles hinted at a view of homosexual oppression resting primarily on homosexual cultural invisibility, suggesting his reliance on an identity political logic. Owles claimed that "we" are aware of the diversity of homosexuals: "We ourselves know that there are all types of gay people, with all types of interests, and from all types of backgrounds."[23] Expression of this diversity is thus positive as it has the consequence of dismantling stereotypes of gays.

Owles then boldly asserted that the diversity he described

> is our strength, not a weakness. There is room in the gay liberation movement for every gay person to make his or her own type of con-

tribution toward creating a society and a world in which we will all be free to be ourselves.[24]

Movement diversity was defined as strength, not weakness. Owles argued for the movement to embrace diversity instead of trying to resolve or deny it.

That Owles relied on an identity political logic is evident in his assertion that the goal of gay politics is "creating a society . . . in which we will all be free to be ourselves." It was *this* vision of change that made it possible to see diversity as strength. From a political worldview in which the ultimate end is individual self-expression, the presence of diversity is evidence of movement toward that goal. In a worldview in which the end goal is eliminating discriminatory law, the presence of ideological diversity could be seen as hindering the likelihood of achieving policy change. Thus, framing diversity as strength is made possible within an identity political logic.

Defining diversity as strength makes sense within a political logic that sees change as emerging out of the aggregation of individual actions. In closing, Owles restated his commitment to a movement composed of multiple and varied forms of political expression:

> The way we will build an effective national movement is by every gay person making his or her own particular contribution, and by gay individuals and organizations working together when possible.[25]

With diversity defined as strength, gay pride, gay rights, and sexual expression all became perfectly acceptable forms of gay politics. All furthered the gay movement.

In order for gay identity to be meaningful, activists also needed to define a minimal set of shared characteristics. After all, the term "identity" implies likeness as well as individual uniqueness. The first premise was that gay men and lesbians had a core of shared experience simply because of shared same-gender sexual attraction. The experience of growing up "closeted," combined with the subsequent experience of developing a gay identity, joining a gay community, and coming out to family, friends, and coworkers was presumed to produce feelings of commonality. The second premise was that supporting gay rights logically followed the adoption of a positive, public gay identity. While it was understood that ideological consensus was impossible, gay rights were seen as a lowest common denominator set of political goals. Such activists as Owles went to great lengths to emphasize that the gay rights agenda fit with political philosophies across the spectrum. Gays from the political right or left could endorse gay rights. A third point of agreement placed participation in a liberated, active sexual subculture at the center of gay male identity. But because a diverse movement would be built out of the aggregated contributions of all gay individuals, however they defined their contribution to the collective project, even those who disagreed with gay rights or with the role of sex in gay life could find a place in the movement.

Displaying Unity through Diversity: The Gay Freedom Day Parade

The creation of the gay freedom day parade illustrated that an identity movement that defined itself in terms of its diversity could produce large collective action events. That the founders of the event commemorating the Stonewall riots eventually arrived at "parade" for the form of the event, after initially calling for a "demonstration," illustrated the emerging dominance of an identity logic. In turn, the immediate success of the parade contributed to the consolidation of the gay identity movement.

The annual freedom day parade was born at the Eastern Regional Conference of Homophile Organizations in the fall of 1969. Activist Craig Rodwell proposed that the Stonewall riots be commemorated with an "annual reminder."[26] The resolution establishing "Christopher Street Liberation Day" read as follows:

> We propose that a demonstration be held annually on the last Saturday in June in New York City to commemorate the 1969 spontaneous demonstrations on Christopher Street and this demonstration be called CHRISTOPHER STREET LIBERATION DAY. No dress or age regulations shall be made for this demonstration. We also propose that we contact Homophile organizations throughout the country and suggest that they hold parallel demonstrations on that day.[27]

The "annual reminder" was originally intended to be a "demonstration," not a "parade" or "celebration."

In preparation for the first event, which was to take place on June 28, 1970, in New York, activists struggled to find a form for the event that could motivate the participation of a diverse constituency. Disagreement over the shape of the event was fierce. The Gay Activists Alliance, Marotta explains, wanted "to make homosexuals aware of the need to exercise political power and to confront politicians and public officials with evidence of the gay voting bloc. Instead of a picnic in the park, they wanted a program of speeches by political leaders and politicians."[28] In contrast, Craig Rodwell and others wanted to emphasize the importance of "affirming liberated gay life styles and celebrating gay community."[29] The victory of the identity affirmation perspective was evident in the Christopher Street Liberation Day Umbrella Committee's welcome message:

> Welcome to the first anniversary celebration of the Gay Liberation movement. We are united today to affirm our pride, our life-style, and our commitment to each other. Despite political and social differences we may have, we are united on this common ground: For the first time in history we are together as The Homosexual Community.[30]

All references to "demonstration" were dropped and replaced by the language of "celebration" and "pride." The language of "political and social differences" and "unity," which would become ubiquitous, emerged. While this first event did not include floats and more closely resembled a march than a parade, it was certainly not a political demonstration as it was originally conceived. Until the day of the event, it was unclear whether gay organizations would support the event. By the time of the march, every major gay political group in New York had signed on as a sponsor.[31] The use of essentially the same welcome message the next year suggests that key activists felt that the framing worked to motivate the participation of the whole community.[32]

The first San Francisco gay freedom day parade, called "Christopher Street West," was held in 1972 with about fifty thousand participants.[33] Organizers were aware of the implications of the different possible formats for the event:

> More speakers had not been allowed in an attempt to avoid political or protest activities and to keep the parade from becoming a demonstration. It had been the Christopher Street West S.F. committee's contention that a demonstration as such in San Francisco would prove a flop and would alienate most gay community members here. Their contention was supported by gay community leaders who had been involved in the parade, who commented to the *Advocate* that only a non-political Gay Pride celebration would be able to unite all spectrums of the community.[34]

Leaders were committed to unifying the community and were convinced that a parade was precisely the right format to accomplish this goal. They felt that the "nonpolitical" character of a parade would make it appealing to all parts of the community.

San Francisco's first freedom day parade was quite successful. The format of a parade and the goal of a gay pride celebration enticed a diverse group to participate in the event. According to the *Advocate*:

> Almost every spectrum of the gay community was pulled together in the parade, including every San Francisco gay organization except the Daughters of Bilitis, the Council on Religion and the Homosexual, and the Gay Sunshine Collective, some of whose members participated as individuals.[35]
>
> Drag queens, gay businesses, entertainers, religious groups, prison groups, gay organizations, reigning "royalty," leather men, radicals, street people, conservatives, lesbians, and "hunky guys" were all represented in parade contingents.[36]

There were some who were critical of the turn away from radical politics toward a politics of identity display. The *Advocate* mentioned that "isolated and small groups of radicals . . . began shouting that they had been denied the right to address the crowd."[37] These radicals were already in the minority by 1972.

Since it took the form of a "pride parade" there has been little debate within the community about the assumptions underlying the event. That is not to say the staging of the parade has been without conflict. There have been many battles about the parade.[38] However, the conflicts have not generally been about whether the parade should exist or whether the event should be a political demonstration. The value of the parade is usually accepted as given. That the event was originally intended to be a political demonstration has been forgotten. Conflicts about the parade have typically reinforced the sense of its inevitability. Most of the conflicts have been about issues of inclusion (of bisexuals and transgendered people) or status within the event (the ordering of contingents and locations of booths). And of course, there have been conflicts about the public representation of sexual diversity: Should we highlight those who are most different from mainstream society (drag queens, people into S/M)? Or should we emphasize those who are ever so conventional (lesbian/gay parents, employees, bicyclists)? Every so often some group complains that the parade has become too much of a "party." But even those who think the parade should be more political rarely suggest that the parade be transformed into a demonstration.

Activists discovered a form of collective action that conveyed both unity and diversity. The fit between the parade as a form and the message displayed was perfect. A parade by definition involves display, and the form of the parade worked beautifully to display newly visible collective and individual identities. Even if one participated with a different intention, the audience tried to "read" one's identity. By convention, parades consist of identifiable groups or contingents. When the contingents were different from each other, the event was more successful as an exhibition or show. By participating in the same parade, the contingents appeared unified.

To participate in the parade, individuals needed to form a contingent or to pick a contingent with which to march. The parade demanded the display of both shared gay identities and secondary, modifying identities. That everyone needed a contingent, a secondary identity, constructed diversity as a point of commonality. *Everyone* brought one or more additional identities into the community with them. The demand for display of both individual and organizational identities also produced a continual diversification of the community, as people searched for different variations of gay identity to contribute to the spectacle.

In this new arena, the existence of multiple organizations is unambiguously positive. Gone were the homophile concerns about organizational competition. The more organizations, the more contingents there were to participate in the parade. The more different the contingents were from each other, the better the show. The existence of many organizations was now seen as evidence of community richness and strength rather than as evidence of fragmentation and division.

The structure of the parade and the relationships between organizations can be described as *articulated*. Something that is articulated is expressed in parts, but is also systematically interrelated. Each contingent or organization expresses its position without restraint but does not claim to represent the gay movement as a whole. Organizations were linked by shared gay identity. Beyond this basic point of commonality, participation in the parade and in the movement meant simply accepting the diversity of goals and identities expressed by others. Real political differences were finessed. Groups that disagreed with each other—say a radical group and a Republican group—have usually been separated from one another in the parade. That such politically disparate groups participated conveyed the message that political differences were not threatening. Shared gay identity was asserted to be a more fundamental commonality. By stumbling upon a way to integrate the various aspects of the project, activists solved the final obstacle to the creation of a new kind of movement—a gay identity movement. They forged a field. The next chapter shows that this consensus allowed the movement to grow rapidly in the 1970s.

PART TWO

Consequences of Field Formation

Success: Growth of a Gay Identity Movement in the 1970s

The real achievement of the gay liberation movement was to stimulate the growth of the lesbian and gay community. It is that community, in all its diversity and complexity, rather than a narrowly political movement, whatever its creativity, which has become the real actor on the stage of history.
Jeffrey Weeks, *Coming Out: Homosexual Politics in Britain from the Nineteenth Century to the Present* (1977)

The period from 1970 through 1972 was crucial to the formation of gay San Francisco. By 1973, the goals, identity, and strategies of a gay identity movement had coalesced. The building of gay identity became the central task. The pursuit of gay rights and the elaboration of a sexual subculture were defined as complementary to this project, as they contributed to the expansion of possible ways to be gay.

In the 1970s, the gay community in San Francisco acquired an unprecedented power and visibility. The number of organizations, both nonprofit and commercial, exploded. Most of the organizational growth took place in the Castro, a neighborhood that was rapidly becoming a gay mecca. Gay men from all over the country migrated to the city. Sexual possibilities seemed infinite, with gay bars filled with young men. And in 1977, the community demonstrated its political power by electing Harvey Milk to the Board of Supervisors, making him the first openly gay person to be elected to public office in a major city in the United States.[1]

The dynamism of the gay movement in the 1970s built upon the crystallization of the gay identity movement in the early part of the decade. The crucial cultural work was accomplished *prior* to the beginning of the tremendous growth in the 1970s. The various parts of the project—identity-building, gay rights, and the sexually focused commercial sector—proved to be synergistic. The accomplishments of each fed the others, producing a mutually reinforcing cycle of growth. Expansion in the numbers of gay identity organizations, the forging of the Castro as a gay neighborhood, and the growth of the sexual subculture provided the numbers and spatial concentration that made for a powerful gay rights voting bloc. Protections from repression won by activists devoted to consolidating gay electoral power encouraged further cultural and commercial development. The Gay Freedom Day Parade provided a marvelous opportunity for bars to advertise. The success of bars provided financial support for nonprofit organizations and political campaigns. This chapter documents these synergistic relationships, revealing the peculiar strength and generativity of the gay identity movement.

These successes provoked repression from a fundamentalist religious movement gathering strength in the late 1970s. The effects of this repression were mixed. On one hand, responses to this repression led to further mobilization, ultimately leading to the crystallization of the gay movement on the national level in 1979. On the other hand, right-wing mobilization was able to slow and reverse passage of local gay rights ordinances around the country and continue to keep stigma about homosexuality at high levels.

My claim that the dynamism of the gay movement in the later 1970s resulted from the crystallization of a multifaceted, reinforcing gay identity movement in the early 1970s challenges conventional wisdom. It challenges resource-rationalist understandings of what movements are, where the boundaries of movements lie, the processes through which movements grow, what it means for them to become institutionalized, and the relationship between culture and politics. In order to understand the nature and development of the gay identity-building project even the commercial sector must be considered to be within the boundaries of the gay identity movement. Political process approaches to movements, based on distinguishing between the political and the nonpolitical, miss the importance of the mutually reinforcing relationships among the cultural, political, and commercial aspects of this movement. The presence of these synergistic relationships is implicit in all historical accounts of gay San Francisco, but because of the descriptive nature of these accounts historians have not highlighted their theoretical salience.

My emphasis on the internally generative features of the gay identity-building project also contrasts with a view that sees the success of San Francisco's gay movement in the 1970s as an inevitable response to a positive cultural and political environment. I show that the gay identity movement did not simply benefit from opportunities, but in fact helped *create* those opportunities.

A third way this argument contrasts with conventional wisdom is with respect to the dates that historians of sexuality see as pivotal. Scholars generally credit the contemporary shape and success of the gay movement either to the beginnings of gay liberation (usually dated to the Stonewall uprising in New York in 1969) or to the mid to late 1970s, when the movement's new shape and obvious successes became visible in San Francisco. Scholars who have studied San Francisco have focused on the mid to late 1970s, as it was in these years that the career and assassination of Harvey Milk brought national attention to the city. I argue, however, that by focusing on these two periods, scholars overlook the importance of the years in between the height of gay liberation and the visible ascendance of a dynamic gay community. Earlier chapters showed that the decline of the New Left—not the birth of gay liberation—marked the crucial moment when the field crystallized. This chapter extends and reinforces my earlier argument by showing the importance of that moment of crystallization (1970–72) in the visible successes of the gay movement in San Francisco in the later 1970s and beyond.

The Blossoming of a Gay Culture

In the 1970s San Francisco became a gay cultural mecca. This section describes the cultural transformation of San Francisco in the 1970s—the proliferation of gay identity organizations, the making of a gay neighborhood, the gay migration to San Francisco, and the increased size of the annual Freedom Day Parade. While the movement benefited from unusually hospitable political, demographic, and ecological circumstances, the blossoming of gay culture would not have been possible without the prior crystallization of the gay identity movement. The crystallization of a gay identity movement created a template for organizational growth, a rationale for building a gay neighborhood, and the cultural framework that gave "coming out" its meaning.

A simple chart displaying the growth in the numbers of San Francisco's gay identity organizations provides a systematic view of the cultural blossoming of gay San Francisco (see figure 6.1). The first gay identity organizations formed in 1970. There were twice as many in 1971. By 1973 the numbers doubled again. By 1977 the number of gay identity organizations had doubled yet again. In 1981, the number of organizations had almost tripled from the number in existence in 1977. In 1987, 301 organizations existed. It is no wonder that John D'Emilio has referred to the growth in the number and variety of gay organizations in the 1970s as "almost miraculous."[2]

Gay organizations formed in the 1970s were different from earlier organizations. The crystallization of the gay identity movement produced an organizational template—an implicit set of guidelines for the formation and

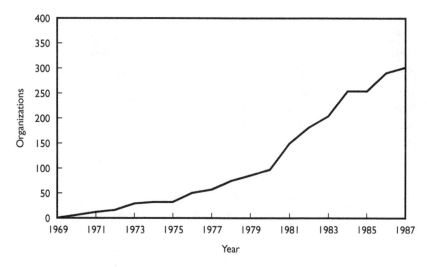

Figure 6.1 Gay Identity Organizations in San Francisco, 1969–87

characteristics of these new kinds of organizations. As described in chapter 5, these new organizations included sexual identity in their organization names, thus asserting membership in the gay identity-building project. This boldness about sexual identity was made meaningful and possible by the new strategy of coming out. These new organizations also proclaimed one or more unique functions or identities in their names, defining their contributions to the diversity of the gay community. In 1969, not one gay organization had this structure. After 1970, almost all new organizations employed this structure. These new organizations made sense only within the cultural context created by the gay identity movement.

Many of these new organizations were located in the Castro neighborhood, which was rapidly being transformed from a newly vacated working-class neighborhood into the first true gay neighborhood in the United States. While homosexual bars and commercial establishments were clustered together in specific neighborhoods of most major urban areas in the United States throughout the twentieth century, the Castro took this spatial congregation to a new level.[3] The Castro became a neighborhood, rather than simply an area frequented for commercial and sexual purposes.[4]

The gay movement developed the *idea* of building a gay neighborhood before the *reality* of the gay neighborhood was achieved. In earlier chapters we saw that gay liberationists engaged in intense debates about the desirability of segregated gay space. Some were opposed to creating or maintaining any form of spatially distinct gay community. They saw the creation of a gay neighborhood as defining the gay community as a minority group vulnerable to discrimination, instead of contributing to the overthrow of a corrupt capitalist society. Other gay liberationists, such as Carl Wittman, in his "Gay Manifesto" (1969), supported gay spaces but viewed the existing areas where bars were concentrated as "ghettos" and criticized their control by capitalists and cops. In contrast to the "ghetto," he envisioned "free territory":

> We must govern ourselves, set up our own institutions, defend ourselves, and use our own energies to improve our lives. The emergence of gay liberation communes and our own paper is a good start. The talk about a gay liberation coffee shop/dance hall should be acted upon. Rural retreats, political action offices, food cooperatives, a free school, unalienating bars and after hours places—they must be developed if we are to have even the shadow of a free territory.[5]

For Wittman, self-governance and the creation of organizations other than bars distinguished "free territory" from a "ghetto." As we saw in chapter 4, San Francisco's gay liberation movement tried to realize Wittman's vision with the plan to take over Alpine County in California. Wittman's vision was utopian, involving complete self-governance. With the demise of gay power and the crystallization of the gay identity movement, gay activists no longer desired a total separation from mainstream American institutions. But the conviction that a spatially concentrated gay world should involve more than just gay bars and bathhouses survived. As the gay movement coalesced around an identity-building project modeled on ethnic identities, the idea that there should be gay neighborhoods made sense.

However powerful this vision, the phenomenon of the Castro in the 1970s would not have been possible without the convergence of this vision with a unique opportunity. Housing stock and storefronts vacated by working-class departures from the Most Holy Redeemer Parish created the possibility of building a concentrated gay neighborhood. Randy Shilts explains, "Single men with excess income began moving in, buying up the old houses, and using their leisure time to renovate them. By 1967, a few gay bars were doing business. By the early seventies, gay business people began leasing the deserted storefronts. The trend became an explosion in 1974."[6] Temporally, the idea of a gay neighborhood preceded the reality. Gay settlement of the Castro began in earnest only in 1972, *after* field crystallization.[7]

The founding of new community organizations and the settlement of the Castro were fueled by gay migration to San Francisco from other parts of the country. Estimating the size of the gay migration is impossible, not least because it cannot be determined whether people moved because they identified as gay or whether they adopted a gay identity only after moving to the city. While the possibility of living an openly gay life in an emerging gay neighborhood certainly motivated some migrants, others came as part of a larger migration of young, single, white, college-educated people to newly available professional jobs.[8] Unconstrained by circumstances that would have limited participation in gay and lesbian lifestyles, such as commitments to families, careers, or communities, these migrants were "biographically available" for conversion to gay identity.[9]

Regardless of whether awareness of same-gender sexual interest preceded or followed migration to San Francisco, what the men and women joining the public life of gay San Francisco shared was the adoption of gay or lesbian identities. The notion of coming out was at the heart of this new gay identity movement. This new rhetoric persuaded people that the psychological benefits of adopting gay identity were considerable, to say nothing about the social and sexual benefits of gay life in the city that had acquired a reputation as the best place on earth to be gay. The intersection of this persuasive new ideology and the large cohort of single young migrants produced a remarkable swelling of the publicly gay population in San Francisco. According to FitzGerald:

> Estimates of the gay population of San Francisco [in 1978] ranged from 75,000 to 150,000. If the oft-cited figure of 100,000 were correct, this meant that in this city of less than 700,000 people, approximately one out of every five adults and one out of every three or four voters was gay. A great proportion of these people—half of them or more—had moved into the city within the past eight years. And most of these new immigrants were young, white, and male.[10]

Karen Heller, citing a 1989 *San Francisco Examiner* article by Richard Ramirez, estimates that "one-third of San Francisco's gay male population had migrated to the city between 1974–78."[11]

The growth in numbers of gay organizations, gay migration, and the new geographical concentration contributed to the size and vitality of the most visible expression of the diversification of gay culture in San Francisco—the annual Gay Freedom Day Parade. While substantial in size since 1972 (the estimated crowd size was fifty thousand), by 1977 the event annually brought around a quarter of a million people onto the streets of San

Francisco. The articulated structure of the event, organized around the theme of "unity through diversity," provided a framework that accommodated massive crowds. And as the event grew larger and more complex, it exemplified the solidity of gay identity more effectively.

As the cultural elaboration of gay life in San Francisco progressed, it was reinforced by gay commercial and political development. San Francisco's increasing number and variety of gay bars and bathhouses served as a major attraction. Men who moved to the Castro in search of social and sexual venues also joined community organizations and participated in other aspects of community life, including the annual parade. In the bars, bathhouses, and other gay commercial establishments, gay men spent money. The money from these commercial endeavors was, in some cases, directed toward the support of nonprofit organizations and electoral politics. The Tavern Guild, an association of gay bar owners, supported the Society for Individual Rights and its selected political candidates. Bars could afford to build elaborate floats for participation in the Freedom Day Parade, thus livening up the parade. Nonprofit and for-profit gay organizations were frequently indistinguishable, both defining their missions in terms of building gay culture and identity. The success of non–sexually oriented commercial organizations, such as gay newspapers, bookshops, hardware stores, and clothing stores, contributed to the institutional completeness of the gay community.

In sum, by end of the decade, gay life in San Francisco had been transformed culturally, organizationally, politically, and sexually. This transformation was not an inevitability. It was a political accomplishment, sparked by the crystallization of a gay identity movement in the early 1970s. The availability of cheap housing, professional jobs, and biographically available young people fueled the sheer size and vitality of the phenomenon, but the ideas came first. The dream of a gay neighborhood preceded the reality. The availability of cheap houses and good jobs provided uncommitted resources. Resources, however, are passive. They are not always exploited. The movement of white middle-class families to the suburbs in the 1960s and 1970s was a national phenomenon, but not every city saw a gay migration of similar scale. While there was some gay migration to other cities (after all, the cultural project was national, not just local), none was as massive as the migration to San Francisco. The opportunity to build a gay neighborhood was more fully exploited in San Francisco because the movement was more developed. The crystallization of the gay identity movement in the early 1970s made the tremendous successes of the gay identity-building project possible.

The Explosive Growth of the Commercial Sector

The emergence of a "sexual free-for-all" was perhaps the most visible change in San Francisco gay life in the 1970s. Frances FitzGerald observed:

> By 1978 the Castro had become the most active cruising strip in the city—and perhaps in the country. Even in the daytime there were hundreds of young men out cruising in the bars, the bookshops, the restaurants, and the stores—even in the vast supermarket some distance down Market Street. At night the bars were jammed—there were lines out on the sidewalks—and cars had trouble getting through the crowds of men. The scene was mind-boggling to newcomers: the openness of it and the sheer turnover.[12]

Figure 6.2 suggests the energy of the Castro in the last 1970s. The growth of the sexual subculture has generally been seen as irrelevant to, or even possibly destructive of, the gay identity movement. I argue that the sexual subculture was not destructive of the gay identity movement. Instead, it reinforced the successes of the more conventionally political aspects of the movement. In turn, political and cultural successes also fueled the growth of the sexualized subculture.

The synergistic relationship among the various aspects of the gay identity-building project is illustrated by the growth of the various kinds

Figure 6.2 Men in the Castro district in 1976. Courtesy Rink Foto.

of lesbian/gay organizations. The growth of the gay male sexual subculture in the 1970s paralleled the proliferation of other gay organizations. Figure 6.3 shows the growth of lesbian/gay organizations, divided into commercial organizations focused on sex (bars, bathhouses, sex clubs, and sexually oriented stores) and nonprofit organizations. Sexually focused commercial organizations peaked in number in 1979 with more than 200. The growth of the nonprofit sector in the 1970s suggests that the growth of sexually focused commercial organizations was not at the expense of nonprofit organizations. That commercial, political, and nonprofit organizations participated in the annual parades and were listed in community resource guides confirms that participants viewed these organizations as part of the same project.

These connections between the commercial and cultural aspects of gay life were not inevitable. At the peak of gay liberation it was not clear that gay bars were going to be viewed as part of the movement.[13] In the eyes of gay power activists, gay bars were not part of a "liberated community." These radicals complained that bars were capitalist, that the profits went to the Mafia, and that they cultivated an alienated, objectifying male sexuality. This antipathy toward the bars manifested itself in debates about whether bars should be allowed to participate in the very first commemoration of the Stonewall uprising.

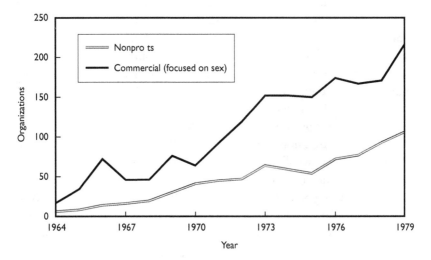

Figure 6.3 Lesbian/Gay Nonprofit and Sexual Commercial Organizations in San Francisco, 1964–79

The consolidation of the gay identity movement pushed ambivalence about gay bars to the margins. The sexual subculture appealed to a diverse constituency of gay men. Protecting gay bars was central to gay electoral politics in San Francisco. Clendinen and Nagourney claim that "gay politics in San Francisco, as in L.A. and New York, had been formed almost entirely in reaction to the continuing crackdown by authorities on gay bars and gay male sexuality."[14] The Tavern Guild, composed of gay bar owners, devoted itself to the task of protecting gay bars and their patrons. Thus, the explosive growth of gay bars and the surrounding sexual culture was, quite directly, the realization of a goal of gay politics. The pursuit of gay rights was, to a large extent, the pursuit of the right of gay men to have sex with each other without the interference of the law.

The cultural accomplishments of the gay identity movement also reinforced the growth of the sexual subculture. The vision of a positive gay identity and the promise of the psychological benefits of coming out brought people into the community. Gay men came to participate in San Francisco's gay identity-building project because of what it promised in terms of a whole gay lifestyle and culture, of which the availability of sex was certainly a central part.

The commercial subculture was not simply a beneficiary of political and cultural aspects of the gay identity-building project; the commercial subculture was also a major source of energy for the rest of the gay identity project. Businesses generated revenue. When these businesses were owned by gay men, which they increasingly were, this produced a consolidation of economic power that translated readily into political influence. For example, the Tavern Guild was a major contributor to political campaigns.

The intensification of the sexual subculture increased the spatial concentration of gay men. FitzGerald describes bars and streets literally jammed with men. According to social movement theorists, this kind of intense interaction is the perfect precondition for social movement mobilization—dense connections among a homogeneous group.[15] The political potential of these crowds of gay men was illustrated by the collection of over one-third of the northern California signatures McGovern needed to get on the ballot in one night of canvassing San Francisco's gay bars by the Alice B. Toklas Democratic Club in 1972.[16] And in 1977, men poured out of bars into the streets reacting in outrage to the defeat of a gay rights ordinance in Dade County, Florida.

Participation in the gay sexual world also built gay identity by creating a distinctive world of shared experience. It provided a simple answer to the question: What do gay men have in common? Why, sex, of course. Karen Heller describes the way the *collective* experience of sexual pleasure affirms both individual and collective identity:[17]

> Anonymous sex in places where homosexuals could congregate freely without fear, such as bathhouses, allowed for the transcendence of the personal burden of being gay. . . . Thus, for many gay men, anonymous sex in a communal setting, such as a sex club or bathhouse, had become kind of a dominant symbol, which linked them together impersonally, yet profoundly, through an experience of communitas.[18]

Participation in the sexual subculture was fun, it provided motivation to relocate and to identify as gay, and it heightened investment in the fate of the community. Clendinen and Nagourney have described the Castro as "a community based on pleasure, not politics."[19] But it was a community of pleasure made possible by decades of political organization. Participants would prove to be as passionately devoted to the defense of this lifestyle as they were to participation in it.

D'Emilio and Altman are correct when they recognize the entangled nature of the commercial subculture and gay identity. According to Altman "No other minority has depended so heavily on commercial enterprises to define itself: while the role of movement papers, dances, and organizations has been significant, it has been overshadowed, especially for gay men, by the commercial world."[20]

Culture, Sex, and the Ascendance of Gay Political Power

More than any other single event, the election of Harvey Milk to the San Francisco Board of Supervisors in November 1977 signaled the ascendance of gay electoral power in San Francisco.[21] Explanations of the growth of gay political power in San Francisco usually emphasize highly fortuitous changes in San Francisco's economy and demography. In this section, I argue that these changes were only part of the story. Without the prior crystallization of the gay identity movement, the gay movement would not have been able to transform economic and demographic changes into political opportunities. The cultural and sexual aspects of the gay identity movement also contributed to the growth of political power by increasing the size and concentration of a gay voting bloc.

The single most important reason why the gay movement acquired political power in San Francisco in the 1970s was that it was able to play a crucial role in advancing the careers of a cohort of ambitious liberal politicians. Liberal politicians discovered that the gay community represented an organized, reliable voting bloc, leading them to be highly solicitous of this important constituency. This mutually beneficial relationship between the gay community and liberal politicians not only contributed to the growth of gay political power, but played a pivotal role in the political careers of some of California's most powerful politicians (e.g., Dianne Feinstein and Willie Brown). This relationship depended upon two conditions: that the liberals were actually viable candidates and that the gay community could deliver votes.

The viability of liberals as political candidates was enhanced by changes in the demographics of the city. In the 1960s San Francisco underwent a profound transformation from an industrial city with a heavily blue-collar population to a financial center with a much more professional population.[22] Much of the traffic of the port of San Francisco moved to Oakland. The factories and warehouses south of Market Street closed down. Blue-collar workers followed their employment and left the city, emptying neighborhoods such as the Haight and the Castro. To stabilize the city's economic base, Mayor Joseph Alioto and other influential politicians pushed to build the financial sector and to make San Francisco appealing for tourism and for corporate headquarters. These new businesses lured white-collar workers, professionals, and service industry personnel to the city—young people with college educations. FitzGerald describes how Alioto "changed the city and at the same time swept away the very base of his own power. As manufacturing left, so did his supporters."[23] The young professionals moving to the city were more liberal, improving the electoral prospects of liberal politicians. But liberal politicians needed to reach these votes. They needed organized voting blocs. As it happened, the gay movement was able to provide such a bloc.

The gay community *entered* the 1970s able to deliver votes. In fact, liberal candidates quickly realized that they could not win elections without garnering gay support. The gay movement was able to deliver these votes only because of the history of homosexual organizing in the city and the more recent crystallization of the movement. In chapter 4, I showed that as the 1960s drew to a close the Society for Individual Rights remained strong. San Francisco's most established homophile organization had survived the challenge of gay liberation, abandoned its reticence about public display, and emerged from the 1960s espousing a politics of gay rights and gay pride. And given its homophile roots, SIR had no ambivalence whatsoever about leaving behind the radical, multi-issue, revolutionary politics of the New Left. Working within the established political system was, as far as SIR was concerned, *the* way to improve life for homosexuals in the city.

Dianne Feinstein was the first to realize the benefits of courting the gay vote. Running for the San Francisco Board of Supervisors, her first political office, "she so charmed the men of SIR when she showed up at a candidate night in 1969 that they outdid themselves in creating a gay vote for her at the polls that fall."[24] Feinstein not only got elected, she won more votes than any other candidate elected to the Board of Supervisors that year, making her president of the board.[25] Attributing her success to the gay vote, Feinstein continued to cultivate the gay male community. The gay vote played a crucial role in returning Feinstein to the presidency of the Board of Supervisors in 1973.[26]

Richard Hongisto, a liberal police officer, also sought the support of the gay movement. In fact, it was gay leader Jim Foster who suggested to Hongisto that he run for sheriff in 1971.[27] In his campaign, Hongisto ran on issues near and dear to the hearts of gay men—reforming California's laws on sexual conduct. The Tavern Guild provided financial support for Hongisto's campaign.[28] Hongisto won the election. According to Clendinen and Nagourney, "the new sheriff-elect made no bones about who had put him into office. His 'biggest single source of support was gay and lesbian,' he told people. 'Hands down.'"[29]

From 1971 onward, the gay voting bloc was a factor in all San Francisco elections. This reality was hard to miss when the *San Francisco Chronicle* reported in October 1971 that

> San Francisco's populous homosexual community, historically non-political and inward looking, is in the midst of assembling a potentially powerful, political machine. A sustained and determined effort is underway to raise money and political consciousness, organize precinct workers, distribute campaign literature and pursue all other avenues classically associated with the development of political muscle.[30]

San Francisco's politicians were certainly highly attuned to this fact. In 1975, according to Clendinen and Nagourney, "Dianne Feinstein's campaign manager told the *Los Angeles Times* [that the gay vote was] probably the largest liberal voting bloc in the city."[31] The result, the *Times* story said, was that the city's "politicians are rushing virtually en masse toward what they see as a rich new source of campaign strength."[32] Politicians appealed to SIR and to the Alice B. Toklas Democratic Club, formed by Jim Foster in December

1971,[33] for endorsements. Candidates participated in the Gay Freedom Day Parade. Clendinen and Nagourney report that "one candidate told a crowd assembled by the Gay Voters League at Bo-Jangles, a dimly lit gay bar in the Tenderloin, that in September, 'I rode in the Gay Freedom Parade and am *proud* of it.'"[34]

When liberal candidates competed for office, the gay community could select among multiple candidates vying for their loyalty. In 1975, Moscone and Feinstein competed for the gay vote in the mayoral election. In spite of Feinstein's long-standing relationship with the gay community, she did not win the endorsement of the Alice B. Toklas Democratic Club. George Moscone secured gay support with his role in the 1975 passage of consenting adults legislation in the California state senate.[35] Clendinen and Nagourney report that as majority leader of the state, Moscone

> called in every important political chip. The Senate had deadlocked in a tie, 20–20, and Moscone had literally held it there by locking the doors of the chamber until the lieutenant governor could fly back from Denver and arrive to break the tie by voting with Moscone.[36]

In a runoff against conservative John Barbagelata, Moscone won by 4,400 votes.

Moscone credited gays with his victory. He gratefully responded with political appointments to gay movement leaders. Moscone appointed Harvey Milk to the Board of Permit Appeals. Milk was a logical choice. In 1975, Milk "had very nearly won his second race for supervisor, coming seventh in the citywide voting for all candidates for a six-person board."[37] This made him "the city's principal,—if not yet elected—gay politician."[38] The near-victory of the 1975 campaign revealed that Harvey Milk would win if he could "run for office in the precincts where he was strong, and not the rest of the city."[39] In 1976, Harvey Milk, in a challenging feat of coalition building, persuaded labor unions and neighborhood organizations to work with gays to mount a grassroots campaign to get district elections on the November 1976 ballot.[40] Newly elected mayor George Moscone campaigned for the initiative. Districtwide elections were approved in 1976, clearing the way for Milk's successful campaign in 1977.[41]

By playing a deciding role in electing Moscone and other liberal politicians, the gay movement actively reshaped its political environment. The ability of the gay movement to remake its environment in this way rested not only on the power of its political organization, but also on the size and concentration of its constituency. Those devoted to electoral politics did not control the growth and concentration of the population. Gay migrants moved to the Castro because of its social, cultural, and sexual possibilities— not simply to contribute to a gay voting bloc. But once they became part of this spatially concentrated gay world, they were likely to vote for gay-friendly candidates.

The Paradox of Success: Backlash and Response

By the late 1970s, it was becoming difficult for mainstream Americans to overlook the astonishing vitality of gay communities in major urban areas in the United States, particularly in San Francisco. The sheer size of the migration to San Francisco, the phenomenon of the Castro, the energy of the sexual subculture, and the political power of the gay community demanded attention. Some observers were not happy with what they saw. Their disapproval of the successes of the gay movement provoked a backlash.[42] Like other waves of repression, this backlash had complex consequences. On one hand, the process of mobilizing against these assaults brought the gay movement to a higher level of organization, leading to the crystallization of the movement at the national level in 1979. On the other hand, this repression, particularly when it took the form of political assassinations, took a toll on the movement.[43]

In January 1977, Dade County, Florida, passed a gay rights ordinance.[44] Claiming that "no one has the human right to corrupt our children," Anita Bryant, a former Miss America and spokeswoman for the Florida orange industry, formed a coalition to repeal the ordinance.[45] The Save Our Children campaign displayed footage of the Gay Freedom Day Parade to show that San Francisco was "a cesspool of sexual perversion gone rampant."[46] Horror about the growth of the gay community in San Francisco was clearly an inspiration for the Miami campaign, which explicitly made the connection with its appeal, "Don't let Miami become another San Francisco."[47] Bryant's group collected signatures to put the ordinance to the voters as a referendum. In spite of national organization in support of the gay rights ordinance, Dade County voters elected to repeal the gay rights ordinance on June 7, 1977.[48]

While a demoralizing defeat for the gay movement, it had positive consequences. Bryant's campaign indicated that gays had succeeded in becoming a new political actor on the American scene. By defining gay life as a threat worthy of attack, antigay activists acknowledged that the gay movement could no longer be dismissed as a joke. Everyone, sympathetic or hostile, would have to contend with the reality of gay identity and gay communities.

Bryant's campaign not only recognized gay identity, it also contributed to its institutionalization. By recognizing and publicizing gay identity, Bryant participated in creating her enemy. In cultural struggles like this one, all press is, in a sense, good press. By generating media coverage the backlash further disseminated gay identity and the gay rights agenda. Harvey Milk pointed this out in an address to the gay caucus of the California Democratic Council on March 10, 1978:

> In the week before [the] Miami [vote] and the week after that, the word homosexual or gay appeared in every single newspaper in this nation in articles both pro and con. In every radio station, in every TV station and every household. For the first time in the history of the world, everybody was talking about it, good or bad.[49]

Bryant's campaign not only affirmed the reality and solidity of gay identity, it also reminded gay men and lesbians that the freedoms they experienced in San Francisco and other urban centers were localized and fragile. Seeing themselves through the eyes of hostile outsiders led them to see that their safety in urban centers could not be assured without thinking nationally about the protection and extension of gay rights. This growing recognition of the need for national organization was reflected in the *Advocate* of April 20, 1977. Publisher David Goodstein proclaimed that "if the orange juice cow and her bigoted cohorts have their way in Dade County, you can rest assured they'll bring their hate crusade to your front door in Los Angeles, New York, San Francisco, Chicago or wherever you think you're living in relative safety."[50]

This new realization was, according to Clendinen and Nagourney, a "turning point for gay men and lesbians who years later would trace their own coming out or interest in gay politics to the Anita Bryant victory. In the days after the repeal, there were marches in cities large and small."[51]

This recognition of the fragility of urban gay lifestyles impressed itself not only on seasoned politicos, but also on gay men whose main form of participation in gay life was in the bar scene. When gay men in San Francisco bars and clubs heard about the Dade County vote, they congregated at the intersection of Market and Castro. Chanting "Out of the bars—into the street!" they marched toward Most Holy Redeemer Catholic Church, then up Market Street, and finally to Union Square, where the crowd numbered more than five thousand.[52] The angry response of the crowd was spontaneous, stunning gay leaders, who had envisioned a silent candlelight vigil on Castro

Street. The event revealed the political potential of a densely concentrated community that was presumably concerned only with pleasure.[53]

The struggle over the gay rights ordinance in Florida not only mobilized the gay movement, it also mobilized the right. It had immediate consequences in California. As D'Emilio explains:

> The day after the Miami vote, John Briggs, an ultraconservative state senator from Orange County with aspirations for higher office, announced plans to introduce legislation to prohibit gays from teaching in the public schools. When it became obvious that the legislation had no chance of passage, Briggs shifted tactics and mounted a campaign to have his proposal placed on the ballot as a statewide initiative. By early 1978 it was clear that California voters would have to decide in November whether lesbians and gay men, as well as anyone who publicly or privately advocated or encouraged homosexual conduct, should be dismissed from jobs in the public school system.[54]

The Briggs Initiative was closer to home. In June 1978 Harvey Milk and other gay leaders were convinced that Californians would vote for the Briggs Initiative in November.[55] Nonetheless, they organized to defeat the initiative. At the Gay Freedom Day Parade in June 1978, amidst the bar contingents and the Dykes on Bikes, people carried signs against the Briggs Initiative (figure 6.4). The event reveals the power of the melding of the cultural and political characteristic of the gay identity movement. Shilts called this parade "the signal event of the gay emergence in San Francisco during the late 1970s."[56] With an estimated 350,000 people, Shilts speculates that this may have been the largest single political gathering in San Francisco, and perhaps in the United States, in the 1970s. Harvey Milk spoke at the rally at City Hall.[57] The celebratory aspect of the event, that it was a parade, not a political rally, drew many more people than would have attended a "No on Briggs" march. That the parade was a way of standing against the Briggs Initiative also swelled the size of the event. The sheer size of the event delivered a political message.

The Briggs Initiative was defeated in November 1978. Funded by affluent Los Angeles gay activist David Goodstein, the anti-Briggs campaign had hired an experienced political consultant, Don Bradley. The campaign engaged in fund-raising, television commercials, and a speakers' bureau and tried to influence newspaper content. It registered voters, made phone calls, painted picket signs, and drove people to the polls. And, most critically, campaign leaders David Mixner and Peter Scott found a way to use personal connec-

Figure 6.4 Supervisor Harvey Milk rallied against the Briggs Initiative in San Francisco's 1978 Gay Freedom Day Parade. Courtesy *San Francisco Chronicle,* June 25, 1978.

tions to gain a private meeting with Ronald Reagan, who had already been tagged as a presidential contender. In discussion with Reagan, they framed the issue in terms of privacy issues and the potential for blackmail. Reagan's political committee opposed the initiative, which effectively turned the tide.[58]

The battle against the Briggs Initiative strengthened the gay movement through development of the political and organizational infrastructure. Clendinen and Nagourney point out that "they had shown they could do this; they had raised $800,000, developed an effective campaign theme, and produced television commercials and endorsements."[59] This victory, "the greatest electoral victory the gay rights movement in the United States had known," conferred an "aura of historical celebrity on Harvey Milk."[60]

At the party celebrating the defeat of the Briggs Initiative, Harvey Milk called for a gay march on Washington in 1979. The idea of a gay march on Washington had been circulating through political circles since the spring of 1978, arousing little enthusiasm. Sentiment about a national march on Washington changed dramatically after Supervisor Dan White assassinated Harvey Milk and Mayor George Moscone on November 27, 1978, less than three weeks after the Briggs Initiative was defeated. When White received a verdict of voluntary manslaughter instead of murder in May 1979, gays responded with outrage in what came to be known as the "White Night riots." Figure 6.5 shows onlookers watching police cars that were set ablaze by furious gays.[61]

Milk's assassination consolidated support in favor of a national march on Washington.[62] The march, attended by 25,000 people, was held in October 1979 (figure 6.6). The *San Francisco Chronicle* marks this event as the "coming out of the movement on the national political agenda."[63] The process of organiz-

Figure 6.5 Observers watching police cars burn in the White Night riots, May 21, 1979. © 1979 by Daniel Nicoletta.

ing the march required tremendous energy and commitment, producing "an increasingly national sense of gay solidarity."[64]

The consolidation of the gay identity movement in San Francisco in the early 1970s made possible the ascendance of Harvey Milk and the other successes of gay San Francisco in the 1970s. These successes, in turn, provoked repression, in the form of the campaigns by Anita Bryant and John Briggs. Repression led to defensive organization on the part of the gay movement. And in the case of the Briggs Initiative, it gave the movement its biggest electoral success and enhanced the political power of San Francisco's first elected gay politician. Increased success, in turn, provoked further repression: the assassinations of Harvey Milk and George Moscone by Dan White. Repression, in turn, crystallized commitment to organize a national march on Washington in 1979. The process of mobilizing for this march, and its successful result, consolidated the gay movement on the national level. Thus, the cycle of action and reaction had the consequence of ratcheting up the level of organization of the gay movement. This cycle built upon the consolidation of the gay identity movement in the early 1970s.

While responding to antigay organizing led to further movement crys-

Figure 6.6 The first lesbian and gay march on Washington, October 14, 1979. © 2002 JEB (Joan E. Biren).

tallization, the backlash took a deep toll as well. The assassinations of Milk and Moscone eliminated irreplaceable political leaders and effectively ended an era in San Francisco politics. In addition, the efforts to repeal the Dade County gay rights ordinance and to pass the Briggs Initiative were only the first of many attacks on gay rights. This assault would prove to be sustained, well funded, and well organized. Antigay activists were passionate about their cause. The campaign grew to be national in scope and was energized by strong feelings about other issues, such as abortion. These campaigns were difficult to counter in the 1980s, in a political climate shaped by the election of Ronald Reagan in November 1980.

The crystallization of the movement in the early 1970s yielded visible successes later in the decade. Movement crystallization established the groundwork for large numbers of people to come out, the proliferation of lesbian and gay organizations, gay migration to San Francisco, the growth of a gay neighborhood, the expansion of the sexually focused commercial sector, and the consolidation of gay electoral power. Synergistic relationships

among the cultural, political, and commercial aspects of the movement contributed to its dynamic growth. These successes provoked repression, which,
ironically, contributed to further development. The development of the gay
identity movement in the 1970s was not only a story of growth fueled by internal unity. Tensions around issues of race, class, and gender were brewing
under the surface. Chapter 7 examines the ways the gay identity movement
marginalized white lesbians and lesbians and gay men of color.

SEVEN

Exclusions: Gender, Race, and Class in the Gay Identity Movement, 1981–1994

We're fine for show during Gay Pride Week when a little color is needed.
Thom Beame, "Racism from a Black Perspective" (1983)

We only have one thing in common. . . . We are on the same side of the civil rights issue.
Christine Jarosz, white lesbian, interviewed for the 1997 documentary *Pride Divide,* on relationships between lesbians and gay men

I didn't see any of them as cause issues.
Jim Kepner, white male gay activist, interviewed for *Pride Divide,* on why he did not support issues of concern to lesbians in the early 1970s

I don't want to be a part of a movement that once the sexual orientation issue is answered will leave me . . . to fend for myself as an African American and as a woman.
Nadine Smith, African American lesbian, interviewed for *Pride Divide,* on the race and gender politics of the gay movement

Through the 1970s, as the crowds turning out for freedom day parades in San Francisco swelled to hundreds of thousands of people, it appeared that the gay identity movement was indeed both unified and diverse. But behind the scenes many lesbians and gay men complained that the vision of a diverse, inclusive community belied the reality of their experiences. White lesbians, gay men and lesbians of color, less affluent gays, and others experienced the 1970s as a time of exclusion from an increasingly powerful white middle-class male gay political project. Lesbians found that issues of importance to them, such as how to preserve custody of their children, were considered peripheral to the gay rights agenda.[1] Gay men of color were discriminated against in the predominantly white bar circuit of the 1970s through such tactics as the selective demand for multiple forms of identification at clubs.[2] Lesbians of color felt that lesbian separatism ignored their need to maintain alliances with men of color.[3]

Thus, we are faced with a paradox. I claimed that the gay identity movement crystallized in the early 1970s, enabling the growth of the movement in the 1970s. But white lesbians, gay men and lesbians of color, street gays, and radicals would have said that they did not sign on to any such consensus.[4] In what sense is it meaningful to talk about a consensus if these groups disagreed with the direction of the movement? I claimed that this new gay identity project prided itself on its diversity. But with the proliferation of white male "clones" in urban centers and the dominance of young white men in gay culture and politics, gay life in the 1970s seemed to be about homogeneity, not diversity. Was the rhetoric of "unity through diversity" wishful thinking at best or, at worst, an empty, hypocritical slogan?

The key to understanding this paradox is focusing on the nature and limitations of the consensus and the kind of diversity with which the project was concerned. In chapter 5 we saw that the agreement reached in the early 1970s was primarily a new level of accord among white, middle-class men. A celebration of diversity was part of this new consensus, but the forms of diversity with which activists were most concerned were *ideological and sexual diversity among white, middle-class men.* Even getting this demographically homogeneous group organized around an identity was an enormous political accomplishment. Thus, while the pride-rights-sex synthesis presented itself as universal, it emerged from the particular experiences of a cohort of American middle-class urban white men. By interpreting the movement's claims of universality and diversity more broadly than the original founders' (not fully conscious) intentions, those leveling accusations of exclusion had legitimate grievances.

This ambiguity set in motion decades of conflict about the movement's inclusivity, universality, and representativeness. The movement understood itself as in the general interest of all people engaged in nonnormative sexuality, while concretely embodying the evolving interests of middle-class, white gay men. During the 1970s white lesbians devoted themselves to elaborating a separate lesbian feminist movement, not directly confronting the masculinist premises of the gay identity movement until the late 1970s. By the early 1980s, lesbians of color began challenging the assumptions about race implicit in a lesbian separatist politics. Challenges by gay men of color to the racial exclusivity of the gay identity movement were slowest to develop, not fully taking shape until the late 1980s. Achieving racial inclusivity involved more fundamental challenges to the core assumptions of the political project.

While the nature of the exclusions and contradictions discussed here are particular to this field, that field formation produces exclusions and internal contradictions is a general property of fields. Even the most ambiguous and inclusive of fields must be able to establish boundaries. It is not a question of whether exclusions will be created, but rather of who and what will be excluded. Thus, field formation involves power. By establishing the "rules of the game," field formation makes collective action along some lines much easier, but also makes action according to other logics less possible.

Universal and Diverse? Or Particular and Homogeneous?

There is room in the gay liberation movement for every gay person to make his or her own type of contribution.

white gay activist Jim Owles (1971),
quoted in Laud Humphreys, *Out of the Closets*

Gay liberation, when we get right down to it, is the struggle for gay men to achieve approval for the only thing that separates them from the "Man"— their sexual preference.

Canadian lesbian activist Marie Robertson,
"We Need Our Own Banner" (1982)

How did the gay identity movement develop a sincere understanding of itself as universally representative and diverse while simultaneously becoming intensely particular and homogeneous? The founders believed that each element of the consensus—gay pride, gay rights, and sexual self-expression—benefited all gay people equally, regardless of race, class, or gender. The assumption that all would benefit equally from such a movement relied on what Steven Seidman has referred to as the assumption of a "unitary" gay experience, that is, the idea that "the meaning and experience of being gay are socially uniform."[5]

The movement assumed that coming out was positive and that this was a goal that all gay people supported regardless of race, class, or gender. Gay identity was defined as a "master" identity. Activists drew parallels between the experiences of ethnic minorities and gays and defined gays as an ethnic group.[6] They assumed that it was necessary for individuals to make a break with past social and familial roles in order to adopt new roles within gay communities. They assumed that all gay people, regardless of social origins, experienced breaking with a community of origin, adopting a gay identity and joining a gay community in the same way. The belief in the psychological

and political benefits of coming out held a central, unquestioned, almost sa-
cred place at the core of the gay identity movement.

The unquestioned nature of this assumption made it difficult for those
who were not white, middle-class men to articulate that coming out was not
always experienced as unambiguously positive. Social origins shaped the likelihood of and the experience of coming out and joining a gay community.
For women, making a break with the heterosexual world and joining a lesbian world often involved giving up economic security. Women's economic
security has often depended on alliances with men. For people of color, making a break from communities of origin and joining a gay community often
meant losing the protection of an ethnic/racial community and attempting
to fit into an unfamiliar, hostile white world. In the 1980s gay people of color,
such as Isaac Julien and Kobena Mercer, began to assert that coming out felt
"totally ethnocentric as it ignored the fact that black lesbians and gay men
need our families, which offer us support and protection from the racism we
experience on the street, at school, from the police, and from the state."[7] Sociologist Tomás Almaguer argued that membership in the privileged racial
group was necessary for the development of gay identity as master identity;
for gays from other groups, racial/ethnic identity often felt primary.[8] Gay
identity was unproblematic only for those who either had no prior commitments to identity-based communities or were in a position to abandon their
prior commitments.

Given the vibrancy of race and gender movements, gay white men were
well aware that women and people of color had grievances (which they believed should be dealt with in the context of separate movements). But just
as they assumed that coming out had the same meaning for all, they assumed
that discrimination based on sexuality was shared. They assumed that a gay
rights agenda would benefit all gay people, regardless of race or gender, in the
same way and to the same extent. Because they assumed that the policy
changes they sought would benefit all gay men and lesbians, they felt that
they were fighting for the rights of gay men and lesbians in general, even
when their organizations were composed nearly exclusively of white men.

But race, gender, and class intersected with sexuality in ways that produced substantially different experiences of discrimination, and different priorities among the rights that the movement could pursue. For example,
when lesbians lost custody of their children, it was because of sexuality, not
gender. Thus, gay custody rights were a "cause" issue, in the narrowest sense,
in that it involved battling a form of discrimination that occurred specifically

because of sexual identity. Gay men did not prioritize the defense of custody rights because fewer of them were vulnerable to the loss of custody of their children. Similarly, lesbians were far less vulnerable than gay men to being arrested for having sex in public places. However, the gay identity movement defined the defense of public sex as a general gay rights issue, while custody issues were defined as a peripheral women's issue.

A single-issue focus on gay rights was central to the gay identity movement. For women and people of color this focus meant setting aside issues that were as important, if not more important, to improving the quality of their lives. Lesbians were invested in political issues that affected them as women, such as equal opportunities in employment, reproductive rights, and violence against women.[9] Gay men of color often felt that it was important to address issues of economic inequality.[10] For white men a single-issue agenda allowed a concerted focus on precisely the aspects of society that prevented them from having every privilege and right granted to other middle-class, white men in American society.[11]

The gay identity movement also assumed that the protection of venues for sexual expression was equally important to all those interested in same-gender sexuality. The gay identity movement endorsed all consensual sexual practices, including impersonal sex, the use of pornography, sadomasochistic sex, prostitution and other forms of commercial sex, and erotic styles that some saw as having racist and fascist connotations.

But race and gender sometimes provided lesbians and people of color with a different perspective on sex. Women's gender socialization led many lesbians to find the intensifying gay male sexual subculture mystifying and distasteful.[12] In addition to this aesthetic reaction, lesbians also criticized impersonal sex on ideological grounds. Feminists felt that women had been harmed by conventional constructions of desire and were interested in uncovering the sources of desire and transforming it. For example, instead of simply expressing and displaying sadomasochistic desires, some feminists advocated analyzing, working through, and eliminating such desires.[13] Gay men of color mused about whether "such sexual libertarianism and individualism is itself based on certain racial privilege."[14] They criticized sexual tastes they saw as racist, the lack of images of men of color in gay publications, and fetishizing of men of color by white gay men.[15]

Above, we saw that the gay identity movement was not as universal as it represented itself to be. And it was diverse only in the sense that it linked people with diverse political ideologies and sexualities. Its articulated structure, and the conviction that positive social change grew out of the diverse and even contradictory activities of gay people, provided it with the capacity to produce and display an astonishing variety of gay organizations. But there were definite limits to the kind of diversity that the movement could accommodate. Movement diversification was highly structured around the modification and elaboration of the core gay identity. The gay identity movement encouraged the production and display of all secondary identities, but rejected diversification that threatened the core agreements binding together the project, the most fundamental of which was the belief in a positive, public, socially uniform gay identity. Thus, lesbians and gays of color could be easily accommodated when they were willing to treat racial identity as secondary, of no more or less importance than the choice of a hobby. The gay identity movement could not so easily include people of color when they refused to subordinate racial/ethnic identity to sexual identity or when they insisted that racial identity changed the very meaning of gay identity.

Ironically, the identity logic that produced a commitment to gay identity simultaneously heightened the salience of identity in society in general and created equally compelling commitments to racial, ethnic, and gender identities—identities that, like sexual identity, are under constant political reconstruction. The intensified commitment to identity in all of these various movements made the emergence of critiques of exclusion inevitable. In this context, it was unlikely that people of color would be willing to treat racial or ethnic identity as secondary. The proliferation of movements offering competing master identities created competition for the loyalties of individuals with multiple possible allegiances.

Given that identity politics presumed that psychological health depended upon the open expression of and positive recognition of identity, individuals experienced the demand that they privilege one part of the self over others as a demand to "closet" or "repress" aspects of the self. Not surprisingly, these individuals came to demand the freedom to express all aspects of their selves at the same time. They did not want to be out about sexual identity at the expense of being closeted about race, ethnicity, or gender. When individuals found that they could not express these other salient identities in the context of gay organizations, they drew on the rhetoric and language of identity politics to criticize this repression. For example, white lesbians said, "You claim the gay movement is universal and diverse, but it doesn't reflect the specific concerns of lesbians. Men and women are fundamentally different. Women have different concerns. Unless we can express ourselves, we won't feel comfortable in this movement." Likewise, people of color argued, "You claim the movement is universal and diverse, but it does not include gay men or lesbians of color. Our racial identities are as important to us as our sexual identities. Unless we can express both sexual and racial identities, we won't feel comfortable. We should be able to express the entirety of our selves within this movement."

Lesbian Feminism as a Separate Project

Given the dynamism and analytical sophistication of the women's liberation movement in the early 1970s, we might have expected lesbians to confront the male biases embedded within the gay identity movement early in the 1970s. But they did not. Instead, lesbians focused on building separate women-centered communities. The intersection of lesbianism and feminism produced a lesbian feminist analysis that emphasized commonalities with heterosexual feminists and differences from gay men. Lesbian feminists argued that "considering the centrality of lesbianism to the Women's Movement it should now seem absurd to persist in associating lesbian women with the male homosexual movement. Lesbians are feminists, not homosexuals."[16] Emerging from such groups as the New York Radicalesbians, which collectively authored the manifesto "The Woman-Identified Woman" in 1970,[17] this perspective argued that directing energies toward men was counterproductive.[18] The notion of shared gender as a basis for solidarity provided the engine of a dynamic, vital lesbian feminist movement. Lesbians, in Marotta's words, came to "think of themselves as a special political breed committed to both gay and women's liberation."[19]

Lesbian feminism resolved the contradictions between loyalty to a gender-based movement and loyalty to a sexuality-based movement. By claiming that lesbianism was central to feminism, lesbians did not have to choose which aspect of their identities was more central. By living a lesbian life, one was living as a feminist.[20] It placed heterosexual feminists in the interesting position of being disloyal by continuing their relationships with men. In order to illustrate gender loyalty, some feminists who had previously considered themselves heterosexual came to identify as lesbian. Lillian Faderman quotes a radical feminist "who divorced her physician husband in 1974 to become a lesbian" as describing lesbianism as "the only noble choice a committed feminist could make."[21] Defining lesbian identity as an issue of gender loyalty as well as a description of erotic interests intensified concern about loyalty and authenticity within lesbian communities.[22]

The turn away from the gay identity movement was pragmatic, as well as ideological. Lesbians were well aware of the gendered nature of homosexual experience and of gender differences in priorities. Lesbian activists such as

Del Martin and Phyllis Lyon had tried hard to get men to recognize lesbian issues. Women in the homophile movement and gay liberation had experienced gay men's outright sexism, been asked to make coffee and copies, treated as tokens, and excluded from leadership positions. These negative experiences, combined with parallel experiences in the women's movement, convinced lesbians that attempting to transform the gay identity movement was a waste of time in the early 1970s. Del Martin, a founder of the Daughters of Bilitis, described her decision to turn away from the gay movement in a statement published in the October 1970 issue of the *Vector*.[23] Lesbian assessments of the prospects for success at this moment were probably accurate. White gay male leaders were oblivious to the concerns expressed by women. Interviewed in later years, some of these leaders, such as Jim Kepner, express regret for their lack of concern.[24]

Lesbian feminism shared with the gay movement a wholehearted commitment to pride, coming out, and community building. Like gay men, lesbians saw sexual identity as a master identity and coming out as healthy, therapeutic, and politically important. Lesbians also set about institution building. Women-only spaces such as community centers, theater groups, music festivals, and collectives of all kinds emerged.[25] The intellectual vitality of this project was reflected in a stream of lesbian feminist theorizing.[26] The flowering of lesbian culture in the 1970s has been described as a "cultural renaissance."[27] Women's music festivals played a similar role in lesbian communities as gay freedom day parades in gay communities. Figure 7.1 displays the growth of lesbian and feminist organizations in San Francisco from 1964 through 1994.[28] The overlap between lesbian and feminist organizations was such that it was often difficult to distinguish feminist organizations open to heterosexual women from exclusively lesbian organizations. The number of organizations hovers around ten through the middle 1970s and then begins to increase. In 1978, eighteen women-only organizations are listed. The number more than doubled by 1982. In 1991, the number peaks at eighty-eight, after which it declines. Lesbian organizations included: *Dykespeak,* a lesbian newspaper (1993–); San Francisco Lesbian Archives (1983–84); San Francisco Lesbian Chorus (1982–93); Lesbian and Bisexual Rights Task Forces of NOW (1984–); San Francisco Lesbian Avengers, a radical political group (1983–); the Full Moon Coffeehouse, an early lesbian-feminist coffeehouse (1975–78); Black Lesbian Support Group (1991); and Vietnamese Lesbian Bisexual Group (1992–).

Lesbian feminism avoided the masculinist assumptions of the gay identity movement and thus implicitly critiqued the gay movement by showing

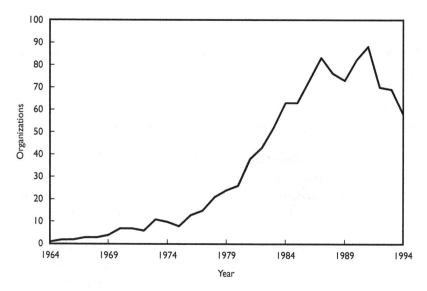

Figure 7.1 Lesbian and Feminist Organizations in San Francisco, 1964–94

what a sexual identity–based movement would look like if it centered on women's experience. Lesbian feminism differed from the gay identity movement even in terms of institution building. Lesbian feminism retained more of the New Left critique of conventional organizational forms and a deep commitment to building nonauthoritarian, nonhierarchical organizations. Combined with a more intense and dyadic gender style of socialization, this meant less emphasis on the kinds of formal organizations gay men formed. Lesbian organizations were fewer in number, less densely concentrated in urban areas, less likely to be for-profit, and more likely to be smaller and more informal. Wolf described San Francisco's lesbian community between 1972 and 1975 as a "series of overlapping social networks, in which friendship groups focus[ed] around pair relationships or special interests."[29] Taylor and Whittier employed Melucci's concept of "submerged networks" to describe lesbian feminism, arguing that "the lesbian feminist movement does not mobilize through formal social movement organizations."[30] Rather, it consisted of "a decentralized network of primarily local, autonomous groups lacking formal organization."[31] The residential segregation of lesbians in distinct urban neighborhoods was not as dramatic as that of gay men. Much of the lesbian cultural renaissance took place in rural communes or in smaller towns. The only lesbian publications produced in San Francisco were those of Daughters of Bilitis.[32] The *Amazon Quarterly* (1972–75) was published in Oakland; *Lesbian Voices* (1974–81) in San Jose; the *Rubyfruit Reader* (1976–78) in Santa Cruz; and *Mama Bears* (1984–) in Oakland.

Fewer commercial organizations, less visible nonprofit organizations, and less residential segregation meant that lesbians did not present a coherent, well-financed voting bloc. Lesbians were peripheral to the rapid consolidation of gay electoral power in San Francisco in the 1970s. Initially, lesbians did not worry about this lack of mainstream political influence because they were skeptical about the value of gaining power within institutions they saw as deeply flawed.[33] The gay identity movement had jettisoned claims to being a movement engaged in a redistributive politics. Not so lesbian feminism. Issues of economic and social injustice continued to be of central concern.

Lesbian feminism did not produce anything like the public sexual subculture produced by men. The comparatively tiny lesbian bar scene might be partially explained by antagonism toward capitalism and low levels of financial resources. But the primary reason for this difference was that women's gender socialization did not incline women toward the anonymous, objectifying sexual encounters that were central to the bar culture. Feminism was critical of sexual objectification, which they saw as an aspect of men's sexuality that had caused women to be treated as less than fully human. While gay power activists had briefly entertained a critique of gay male sexuality at the height of gay liberation, gay men had rejected this critique. Most gay men had no interest in reconstructing their sexuality. They simply wanted freedom of sexual expression. Lesbian feminism, however, did not relinquish the ambition to transform sexuality. Instead of gay male celebration of sexual variation, lesbian feminists devoted themselves to identifying problematic forms of desire (i.e., butch/femme, S/M, pornography), analyzing the underlying sources of these forms of desire, and developing agendas for reshaping sexuality in ways consistent with a feminist vision.

The gay identity movement was built around pride, rights, and sexual expression, while lesbian feminism espoused pride, social justice, and sexual self-transformation. The emphasis on justice and sexual self-transformation instead of rights and self-expression led lesbians to police each other's lifestyles and political beliefs. Commitment to developing a feminist analysis and a multi-issue social justice politics meant that lesbian feminism was not interested in bridging ideological diversity. Because lesbian feminism believed in the existence of a preferable form of sexuality, it could not tolerate the sexual diversity accommodated within the gay movement. If "unity through diversity" summed up the gay identity movement, "the personal is political" summed up lesbian feminism. While both built on the logic of identity politics, they did so quite differently. Gay men *expressed* identity, while lesbians *transformed* it.

Lesbian feminism did not produce the synergistic growth or mainstream visibility of the gay identity movement. By the end of the 1970s, women found themselves unable to live up to what they experienced as increasingly restrictive community standards. They tired of attempting to transform their psyches and sexualities. Some lesbians became intrigued with the freedom to express sexual and ideological diversity cultivated by gay politics. Years of relatively unsuccessful efforts at mobilizing for social justice in an inhospitable social context also took its toll.

While lesbian feminism did not produce the formidable political, cultural, and economic edifice the gay identity movement produced, it produced a rich political conversation. Its existence provided an analysis of how the gay identity movement would need to be transformed to take on lesbian issues. It kept alive a sexual politics committed to a broader social justice agenda. It developed awareness of issues of racial exclusion. Its existence highlighted the exclusions of both women's and gay movements.

Integrating Lesbian Concerns into the Gay Political Project

Some lesbians continued participating in the gay identity movement throughout the 1970s.[34] Lesbians with identities as sexual nonconformists who felt uncomfortable with the submersion of the erotic aspect of lesbianism typical of lesbian feminism were particularly likely to stay involved in the gay movement.[35] Lesbian participation in the gay identity movement was reflected in the steady accumulation of gender-integrated gay organizations. These organizations grew at just about the same rate as exclusively lesbian organizations. Gender-integrated organizations of the 1970s included such organizations as the Metropolitan Community Church (1971–), San Francisco Gay Rap (1972–73), Achavah Jewish Gay Union (1973–89), and Gay Teachers and Schoolworkers (1978–88). Lesbians also participated in the Gay Freedom Day Parade before its name was changed to include "Lesbian" (see figure 7.2).

Because the term "gay" was commonly used to refer to both men and women, it is difficult to assess lesbian participation in the gay movement in the 1970s. Organizations composed of gay men could and did represent themselves as including both gay men and lesbians even when lesbian participation was minimal or nonexistent. For example, in 1973, the mission statement of the San Francisco Gay Rap acknowledged that "in practice it's mostly attended by men, but gay women are welcome also." The ambiguity

Figure 7.2 Lesbian marchers in San Francisco's 1977 Gay Freedom Day Parade, four years before "lesbian" was introduced into the name of the parade. Courtesy Rink Foto.

of the term "gay" tended to make women invisible and implied that lesbian concerns were identical to gay men's concerns.

Lesbian criticism of the gay identity movement heated up in the late 1970s. Lesbians turned back to the gay identity movement as lesbian feminism became less vibrant, while the emergence of the antigay backlash alerted gay men to the need to be more receptive to lesbian demands. Gay men had to be forced to see the gendered nature of homosexual experience. They assumed the typical homosexual person was male and viewed gay men's problems as generic to gay life while viewing lesbian issues as particularistic. When lesbians turned their attention back to the gay movement, they pushed for inclusion of the term "lesbian" in organization names. Simply by demanding that "lesbian" be included in organization names lesbians asserted that: (1) women's experience of being gay was different; (2) it was both as universal and as specific as men's experience; (3) lesbian issues were of equal importance; (4) one could not claim to represent lesbians without including "lesbian" in the organization's name; and (5) organizations that claimed to represent lesbians had to have lesbians as members and leaders.

In June 1980 a group of lesbians called the Gay Freedom Day Parade a male-dominated event and requested that women not participate.[36] Controversy over the 1980 parade was not just about women's invisibility but also about the low participation of third world and disabled people and about the administration of the parade. Concerns were expressed about "finances, speakers, monitor policies, . . . outreach, general production and internal procedures of the Gay Freedom Day Parade Committee."[37] In spite of the conflict, the 1980 parade went off as planned. In August 1980, as the parade committee began planning the 1981 event, the group of dissidents again made an "effort to recapture our parade," urging a series of structural changes that would democratize the organization.[38] By October, the dissidents felt that they could not achieve representation in the current parade structure. They organized a competing parade committee. The new, competing parade committee called itself the "Lesbian/Gay Parade Committee." In December, the two parade committees agreed to arbitration in order to merge.[39] In February 1981, the parade unified under the new name and with a new structure.[40] On June 4, 1981, the *Bay Area Reporter* ran a front-page article informing the community of the new name and the details of the event scheduled for June 28. In the June 18 issue the *Bay Area Reporter* reported that it had received letters and phone calls from gay men expressing concern that "lesbian gays are in charge and, presumably male gays can participate only on the sufferance of lesbian gays."[41] The newspaper clarified the meaning of the new name:

> Judging from the letters and phone calls received at *B.A.R.* clarification is needed regarding the name of this year's event. The event is the Lesbian/Gay Freedom Day Parade and Celebration. Emphasis is made on the slash between the words "Lesbian" and "Gay." The title is not intended to discourage participation by men but to encourage participation by women. This year, many men have expressed concern that this event was for women and not for men. This is not the case and for any Gay man to assume this is to make an error in judgment. As it has always been, the San Francisco event is an expression of pride by Lesbians and Gay men.[42]

The reaction on the part of men partly revealed the novelty of the use of the slash between "lesbian" and "gay" as a way of indicating inclusion of both women and men. But men's reactions also suggested a lack of comfort with the new visibility and symbolic equality of lesbians denoted by the term "lesbian/gay."

Many other organizations added the term "lesbian" to their names in the early 1980s. In 1980, the Harvey Milk Gay Democratic Club became the Harvey Milk Lesbian/Gay Democratic Club. The Gay Law Students Association at Hastings became Gay and Lesbian Students at Hastings College of Law. The Gay Rights Chapter of the American Civil Liberties Union became the Lesbian and Gay Rights Chapter of the American Civil Liberties Union. As new organizations were founded in the 1980s, they identified themselves as both "lesbian" and "gay" if they intended to represent both men and women.

Lesbians won symbolic equality with gay men, but the inclusion of "lesbian" in the names of organizations did not demand much of gay men. The reference to the communities as lesbian "and" gay, or lesbian "slash" gay indicated the existence of two culturally and politically distinct worlds, but did not require the creation of a gender-neutral homosexuality. On other issues, lesbian inroads were slower. Men were slow to incorporate lesbian issues in a gay rights agenda, and slow to cede leadership positions to lesbians.

The AIDS epidemic introduced a "new spirit of cooperation and solidarity between lesbians and gay men."[43] Motivated both by personal ties to gay men and (sometimes ambivalent) political solidarity with the gay movement, many lesbians devoted astonishing amounts of energy to fighting the epidemic.[44]

The AIDS epidemic changed the balance of power between gay men and lesbians. It provoked a fundamental reassessment of the role of sexual expression in gay lives, making lesbian critiques of gay sex seem less absurd.[45] AIDS also made the economic and familial issues that lesbians were concerned with seem more relevant. By turning the attention of gay men to AIDS work, and by taking the lives of a cohort of activists, AIDS may have produced a leadership vacuum into which lesbians stepped.[46]

Challenges by Gay Men of Color

In the 1970s men of color were situated in a less powerful position relative to the dominant gay white male political project than were white lesbians. Lesbian feminism provided a cultural vantage point for a gender-based critique of the masculinist biases of the movement and a place to retreat where being both gay and female was celebrated. Unlike women, who responded to gay men's sexism by exiting into a world in which gender and sexual identities were equally salient, in the 1970s people of color were not able to retreat into a world in which both their racial and sexual identities were recognized. Nonwhite gay spaces were few and far between. Gay men of color faced a hard choice. They could live with racism in the gay world, or they could re-

ject participation in the gay community and lose access to the only spaces in
which they could safely be gay.

The racism encountered in the gay world was often quite blatant, utterly
at odds with the gay movement's claims of "diversity."[47] Particularly painful
for gay men of color was social exclusion from white gay spaces. Joe DeMarco
described experiences of racism in bars in Philadelphia:

> The most visible form of discrimination in the gay community is at
> the bars—our most public and popular gathering places. Carding is
> the practice of demanding a Liquor Control Board (LCB) card at the
> door of a bar before entrance is permitted. This routine is meant to
> keep people under the age of 21 out of the bars. But, as it is most
> frequently used, the LCB card is a means of keeping Black gays out of
> White gay bars—because only Black patrons are asked to produce
> their cards.[48]

Thom Beame, in an anthology on black gay men, talking particularly about
San Francisco, explained that

> there's a lot of lip service and rhetoric on liberal posture, but there's
> very little that addresses issues like jobs for minorities in gay establish-
> ments or genuine efforts to involve us politically and socially.[49]

This treatment reduced the loyalty of gay men of color to the gay identity-
building project. They asked:

> Why should we believe in White middle-class gay liberation when we
> are as systematically excluded by them as we are by White straights?
> Gay power means White gay male power.[50]

Even when gay men of color were accepted within the white male gay
world, it required the subordination of racial identity to sexual identity.
Thus, for men of color adopting a gay identity often meant abandoning or
trivializing racial or ethnic identification. Charles Fernández, in a 1991 piece
in *Out/Look*, described how he repressed his Latino identity in the effort to construct a gay identity.[51] The cultural logic of the gay identity movement was
such that subordination of racial or ethnic identification was necessary in order to develop full-fledged membership within the gay movement.

People of color often found that downplaying of racial/ethnic identification felt inauthentic.[52] Yong Lee found that participation in predominantly
white gay organizations produced "a feeling of schizophrenia."[53] As one
Latina lesbian explained, "I'd go to one group and I'd be this person, I'd go to

another group and I'd be that person, that's when I started really seeking Latina lesbians, probably through this process I feel like I'm more together."[54]

Many people of color found that attempting to make a place for themselves within the gay identity movement was simply too difficult and too painful. Instead, they retreated to privatized lives within their ethnic and racial communities. Given the tiny number of organizations of gay people of color founded before 1980 (only eleven), it seems that the "flight" response was quite common. The few racially specific gay organizations founded before 1980 included the Native American Gay Rap Group (1972–73), the Black Gay Caucus (1977–78), the Gay Latino Alliance (1977–94), Gay Asian Support Group (1978–81), and the Third World Lesbian Caucus (1977–79). Figure 7.3 shows Gay American Indians in the parade in 1985. It was not until the 1980s that the numbers of these organizations reached the double digits (see figure 7.4).

On October 14, 1979, at the first national lesbian/gay march on Washington, lesbian and gay people of color began to coalesce.[55] In the 1980s, lesbian and gay people of color published articles and a variety of edited collections

Figure 7.3 Gay American Indians in San Francisco's 1985 Lesbian/Gay Freedom Day Parade. Courtesy Rink Foto.

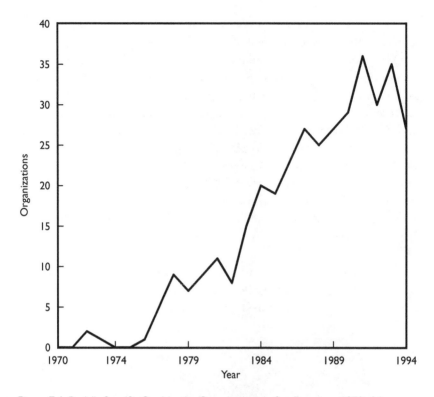

Figure 7.4 Racially Specific Gay Identity Organizations in San Francisco, 1970–94

that articulated the ways that the gay identity movement assumed that its members were white. Gay people of color began to write about how assumptions of the gay identity movement, such as the centrality of coming out, were premised on the assumption of whiteness. They began to suggest that being out may not be a universal barometer of mental health and that sometimes privacy about sexual identity might indicate commitment to social roles within an ethnic community rather than an indication of low self-esteem.[56]

Lesbians of Color Critique Lesbian Feminism

As a Black lesbian feminist comfortable with the many different ingredients of my identity, and a woman committed to racial and sexual freedom from oppression, I find I am constantly being encouraged to pluck out some one aspect of myself and present this as the meaningful whole, eclipsing or denying the other parts of self. But this is a destructive and fragmenting way to live. My fullest concentration of energy is available to me only when I integrate all the parts of who I am, openly, allowing power from particular sources of my living to flow back and forth freely through all my different selves, without the restrictions of externally imposed definition.

Audre Lorde, *Sister Outsider* (1980)

Lesbians of color developed critiques of the racial assumptions of the gay movement in reference to lesbian feminism. These evolved into a sophisticated analysis not only of lesbian feminism, but also of the limitations of identity politics more generally.

Torn between allegiances to multiple communities, lesbians of color questioned the viability of these movements based on one master identity category. Lesbians of color were particularly critical of lesbian separatism, which required a complete break from a community of origin. Barbara Smith argued that such a politics could "only viably be practiced by women who have certain kinds of privilege: white-skinned privilege, class privilege."[57] She argued that such a politics "impede[d] the building of alliances with men of color."[58]

As members of multiple identity categories, but marginal to all, lesbians of color found that they were uncomfortable everywhere. In a speech in 1988, Gloria Anzaldúa explained that

> being a mestiza queer person, *una de las otras* ("of the others") is having and living in a lot of worlds, some of which overlap. One is immersed in all the worlds at the same time while traversing from one to the other. . . . Moving at the blink of an eye, from one space, one world to another, each world within its own peculiar and distinct inhabitants, not comfortable in anyone of them, none of them "home," yet none of them "not home" either.[59]

One response to this lack of comfort, exemplified in the comment of the Latina lesbian above, was to create specialized groups for lesbians of color (see figure 7.5). Theorists like Gloria Anzaldúa, Bernice Johnson Reagon, and Barbara Smith rejected this solution. Instead, they criticized the political usefulness of the search for "womblike" spaces.[60] Reagon, in a 1981 presentation at the West Coast Women's Music Festival in Yosemite National Forest in California, pointed out that even if that safe space is comfortable and organized the way one thinks society should be, it is not really the world. In her view, getting it right in a safe, homogeneous space has little bearing on changing the world. She rejected the "prefigurative politics" embedded within the gay identity movement. Reagon proposed a politics of coalition.

Figure 7.5 African American lesbians in San Francisco's 1982 Lesbian/Gay Freedom Day Parade. Courtesy Rink Foto.

Coalition politics addressed the other problem that lesbians of color had with both the gay identity movement and lesbian feminism. The gay identity movement was resolutely single issue. While lesbian feminism took on both sexuality and gender issues, expanding feminism to address race issues was much more difficult. Many lesbians of color were drawn to multi-issue social justice politics. In the 1980s and 1990s lesbians of color approached building a multi-issue multiracial movement with far less naïveté than activists at the peak of the New Left.

Coalition politics can be seen as a return to the vision of a multi-issue, multiracial social justice politics of the New Left, but with the knowledge that enlisting cooperation across identities would be painful and probably possible only for specific short-term projects. In contrast to the search for comfort and recognition of identity politics, coalition politics, as described by Reagon, was "threatening to the core."[61] This thinking about political strategy by lesbian feminists contributed to the production of queer politics in the late 1980s and 1990s and structures the strategy and approach of progressive lesbian/gay politics to this day.[62]

This chapter showed that the crystallization of the gay identity movement, while claiming to be both universal and diverse, was quite particular and homogeneous. Race, gender, and class exclusions were built into the gay identity movement. But the logic of identity also operated to make white lesbians, gay men of color, and lesbians of color highly aware of and critical of their exclusion, leading them to challenge the movement. In the 1970s these challenges met with limited success. The next round of challenges to the exclusivity of the gay identity movement would take place in a world transformed by the AIDS epidemic, which, as we see in the next chapter, threatened the very nature and existence of the gay identity movement.

EIGHT

Challenge: The Effect of AIDS on the Gay Identity Movement, 1981–1994

*Everything was in jeopardy. It was not at all clear how gay people would
respond [to AIDS]. Would we stay together? We had political power because
we all came to live [in San Francisco]. Why was it that we lived here? Was
it only for sex? If we couldn't have sex, would we still want to live together?
Would we have a community? What about all these things that had been
created in less than a decade? The churches, all the social institutions. Would
they survive? Would we pull together or would we fall apart? I was very
frightened.*

Cleve Jones (interviewed in 1994–95 by
Benjamin Heim Shepard in *White Nights and Ascending Shadows*)

In 1980, the gay identity movement in San Francisco was culturally vibrant
and politically powerful, despite the tensions around race and gender discussed in the last chapter. The synergistic character of the pursuit of gay
pride, gay rights, and sexual pleasure had produced a gay world unimagin-
able even ten years before. Journalist Randy Shilts identified 1978 as "the year
when the Castro clone style reached an almost Platonic perfection."[1] In 1979
there were more gay bars in San Francisco than at any other time.[2] Annual
freedom day parades had swollen to enormous proportions. A continuous
stream of new organizations elaborated on gay identity. The gay movement
had exhibited its political muscle through successfully countering a frontal
assault on gay rights in the form of the 1978 Briggs Initiative and electing its
own Harvey Milk to public office. But the Briggs Initiative, the assassination
of Milk and George Moscone, and the election of Ronald Reagan as president
were only the first challenges of what would prove to be a very difficult decade.

In 1981, gay men in New York, Los Angeles, and San Francisco began to
be diagnosed with diseases "that in the past had occurred only in individuals
whose immune systems had been severely compromised."[3] By the time
health and government officials settled on Acquired Immune Deficiency

Syndrome (AIDS) as the name of this new disease in mid-1982, seventy-two San Franciscans had been diagnosed; sixty-nine had died.[4] While epidemiological patterns suggested that the causative agent was transmitted through bodily fluids, the virus was not isolated until January 1983 by Luc Mantagnier and colleagues at the Pasteur Institute in Paris.[5] In San Francisco, the toll of the epidemic steadily mounted. Responding to the increasing numbers of deaths, the *Bay Area Reporter,* a local gay paper, began to print death notices in May 1984.[6] The number of new AIDS cases diagnosed in San Francisco increased each year, peaking at slightly more than three thousand in 1992, after which the annual number of new cases dropped sharply. Over time, the proportion of new AIDS cases that occurred among gay men declined nationally, dropping from 100 percent in 1981 to 40 percent in 1997.[7] In the early years of the epidemic, death often followed quickly after diagnosis. Gradually, people with AIDS began to live longer, particularly after the introduction of protease inhibitor drugs in 1996.[8]

The AIDS epidemic challenged every aspect of the gay identity movement: the lives and bodies of gay men, beliefs about the healthfulness of gay sex, hard-won pride in gay identity, and the movement's political and cultural organizations. As Cleve Jones, a founder of both the San Francisco AIDS Foundation and the AIDS Memorial Quilt, suggests in the statement that appears as this chapter's epigraph, it was unclear how gay communities would respond. We know now that AIDS did not destroy the gay movement. The community weathered this crisis, although not unchanged. How was the movement able to survive this challenge? What features of the movement inhibited and facilitated effective responses? What did the early concentration of the disease among gay men mean for how both gay communities and the rest of society responded to the disease? What were the consequences of the disease for the gay identity movement?

Any calamity on the scale of the AIDS epidemic produces a voluminous literature.[9] I focus here on how the crystallization of the gay identity movement in the early 1970s shaped responses to the epidemic and how in turn responding to the epidemic changed the movement. As a successful field formation project, the gay identity movement established identities, distributions of power, and taken-for-granted assumptions. Field formation made certain interpretations and lines of action more likely and others less likely. The nature of the gay identity movement produced both debilitating and effective responses to the epidemic. Once it was established that the source of the disease was viral, the character of the gay identity movement enabled it to respond to the epidemic in a more effective manner than other constituencies affected by the disease. But this response exacted a price. I show that an unintended consequence of the gay response to AIDS was the creation of a new, powerful field, which has been referred to as the "AIDS establishment." When gay men and lesbians rallied to take care of their brothers with AIDS, they envisioned themselves as serving their community, not as creating a new sector of the medical health care establishment. This new field, the AIDS field, competed with the gay identity movement for resources. By seeing the response to AIDS as producing a competing organizational field, I counter the view that the response to AIDS further crystallized the gay identity movement by forcing it to "grow up." The gay identity movement in San Francisco had achieved maturity before the onset of AIDS. Even before the first sign of AIDS on the horizon, the gay movement had established itself on the national level, as evidenced by the first national march on Washington in 1979.

Seeing AIDS through Gay Identity

Today, most people believe that a virus transmissible through human bodily fluids is the source of AIDS,[10] but when people first started to become ill in 1981 and 1982, no one understood what was happening. People were confused and fearful. Without definitive knowledge about the source of the disease, how to avoid it, or how to cure it, it was difficult to respond effectively to the epidemic. The earliest efforts to make sense of the disease were filtered through perceptions of its primary victims, gay men. Given the role the gay identity movement played in shaping both internal and external understandings of gay identity, this meant that responses to AIDS developed in light of understandings of gay life disseminated by the gay identity movement. That the gay identity movement was already fully formed prior to AIDS made it difficult for the movement to assimilate information about the disease that ran counter to the core premises of the field.

By 1980, the gay identity movement had succeeded at building gay communities that even those hostile to the gay movement had to acknowledge. This visibility created a target for those with negatives attitudes toward gay men and lesbians, attracting the attention of a growing New Right. In addition, the hardening of the separation between gay and straight life intensified cultural differences, particularly in terms of sexual practices. This divide protected most heterosexuals from knowledge about the sex lives of gay men in urban areas. What heterosexuals saw when they saw gay men getting sick was a disease that targeted a minority whose very existence made them uncomfortable, that seemed to be associated with a way of life that was at best difficult to understand and at worst damnable. These perceptions of gay men led government, medical, and public health organizations to respond ineffectually to the emerging epidemic.

That AIDS first appeared among gay men and other stigmatized groups (Haitians and intravenous drug users) slowed the allocation of funds for research, education, and service. The failures of U.S. institutions to respond adequately to this new disease have been well documented elsewhere.[11] Powerful right-wing politicians and conservative religious leaders justified the lack of response to the epidemic by arguing that gay men had brought this illness onto themselves by their sinful conduct. For example, Patrick Buchanan asserted that "the poor homosexuals . . . have declared war upon nature, and now nature is exacting an awful retribution."[12] While most politicians never made such hateful statements, a lack of empathy for gay men underlay much of the early governmental response to AIDS.

In San Francisco, where the gay community's inroads into the political establishment were the deepest and the gay community's visibility and social power most established, the response to the epidemic was more rapid and generous than in any other city.[13] Shilts reports that by mid-1983 the more than three million dollars the city had spent on AIDS "exceeded the funds released to the entire country by the National Institutes of Health for extramural AIDS research."[14] This suggests the close connection between governmental response to the disease and the value attributed to the afflicted group.

Even when governmental agencies and medical researchers responded to the epidemic in good faith, the success of the gay identity movement at solidifying gay identity impeded the development of an accurate understanding of the nature of the disease. Interpreting AIDS through the lens of gay identity initially blinded policy makers, scientists, and the gay community to basic epidemiological principles: the disease did not respect social identity boundaries. The presence of AIDS in people other than gays was, at first, treated as anomalous, slowing the realization that the source of the illness was viral.[15] As Andriote explains, "Even scientists thought they were dealing with a disease that somehow had a sexual orientation. . . . Researchers continued to look for something unique about gay men in their efforts to deduce the cause of AIDS."[16] Deborah Gould points out that "even health and scientific institutions illogically linked lesbians to AIDS: in 1982–83, the American Red Cross advised lesbians as well as gay men to refrain from donating blood."[17]

Once it was established that the source of the disease was a virus transmitted through human bodily fluids, it became possible to educate people about how to protect themselves from the exchange of fluids during sex. The United States government has never been able to endorse effective prevention programs because to do so would mean talking about gay sex, and perhaps even tacitly condoning it. In the fall of 1987, Republican Jesse Helms convinced the Senate to support an amendment to the Labor, Health, and Human Services Education Appropriation Bill prohibiting the use of federal funds for any AIDS educational materials that "promote or encourage, directly or indirectly, homosexual sexual activities," arguing that such education promoted "safe sodomy."[18]

Gay men were aware of the attitudes of mainstream society as they responded to early news of the disease. The movement was sensitive to efforts to repathologize homosexuality. They knew that many people could not stomach the idea of men having sex with men and that even liberals would be squeamish if they knew exactly how much and what kinds of sex some men were having. They saw the mainstream heterosexual sexual sensibility as prudish and sex negative. On the eve of the AIDS epidemic, writer Edmund White even proposed to an audience including Michael Callen that "gay men should wear their sexually transmitted diseases like red badges of courage in the war against a sex negative society."[19] In this context, initial reports suggesting that there might be something harmful about aspects of the lifestyle of urban gay men seemed merely another round of panicked, irrational responses of homophobic heterosexuals who wanted to scare gay men away from sex. They were aware that heterosexual society was vulnerable to periodic sex panics, during which gay lifestyles would be highlighted as harmful and subject to a crackdown. In the past, these panics had proved to be just that, simply panics. The emergence of a new disease caused by precisely those activities that heterosexuals had the most difficulty accepting seemed simply too convenient. Thus, gay men were quite skeptical of mainstream information about the existence of a disease, its nature, and its possible sources.

Given their previous experiences, gay periodicals acted responsibly by refusing to get panicked about the early suggestions of a "gay cancer." Unfortunately, this skepticism led gay organizations to discredit, minimize, and fail to disseminate important information in the early years of the epidemic. Lawrence D. Mass, a doctor, explains that in the early 1980s both the *Advocate* and the *Village Voice* refused to publish information about the epidemic:

> Not unpredictably, there was pervasive denial of the seriousness of the epidemic in our community. During a period when no other such information was being featured, the *Advocate* declined to publish my "Basic Questions and Answers About AID [acquired immune-deficiency]" and the *Village Voice* killed the big report they had reluc-

tantly commissioned me to do, which I had titled "The Most Important New Public Health Problem in the United States."[20]

San Francisco doctor Marc Conant found it difficult to get gay churches involved in distributing informational brochures, because they felt that the
materials might "panic their parishioners."[21] The motivations of carriers of
the news, even if they were gay themselves or even long-time gay activists,
were seen as suspect. According to Andriote, bearers of bad news were sus-
pected of being "co-opted by the government or some other 'enemy' of homosexuals into participating in a plot that would prevent them from having
sex."[22]

Once it was clear that the phenomenon was real, lack of trust in society's
institutions produced a rash of conspiracy theories. People feared that the illness was not a deadly accident but instead an intentional attack. Ideas about
the form of this conspiracy were wide-ranging, including the possibility that
the disease was caused by some sort of chemical agent "sprinkled like fairy
dust on the floors of bathhouses where barefoot homosexuals would absorb
it through their skin."[23]

As researchers learned more about the nature of the illness and as this information diffused, denial and conspiracy theories both became less plausible. Gay men and lesbians grew afraid, not just of the disease but of the political implications of such a disease. Jim Holm, a gay leader from Seattle,
explained:

> Everything we had—a modicum of civil rights in certain well-
> educated larger cities, some freedom in some places such as the Cas-
> tro to show such minor affectations as holding hands, the acceptance
> by the media of our spokespeople as legitimate news sources, the co-
> operation of friendly straight politicians such as mayors who re-
> strained their homophobic police forces—was seen to be on the
> line.[24]

There was also the fear that perhaps their detractors were right. Maybe having so much sex was not such a good idea. Maybe gay life was unhealthy and
morally wrong. Thus, the disease also challenged the pride and self-esteem
that had been cultivated by the gay identity movement.[25]

These fears fueled the earliest responses to the epidemic: distancing, resistance to governmental regulation of gay men's institutions, and resistance
to changes in sexual practices. Distancing took a variety of forms: avoiding
contact with AIDS organizations, avoiding contact with people with AIDS,
and disassociating oneself from a fast-track lifestyle and from the idea that

one was at risk.[26] Distancing was a way to try to escape shame and guilt, while salvaging pride. Even though the gay identity movement was built on embracing and reversing stigma, a first reaction to this form of heightened stigma was to flee from it, not to embrace it.

In 1983 there was a heated debate in San Francisco about what to do about gay bathhouses. Data suggested that bathhouses were a major site of HIV infection. Many gay men voluntarily stopped going, resulting in the closing of six of San Francisco's twenty bathhouses.[27] But this left about a dozen bathhouses open, presenting San Francisco's gay leaders and public health establishment with a dilemma. In mid-1983 some gay activists urged the director of the city's Department of Health, Mervyn Silverman, to get bathhouse owners to post warnings.[28] This initiated a period of intense debate over the question of whether or not to support state intervention.[29] Some felt that the Department of Health should close the bathhouses, arguing that the threat to the lives of gay men overrode possible violations of civil liberties. Others felt that the Department of Health should stay out of it, but that the gay community should persuade gay bathhouses to comply with emerging safer-sex guidelines. These groups believed that bathhouses should be a site for community education. Still others felt that any regulation, either by the health department or the gay movement, was an infringement of personal liberties and sexual freedom.

As governmental intervention appeared increasingly likely, the opposition became very vocal, sometimes even hysterical. Those who opposed governmental regulation saw it as a dangerous precedent, a slippery slope that could lead to the closure of gay bars.[30] Governmental intervention recalled the police harassment of gay bars that had been a routine part of homosexual life in the 1950s. Lawrence Mass worried that the closure of the bathhouses "could significantly hasten the no-longer creeping pace of fascism against minorities in this country."[31] The *Bay Area Reporter* published a list of sixteen "traitors." Larry Littlejohn, who believed the bathhouses should be closed, was listed as the "traitor extraordinaire."[32] For those who did not want the baths closed, this event signaled a moment when "gay trust broke apart, one tribe willing to sell the other back."[33]

Bathhouses were a cornerstone of gay men's public sexual culture. The efforts to regulate the baths were experienced as attacks on gay men's sexuality and, in the eyes of some, an attack on the heart and soul of the gay community.[34] They believed that "our sex lives lie at the core of our gayness and the integrity of the entire gay community can be undermined by threats to the shared sexuality upon which it rests."[35] The emotions aroused by the debates over the bathhouses were not just about whether governmental intervention was necessary. They were also about how gay men felt about the possibility that their sexual practices might have to change. Gay men wondered whether even the fear of death would make it worthwhile to give up sex. One man writing in response to cautionary advice that appeared in the *New York Native* insisted that: "I refuse to blight my life in order—supposedly—to preserve it."[36]

These early responses, emerging from fears that the gains of the gay identity movement might be lost, were overshadowed by the enormous energies that the gay community directed toward the epidemic in the middle 1980s and the 1990s. The movement came to embrace the epidemic and its victims instead of distancing itself from them. It learned to work effectively with governmental agencies and the medical establishment instead of reflexively distrusting their involvement. The movement learned "how to have sex in an epidemic," moving well beyond the initial visceral refusal to change sexual practices.[37]

Resources, Resiliency, and Anger: Responding to an Epidemic

After an initial period of fear and confusion, the gay identity movement launched an impressive and multifaceted response to the epidemic. It created services to care for those who were ill or dying. It raised funds for research and education. It developed guidelines for safer-sex education and programs to change the sexual behavior of gay men. And beginning in 1987, it launched a campaign of street activism aimed at speeding up the delivery of drugs being developed to treat HIV disease.

While scholars and activists agree that gay communities responded to the epidemic with an impressive commitment to the collective welfare,[38] some think that gay communities were too slow to anger and demanded too little from the government in the early years of the epidemic.[39] That position is persuasive, but it is also clear that gays developed a far more effective response to the epidemic than communities of color and IV drug users.[40] Among gay communities, the response of San Francisco's was the most effective.[41]

The response of the gay movement in San Francisco could not have been so rapid and effective if it had not *already* been mature. That the gay identity movement was most developed and powerful in San Francisco prior to the epidemic explains why San Francisco's response to the epidemic served as a model for other communities around the country and the world. While the response to the epidemic emerged out of and depended upon the develop-

ment of the gay identity movement, the AIDS response quickly began to take
shape as a phenomenon distinct from it.

The Birth of AIDS Services: Stepping into the Trenches

On June 18, 1982, activist Cleve Jones opened the offices of the Kaposi's Sar-
coma Education and Research Foundation on Castro Street, San Francisco's
first organization devoted to responding to the new epidemic.[42] Marc Conant
and a couple of other doctors paid the rent.[43] Randy Shilts documents the
humble beginnings of what would ultimately become a massive organization: "It started with one beat-up typewriter donated by a local gay bartender,
office supplies pilfered from volunteers' various employers, and one telephone that started ringing within an hour of its installation. And it never
stopped ringing."[44] This organization became the San Francisco AIDS Foundation. It was one of many organizations founded to respond to the epidemic. Figure 8.1 displays the growth in numbers of AIDS organizations in
San Francisco. These organizations, which ranged from the huge San Francisco AIDS Foundation to much more modest efforts, such as Pets Are Wonderful Support for People with AIDS/ARC, an organization providing pets to
people with AIDS. Together these organizations "became a model of compas-
sionate, coordinated AIDS services."[45]

Notwithstanding the early distancing from AIDS described above, gay
communities were more willing to be identified with AIDS than other afflicted communities. This may have been partly an accident of the epidemiological patterns: it was simply impossible to deny the association between gay
men and AIDS. But the gay identity movement also had in its arsenal more
than a decade of experience reversing stigma, including that associated with
sexual practices.[46] African Americans and other communities of color, while
accustomed to battling stigma, had less experience responding to stigma that
was so directly sexualized.[47]

Identification with the disease provided the motivation to provide services. Activists made a strong link between "ownership" of the disease and responsibility to "deal with it." For example, Paul Lorch, writing in the *Bay Area
Reporter* in 1983 insisted, "It's our disease (our sickness and dying) and how we
deal with it is our business. What's more, it's our business to deal with it."[48]

But "ownership" of the epidemic was also a double-edged sword. If gay
communities owned the disease too completely, it absolved the government
from the responsibility of responding effectively and providing services.[49]
Gould has pointed out that these feelings of responsibility were a common
emotional reaction to AIDS, provoked by the desire to atone for feelings of

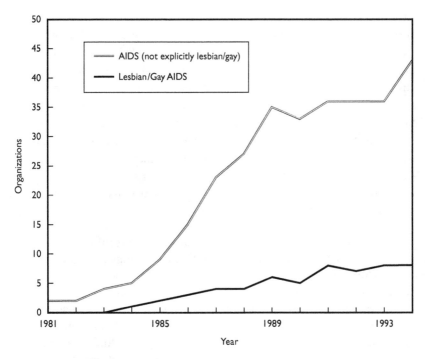

Figure 8.1 AIDS Organizations in San Francisco, 1981–94
Note: Some of the organizations in the not-explicitly-gay category were in fact founded within the gay community but no longer identify themselves as lesbian/gay organizations.

guilt and shame.[50] In New York, gay men asked little of the city, prompting activist Larry Kramer to point out:

> If we quietly take care of ourselves, we are saying not only that the system isn't going to help us, but we're not making the system help us. We're paying twice for the services—what we're paying for the city and state to provide from our taxes, and what we're also giving GMHC [Gay Men's Health Crisis] to do.[51]

In San Francisco, the gay community shared ownership of AIDS with the city. That the city of San Francisco took responsibility, from the beginning, for participation in the delivery of AIDS services, is one of the main reasons, according to Andriote, that AIDS services were better in San Francisco than in New York.[52]

Ownership of the disease was a necessary first step for the development of effective service organizations. But the political and organizational infrastructure in place due to earlier successes of the gay identity movement was also crucial for the development of an effective response. This movement had reached its highest degree of development in San Francisco. The integration of gay men into San Francisco's Democratic political establishment (discussed in chapter 6) meant that elected city officials had instrumental reasons for being responsive to AIDS. Andriote argues, however, that it was the high level of social integration of gay men into the fabric of life in San Francisco that really made a difference. Mayor Dianne Feinstein herself had gay male friends. Peter Nardoza, who worked in the mayor's office at the time, explained that "In [Feinstein's] mind, it wasn't a matter of '*they* are dying.' It was '*we* have a problem.' "[53] In explaining the distinctive character of the AIDS movement, Steven Epstein notes:

> It mattered that gay communities had preexisting organizations that could mobilize to meet a new threat; these community organizations and institutions also provided settings for the face-to-face interactions that are so important in drawing individuals into activism. It mattered, too, that these communities included (and in fact were dominated by) white, middle-class men with a degree of political clout and fund-raising capacity unusual for an oppressed group. And it was crucial that gay communities possessed a relatively high degree of "cultural capital"—that they had cultivated a disposition for appropriating knowledge and culture.[54]

Preexisting organizations included lesbian/gay medical groups and STD treatment centers.[55] Community members knew how to build and maintain organizations (although not necessarily organizations of the size and complexity needed). Geographical concentration made delivery of services and mobilization of volunteers easier. Cleve Jones was able to enlist volunteers by simply stopping people on Castro Street as they walked by.[56] The dense interaction that took place in the community made conveying information relatively easy. And, as Andriote points out, San Francisco was more affluent than New York. That the city was less financially stressed meant that it was easier to get resources directed toward the epidemic in San Francisco than in New York.[57]

Beginning in 1987, AIDS service delivery was supplemented by vocal, angry street activism. ACT UP marks the beginning of a distinct AIDS-related political movement and a shift toward demanding that the government make policy to ensure the health of its citizens[58] (figure 8.2).

Figure 8.2 ACT UP/SF participates in the 1989 Lesbian/Gay Freedom Day Parade. Courtesy Rink Foto.

Remaking Gay Identity: Saving Sex through Safer Sex

The gay identity movement mounted a far-reaching safer-sex education campaign that succeeded at rapidly changing gay men's sexual behavior. After a peak of new infections in 1982, when 21 percent of uninfected gay men in San Francisco became infected, rates of sexually transmitted diseases among gay men plunged dramatically,[59] as did the rates of HIV seroconversion. By 1985 "less than 1 percent of the gay male population was infected [annually] with HIV."[60] Public health officials described this as the "greatest behavior change ever seen in public health" and as a "dazzling success."[61]

Given that many gay men described promiscuous sex as defining of their identities as gay men, how was the gay movement able to accomplish this? What enabled the gay community, particularly in San Francisco, to pull off the most effective behavior change program in history? While initially it seemed that gay men's love affair with sex would make it difficult to get men to change their sexual behavior, ultimately their open, pragmatic, and graphic sexual sensibility enabled a highly effective safer-sex education campaign. While the government was paralyzed by the possibility that encouraging condom use sanctioned nonmarital, nonprocreative sex, the gay community graphically discussed such things as the necessity of using latex gloves and non-petroleum-based lubricants in order to safely engage in anal fisting.

Sex educators in San Francisco anticipated that AIDS was a virus before the virus was actually isolated. They began circulating the information that protection against bodily fluids through the use of condoms was key.[62] Sex educators continued to stay abreast of scientific research on how the virus was transmitted. They developed and refined explicit, scientifically accurate safer-sex guidelines. Developing a clear understanding of how the virus was transmitted allowed them to carefully divide sexual practices into those that were high, moderate, and low risk. The emphasis on risky practices made it possible to distinguish between the *virus* as the source of disease and homosexuality as the source of the disease. If one avoided the riskiest practices one could have multiple partners with relatively low risk.

In addition to attending to how the virus was transmitted, San Francisco's sex educators conducted research on effective ways to bring about behavior change. They quickly realized that knowledge of risk was not sufficient to change behavior. Starting from the premise that gay men were going to continue having sex and that this was good, they focused on distributing information about how to have sex safely. This information was framed in language that appealed to gay men's sensibilities, defining sex as both positive and important, and safer sex as erotic. They also understood that sexual decisions were not made in isolation, but in the context of a community, and made every effort to change the sexual norms of the entire community. Educators developed an understanding of the relationship between low self-esteem and self-destructive behaviors and began to incorporate a focus on gay men's self-esteem into safer-sex education programs. They found that privacy, silence, fear, shame, and guilt led to risky practices, while openness, honesty, and self-esteem produced more positive behavior. The San Francisco Department of Public Health provided funds to implement the programs.[63] There were plenty of lesbian and gay male health educators, both professional and volunteer, with the skills to implement the programs and to do the necessary research.

That gay men had a public sexual culture also facilitated changing gay men's sexual behavior. As those who objected to closing the baths pointed out, public sex is easier to police than private sex. In addition, public sexual venues provide a place to model safer-sex practices.

The richness and diversity of urban gay culture in the 1980s also allowed the efforts to change gay men's sexual practices to be successful. In chapter 6 we saw that while the sexual subculture was surging throughout the 1970s, the gay identity movement was also blossoming in terms of its cultural, hobby, religious, and political possibilities. It offered much more to gay men than opportunities for sex. When the AIDS epidemic emerged, there already existed a full range of resources to assist individuals in the construction of a meaningful gay life that did not rest solely on sexual practices. Those men who might have centered their individual identities around sex in the late 1970s did not have to search far for ways of being gay in which sex played a smaller role.

By the late 1980s, health educators in San Francisco were congratulating themselves on a successful behavior change campaign that they assumed was completed. However, by 1990 it was evident that continual education was needed because of the transience of the population. Younger men and new migrants to San Francisco needed to be educated. Men of color also remained particularly vulnerable to new infection. As a consequence of the declining rate of infection, the epidemic among gay men gradually slowed, except among young gay men and gay men of color, two constituencies whose rates of seroconversion remained high.

AIDS Organizing and the Gay Identity Movement

The thing that annoys me most is the revisionist attitude that gay people didn't discover the bonds of family until AIDS and death forced it upon them. Nothing could be further from the truth. There were, as early as the mid-seventies in San Francisco, gay lawyer groups, gay doctor groups, gay needlepoint groups, gay sports teams, and people forming viable, loving families.

Armistead Maupin

We have seen that the gay identity movement responded to the AIDS epidemic. This response to the epidemic, in turn, reshaped the gay identity movement. While the epidemic was a catastrophe for the gay movement, the movement survived. Cleve Jones's worst fears were not realized. However, scholars and activists disagree about what the response to AIDS has meant for the movement. Some argue that the response of the gay movement to the AIDS epidemic brought a new level of maturity to the movement. In contrast, I argue that, on balance, the consequences of the response to AIDS were negative for the gay movement, at least in San Francisco. As San Francisco author Armistead Maupin suggests, the movement had achieved maturity locally before the onset of the epidemic. The new, powerful organizations created in response to AIDS were not gay organizations, but AIDS organizations. They were organized around a different logic and competed with the gay identity movement for personnel and resources.

The AIDS epidemic has been disastrous for San Francisco's gay community. San Francisco was among the hardest hit of all U.S. cities. The disease decimated entire friendship circles, and in fact a whole generation of gay men. This has had staggering emotional consequences for survivors of the epidemic. David Pattent, interviewed in 1994 by Benjamin Heim Shepard, tells of the loss of over five hundred friends in the previous twelve years, ten to fifteen of whom he comforted as they died.[64] Brad Sherbert tells Shepard of attending "well over" two hundred funerals in six years.[65] Psychologists attending to gay men's mental health developed the term "multiple loss syndrome," akin to post–traumatic stress syndrome, to describe the ways that grief processes shut down when individuals experience too much loss without adequate time to grieve.[66] The loss of a generation has had political and cultural consequences at the collective level. Larry Gross points out, "As the epidemic continued it has steadily killed off (and also burnt out) many [leaders/activists]—an appalling toll of those with activist experience and know-how—and we have few ways to recruit and cultivate activists."[67] The loss of these individuals also meant the loss of the memories of a pivotal generation. Many of the men who died were those who had reached adulthood in the 1970s, developing gay identities just as the movement coalesced.

In spite of this loss, or perhaps because of it, some scholars and activists have searched for positive consequences of the epidemic for the gay movement. Some have found this silver lining in the claim that the response to AIDS provoked the maturation of the gay community from a "lifestyle enclave" into a "genuine community."[68] Steven Murray explains that

> the extraordinary mobilization to lobby for and care for persons with AIDS surely transcends the hedonism and shared leisure of a lifestyle enclave. Contributions of resources—not least, time and energy— by many gay San Francisco men protecting and caring for mortally ill peers show that gay men share more than jargon, costumes, and transient sexual encounters. . . . Whether in fund-raising or in providing services to people with AIDS (and not just gay ones), gay men over the past decade have demonstrated their willingness to take on onerous burdens of caring for others. To put it mildly, it is hard to conceive the gay male response to AIDS as that of a "lifestyle enclave"

with superficially committed individuals concerned only with narcis-
sistic self-gratification or reveling in "the narcissism of similarity" in
consumption patterns.[69]

By illustrating that the connections among gay men transcended those binding together a lifestyle enclave, the response to AIDS proved the responsible
nature of the movement. This perspective tends to see gay men's orientation
to sexuality in the 1970s as "immature" and the shift to care giving as collective movement into responsible adulthood. Al Wardell of the Illinois Gay and
Lesbian Task Force explains:

> Before Stonewall, we were mostly isolated individuals. Since then, a
> community has developed—gay churches, gay choruses, gay athletic
> events. All that had started before AIDS, but dealing with AIDS—
> having to educate ourselves about it, raise money for treatment, set
> up buddy programs, and care for the sick and dying—that has solidi-
> fied it. We did a very fast job of growing up. That has been the miracle
> of the past twenty years.[70]

In this view, the response to AIDS comes to be seen as the crystallizing moment for the gay movement.

The notion that the movement in the late 1970s was irresponsible and
immature is at odds with the understanding of the gay identity movement
that this book describes. We have seen that the gay identity movement in San
Francisco was not underdeveloped, irresponsible, or immature prior to the
emergence of AIDS. At the time, there were only the barest hints of the possible health consequences of promiscuous sexual behavior. Given the state of
knowledge at the time, it was reasonable to believe that sexually transmitted
diseases were simply a nuisance. Gay men's sexual behavior was not an indication of immaturity. The sexual circuit was only part of the gay identity
project of the 1970s. As we have seen throughout this book, the gay identity
movement also involved a successful cultural and political organizing project. The defeat of the Briggs Initiative took place before AIDS appeared on the
scene. Thus, emphasizing the new maturity of the community relies on minimizing the accomplishments of the 1970s.

Deborah Gould argues that the "trope of responsibility" allowed the gay
movement to create distance from the sexual practices of gay men in the
1970s. AIDS brought the sexual practices of gay men to the attention of the
medical establishment and the heterosexual mainstream, which labeled
these practices as "excessive, hedonistic, adolescent, immature, and irresponsible."[71] Not being able to fully reject these external definitions of their behav-

ior produced feelings of shame and ambivalence. Creating distance from the "immature" gay life of the 1970s thus served as a way to seek social acceptance and to rebuild a damaged sense of pride.[72]

Instead of propelling the gay identity movement into a new level of maturity, the response to AIDS produced a competing field, which deflected resources and personnel from the gay identity movement. This interpretation is buttressed by two empirical findings. First, the numbers of non-AIDS-related lesbian/gay nonprofit organizations declined in the late 1980s, while the number of AIDS organizations increased (see figure 8.3).[73] Second, AIDS organizations consistently denied that they were gay organizations.[74] When taken together, these findings are quite suggestive. Alone, the decline in non-AIDS-related gay organizing and the growth of AIDS organizations might be seen as a reallocation of the energies internal to the gay identity movement. The decline in numbers of gay identity organizations looks different, however, when considered in light of the fact that AIDS organizations, after the first few years of the epidemic, did not consider themselves to be gay organizations. AIDS organizations grew at the expense of gay identity organizations. Further investigation reveals why AIDS organizations did not identify

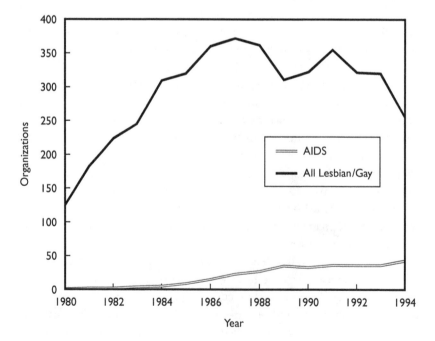

Figure 8.3 Lesbian/Gay Nonprofit and AIDS Organizations in San Francisco, 1980–94

themselves as gay and why the growth of AIDS organizations was so threatening to gay organizations.

While many AIDS organizations originally formed as gay organizations, they encountered strong pressure to leave behind their gay identification. In order to provide services, AIDS organizations required substantial funding. To get this funding, they appealed to government agencies. The pursuit and receipt of large-scale funding reshaped the structure and loyalties of these organizations, reducing their accountability to gay communities. Unlike gay identity organizations, which maintained relatively high autonomy from other fields in society, AIDS organizations became tightly bound to the state and the medical profession. They were subject to intense pressure to conform to conventional organizational forms and practices.[75] As Padgug and Oppenheimer explain:

> The institutions that the gay community was instrumental in creating were, in their methods of operation and ways of viewing the epidemic and the world, molded by the professional and scientific world in which they operated; not surprisingly, when one deals with and utilizes the power and resources of outside forces, one has to play by their rules, at least to some extent. It is significant that earlier attitudes of hostility toward professionals and scientists on the part of gay AIDS service organizations have generally given way to mutual cooperation and the rise of what some have begun to view as an "AIDS Establishment" that cuts across the gay/straight division and has effectively "co-opted" much of the gay political struggle around AIDS.[76]

AIDS organizations became large and highly bureaucratic (figure 8.4). Shepard describes the bewilderment of the gay community at the direction of the growth of AIDS organizations:

> By the 1990s, the volunteers who had lined up in force to serve their communities during the mid-1980s watched the very grassroots organizations they had supported lose sight of their original goals and become bureaucratic monsters. AIDS organizations began putting more effort into courting donors and funds than fighting for their clients.[77]

These organizations became more top-heavy than gay organizations: they had more paid staff, higher administrative costs, and required more resources for organizational maintenance.[78]

Figure 8.4 By the mid-1990s, the San Francisco AIDS Foundation had become a huge organization at the center of a web of various AIDS organizations and services. The 1995–96 version of its *HIV Resource Guide* ran to almost two hundred pages and included referrals to medical, dental, housing, funeral, transportation, legal, and alcohol services. Courtesy San Francisco AIDS Foundation.

The logic of responding to an epidemic is profoundly different than the logic of promoting an identity. Ultimately, as much as the gay community tried to claim the disease, and as much as the heterosexual population associated AIDS with homosexuality, AIDS was *not* a gay disease, and could not be. Viruses do not respect social identity boundaries. Within organizations devoted to battling HIV, the salience of gay identity necessarily retreated in the face of universal human vulnerability to the virus. Thus, the AIDS epidemic produced an entirely new field of organizations.[79]

The growth of the AIDS field proved to be threatening to the gay identity movement. Even though AIDS organizations were not specifically devoted to gay issues, gay men and lesbians had a stake in the success of the battle against HIV. Lesbians and gay men provided the bulk of the staff and volunteers of these organizations, particularly in the early years of the epidemic. Battling AIDS felt like battling for the very existence of a gay community, when approximately 50 percent of gay men in San Francisco in 1988 were HIV positive.[80] Working in AIDS services also provided more career opportunities for gay social service professionals than working in gay identity organizations.

It is difficult to measure the extent of the diversion of gay effort and resources into AIDS organizations. Theoretically, individuals participating in AIDS organizations could have simultaneously worked with gay identity organizations. However, the demands of AIDS work were such that it was unlikely that many people could also participate heavily in non-AIDS-related gay organizing. In 1995, the San Francisco AIDS Foundation reported that "the agency has several hundred dedicated and enthusiastic volunteers donating their time and energy to end this epidemic."[81] AIDS organizations paid staff, while most gay organizations could not. Volunteering for an AIDS organization was often time-consuming and emotionally draining. The San Francisco AIDS Foundation reported in 1995 that "trained volunteers answer more than 10,000 calls every month at the Northern California AIDS Hotline."[82] Arno estimated that the value of AIDS-related volunteer labor for the fiscal year 1985 was $1.2 million.[83]

The competition between gay and AIDS organizations for resources of all sorts (funds, leadership, volunteers, and members) became painfully clear to both AIDS and gay activists in the late 1980s. In an article published in 1990 aptly called "Gay Groups vs. AIDS Groups: Averting Civil War in the 1990s," activist Eric Rofes described this competition.[84] He explains that discrepancies in resources between AIDS groups and gay groups became increasingly obvious in the late 1980s:

Key AIDS groups, conceived within local gay and lesbian communities, rapidly became million-dollar agencies and enjoyed the "goodies" that accompany media limelight. Parallel groups with a specific focus on gay and lesbian health concerns struggled to maintain paid staff and keep doors open. The two quietly began facing off, like boxers entering the ring. Tensions over a perceived shift in community resources have deepened over the past five years because of conflicts over political issues, openness about gay and lesbian participation, sexual liberation, and organizational culture.[85]

Gay and lesbian organizers complained about these disparities:

Gay and lesbian organizers have been critical of AIDS advocates, but primarily behind closed doors, where they'll complain that "all the money is going to AIDS," or that "the community's entire agenda has been swallowed up by AIDS."[86]

AIDS organizers justified their higher level of resources by criticizing gay and lesbian groups. They described gay groups as lacking "professionalism and stability."[87] Rofes also claimed that AIDS groups sometimes warned funders away from gay and lesbian groups, by saying that the groups "were 'well intentioned' but 'unpredictable and radical'—a true funding risk."[88] With many leaders lost to the epidemic, the consequences of the remaining leaders devoting their time to the epidemic were high. When Rofes left his "job at a gay and lesbian service center to work for an exclusively AIDS-focused organization" he "repeatedly heard one version or another of 'Yet another gay organizer sells out to the AIDS bureaucracy.'"[89]

The meaning of gay participation within AIDS organizations changed as the demographics of the disease changed. For years, work in AIDS organizations meant working for gay people, if not directly for a gay cause. Over time, gay people composed a smaller proportion of people with AIDS. Cleve Jones pointed out the strains this caused:

You now have agencies like Gay Men's Health Crisis where a majority of their clients are not gay men. This puts us all through all sorts of changes because, of course, the gay community has this great sense of ownership of the disease and the agencies that were created to fight it. They are often the bases of political power for activists within our community. That's not right or wrong, it's just the way it is. So, things have got to change.[90]

Jones's comment suggests an irony of the epidemic. While AIDS organizations were not gay organizations, and the AIDS establishment competed with gay identity organizations, the power of individuals, often gay men, heading these large organizations, increased.

Thus, the gay response to AIDS did not lead the gay identity movement to "grow up" but instead contributed to the growth of a new, competitive field of AIDS organizations, leading to a decline in the number of gay identity organizations.[91] Paul, Hayes, and Coates are correct in claiming that:

> More than a medical issue, AIDS has wrought a major political, social, and psychological sea change in gay communities. . . . The HIV epidemic has affected practically every aspect of gay life: sexuality, the meaning of being gay, the social structures and modes of participation in the community, the creative output of a generation facing its mortality, and alliance-building between gay activists and other political/social activist groups.[92]

The development of a competing organizational field was certainly a most dramatic change. What did not change was the fundamental logic of the gay identity movement itself. The gay identity movement that survived was smaller (at least on a local level) than before, but it remained organized around the pursuit of rights, pride, and sexual expression. The kinds of non-AIDS-related lesbian/gay organizations created after AIDS were indistinguishable from those formed before the epidemic. The resiliency of the gay identity movement is also suggested by annual freedom day parades, which added AIDS organizations and safer-sex education messages, but continued otherwise unchanged. Bars and other sexually focused organizations continued to thrive. Sex clubs reopened. An active gay male "party" culture lives on. Gay men changed their sexual behaviors, but they did so in a way that was consistent with the sexual sensibility promoted by the gay identity movement. However, continued growth and evolution of the movement, combined with changes in the environment, meant that internal contradictions within the gay identity movement continued to surface in ways that threatened the stability of the project. Chapter 9 discusses the emergence and consequence of challenges that came to the fore in the 1980s and 1990s.

NINE

Continuity and Change: The Gay Identity Movement in the 1980s and 1990s

Queer politics . . . operates largely through the decentralized, local, and often anti-organizational cultural activism of street postering, parodic and non-conformist self-presentation, and underground alternative magazines; it has defined itself largely against conventional lesbian and gay politics.

Joshua Gamson, "Must Identity Movements Self-Destruct? A Queer Dilemma" (August 1995)

The Millennium March has come to symbolize, for its opponents, a movement increasingly run by what is essentially a national, corporate, business-as-usual political lobby, which collects funds while local and state groups struggle against attack.

Joshua Gamson, "The Gay Movement's Long-Simmering Tensions Erupt in a High-Stakes Mud Fight: Whose Millennium March?" (April 2000)

The AIDS epidemic was an environmental catastrophe. However, the gay identity movement has also had to respond to challenges arising out of contradictions within the movement. In the late 1980s, the gay identity movement spun off an angry offshoot, queer politics, that directly challenged the logic of identity. Through a politics of jarring cultural display, queer politics proposed a more complex, ambiguous, and arbitrary notion of sexual identity, harking back to the gay power vision of sexual liberation for all. However, queer politics did not succeed at fundamentally reorganizing the core logic of the gay identity movement. Instead, it was domesticated. It was reduced to simply another of many ways to express gay identity. The queer challenge left the gay identity movement strengthened and organized around the same basic constellation of agreements forged in the early 1970s.

A different sort of challenge to the gay identity movement emerged in the late 1990s. Washington-based interest groups seem to be attempting to exert a top-down hierarchical control over the movement. This new behavior on the part of interest group organizations threatens to disrupt the careful balance between identity and interest group politics that defines the gay identity movement. At this writing, it is unclear whether these trends will lead to a fundamental transformation of the movement.

The appearance of these internal challenges raises questions. If this field has stabilized around a core set of agreements, why do we see these challenges? What forces produce these challenges? What do they mean for our understanding of this field? This chapter argues that queer politics and its domestication were typical of dynamics within stable fields.[1] Describing a field as stable does not mean that it is static. Stable fields are dynamic; they adjust in response to changes in the environment. In this case, internal contradictions within the field, centered on the movement's claims to diversity in the face of the reality of homogeneity, were exacerbated by field growth and changes in the political context. Queer politics was sparked by these heightened contradictions. It did not present a serious threat to the logic structuring the field because it did not provide a persuasive alternative logic to powerful players within the field. However, it did provoke adjustments to the project that neutralized the most serious complaints of exclusion, homogeneity, and particularity. Thus, queer politics is a self-correction typical of a dynamically stable field. These kinds of adjustments, like dipping an oar in the water to slightly adjust the direction of a boat, are necessary because of the inevitability of internal contradictions, changes in the environment, and field growth or decline.

It is not yet possible to tell whether the increasing power of gay interest group politics will produce a fundamental transformation of the logic of the gay movement. Not all challenges lead to reforms that stabilize a field. Internal contradictions may also lead to field transformation. On the one hand, it looks as if contradictions between interest group and identity logics within the gay identity movement may have planted the seeds of the demise of a gay identity movement. The gay identity movement has been highly successful in institutionalizing gay identity, perhaps so successful that it is no longer needed as a protector and carrier of it. The movement successfully created the public collective identity necessary for the pursuit of interest group politics and carefully cultivated and nurtured gay interest group politics within its midst. Meanwhile, there may also have been a more generalized decline in the persuasiveness of identity politics and an increase in the viability of interest group and market logics. On the other hand, there are indications that the gay identity-building project may not be ready for the dustbin of history. Lesbian/gay progressives have mobilized against the increasing domination of

large interest group organizations. Lesbians and gays continue to find participation in the organizations, events, and rituals of this identity-building project to be deeply meaningful. It is hard to imagine people finding freedom
day parades and gay neighborhoods irrelevant to contemporary gay experience.

Emergence and Neutralization of Queer Politics, Late 1980s–Mid-1990s

This section shows how field growth and changes in political context exacerbated tensions internal to the movement, which in turn produced queer politics. Queer politics vacillated between criticizing the logic of identity politics
in general and criticizing the particular character of the identity proposed
by the gay identity movement. It did not present a viable alternative logic
around which the movement could organize. However, it did motivate a re-
laxation of the boundaries of the project and a shuffling of internal hierarchies that neutralized the challenges presented by queer politics.

Creating exclusions is an inevitable consequence of identity politics and
of field formation in general. Organizing around identity necessarily means
drawing boundaries; defining a group of people bound by similarities requires
defining those who are different. Ironically, the gay identity movement made
the assertion of diversity and inclusivity a defining feature of its identity, thus
producing the possibility of having its actual homogeneity and inevitable exclusions pointed out as evidence of hypocrisy. Not all field formation projects, even all identity movements, face this particular Achilles' heel. Most
make no claim to inclusivity.

Lesbians, gay men of color, and lesbians of color had criticized the homogeneity of the gay identity movement in the 1970s and 1980s, producing slight
accommodations by the movement (see chapter 7). But by the late 1980s, the
continued growth and success of the gay identity movement, combined with
changes in the political environment, brought the mismatch between the
movement claims of diversity and the reality of its homogeneity to a crisis
point.

The growth and success of the gay identity movement both raised the
stakes for those groups who had long been aware of exclusion (gay men of
color and lesbians) and by contributing to the consolidation of new constituencies who felt excluded from the gay identity project. The gay identity
movement attracted a variety of people with nonnormative sexual interests
looking for safe space to congregate (or, one could argue, the logic of identity
produced these groups as a natural consequence of its generativity).[2] By the
late 1980s groups such as bisexuals, transgenders, and those into leather,

BDSM (bondage, discipline, and sadomasochism), and fetishes formed size-able congregations on the peripheries of gay worlds in major urban areas. These sexual minorities found the assumptions of the gay identity movement to resonate with their experiences.

These groups gradually clarified that their political fortunes depended upon inclusion within the larger gay identity movement. This became starkly evident to bisexuals when the AIDS epidemic produced a stream of attacks on bisexuals as the source of infection of a "pure" heterosexual community.[3] The gay identity movement initially rejected these appeals for inclusion. From the perspective of a political movement built around promoting gay identity, the very existence of bisexuality and transgenderism seemed threatening. These phenomena threatened to undermine the solidity of lesbian and gay identities.[4] Bisexuality and transgenderism drew attention to experiences of gender and sexuality that did not fit neatly within the categories of gay and straight.[5] Bisexuality raised the disturbing possibility that perhaps sexual desire might be better described in terms of a continuum, rather than in terms of discrete categories. Bisexuality also suggested the notion that, for some people, gender might not be relevant as a basis for sexual attraction. Further, transgendered people introduced the possibility that gender identity, on which lesbian and gay identities were premised, might itself slip away.[6]

Bisexuals and transgenders responded to exclusion by pointing out the hypocrisy of being excluded from the gay movement because of the gender of their lovers or their gender styles.[7] Thus, bisexuality and transgenderism put the gay identity movement in a bind. Inclusion threatened the solidity of gay and lesbian identities and undermined the notion that there was any meaningful boundary between gay and straight. Exclusion revealed the hypocrisy of the movement.

Changes in political context simultaneously led activists to question whether the goals and strategies that characterized identity politics were the most desirable or effective. Universal human vulnerability to AIDS led activists to feel that restricting services to gay people was inappropriate. The slow government response to the AIDS epidemic suggested the need for more confrontational political strategies. The successes of ACT UP at getting "drugs into bodies" suggested that maybe a more radical approach to gay politics could reap similarly dramatic results.

In addition, leftist activists and scholars, as they attempted to come to terms with the successes and failures of the New Left, developed a harsh critique of identity politics in the late 1980s and early 1990s. They saw "identity politics" as misguided, and argued that the movements had gone awry with the sidelining of economic justice concerns in the 1970s. They saw the psychological focus of identity politics as in direct contrast to a politics seeking economic justice. For example, in 1987 feminist Jenny Bourne complained that "identity Politics is all the rage. Exploitation is out (it is extrinsically determinist). Oppression is in (it is intrinsically personal). What is to be done has been replaced by who am I. Political culture has ceded to cultural politics. The material world has passed into the metaphysical."[8] In a similar vein, gay activist Charles Fernández pointed out in 1991 that "While identity politics has politicized new arenas of human experience, taken to the extreme it has resulted in a fragmentation of subjects. It has dead-ended in an overemphasis on identity and personal development rather than liberation, justice, and solidarity."[9] Critics insisted that building and affirming identity was *not* political in and of itself. They criticized the single-issue focus that tended to be associated with identity politics, arguing that this strategy produced reforms benefiting specific groups rather than broad social changes with universal benefits. Critics also pointed to the tendency of those engaging in identity politics to believe that ideology emerged naturally out of identity. Bisexual activist Liz Highleyman explained in 1995 that "people who see the world in terms of identity politics often expect that all people with a given identity characteristic will share certain moral values, political beliefs, and cultural tastes."[10] Highleyman pointed out that those who conflate politics and identity may "define their enemy as 'straight white men' rather than attitudes of homophobia, racism, sexism, and intolerance."[11]

In 1990, the complaints of lesbians, gay/lesbian people of color, leftists, radical AIDS activists, and nongay sexual minorities coalesced in a political current calling itself "queer politics."[12] Queer Nation was founded in New York in April 1990.[13] The San Francisco chapter was founded on July 18, 1990[14] (figure 9.1). Queer politics vacillated between the view that the problems with the gay movement revealed a fundamental flaw with identity politics in general and the more modest critique that there was something wrong with the specific identity promoted by the gay identity movement (too white, too male, too middle-class, too sexually conformist, and insufficiently politically confrontational). Escoffier and Bérubé described the conflict between identity questioning and identity solidification impulses within queer politics:

> Queer Nationals are torn between affirming a new identity—"I am queer" and rejecting restrictive identities—"I reject your categories," between rejecting assimilation—"I don't need your approval, just get out of my face" and wanting to be recognized by mainstream society—"We queers are gonna get in your face."[15]

Figure 9.1 In 1990, Queer Nation's Suburban Homosexual Outreach Project (SHOP) made a trip to the Sun Valley Mall in Concord. Photograph by Paul Miller, by permission of ANG Newspapers/*Oakland Tribune*. Image courtesy GLBT Historical Society of Northern California.

Those who emphasized queer politics as a rejection of categories altogether viewed queer as a kind of anti-identity. As theorist Steven Seidman explained, "queer" was supposed to unify people around a shared resistance to identity categories:

> Under the undifferentiated sign of Queer are united all those hetero-geneous desires and interests that are marginalized and excluded in the straight and gay mainstream. Queers are not united by any uni-tary identity but only by their opposition to disciplining, normalizing, social forces.[16]

But the very name "Queer Nation" suggested a more straightforward en-dorsement of identity building.

During its brief lifetime, the queer movement was dynamic and highly visible. Queer actions resembled the cultural zaps engaged in by New York's Gay Activists Alliance. In its first six months

> Queer Nation conducted over 40 actions, like the kiss-in at the Powell Street cable car turnaround, the retro-chic Queer Be-In at Aquatic Park, and—as part of its Suburban Homosexual Outreach Project (SHOP)—several trips to Bay Area malls, where they staged scenes of everyday urban queer life for gaping audiences unaccustomed to such sights. Queer Nation also spawned several other groups of varying longevity, including LABIA (Lesbians and Bisexuals in Action) and the Castro Street Patrol.[17]

But Queer Nation, as an organization, was short-lived. In San Francisco, it "suspended activities" at the end of 1991.[18]

The brevity of its life flowed directly out of the ambivalence of its politics. Seidman argued that queer politics "offers a thin politics as it problematizes the very notion of a collective in whose name a movement acts."[19] Joshua Gamson pointed out that for gay activists to engage in a critique of identity politics "is an odd endeavor, much like pulling the rug out from under one's own feet, not knowing how and where one will land."[20] Queer politics pre-sented incisive and persuasive critiques of gay identity politics, but did not provide a persuasive alternative to it.

Turning to redistributive politics could have provided a coherent way to reorganize the movement. It was the vantage point that informed many of the critiques of identity politics. And it motivated some participants, like one individual who saw queer politics as "the starting point for bringing together a lot of progressive issues—queer, people of color, women. I thought it might be the kind of rainbow group that would lead all other groups."[21] But the vision of a multi-issue, multiracial social justice movement was a hard sell in the political climate of the 1990s. It was not appealing to the middle-class white men who were still the most powerful players within the gay movement. Instead, the ambivalence of queer politics was resolved in favor of identity politics. The boundaries of gay identity were extended and status hierarchies internal to the movement were restructured.

Some experienced the failure of queer politics to move toward a social justice politics as "very disappointing, because race and gender were really marginalized."[22] The nationalist thread of queer politics made this retreat to identity politics possible, leading those who envisioned queer politics as a way of moving toward a multi-issue, multiracial politics, such as writer-activist Mab Segrest, to argue that "we have opted for the wrong model. We don't need a queer nationalism. . . . We need a queer socialism that is by necessity anti-racist, feminist and democratic."[23]

Gay identity was made over to fit the sensibilities of a new generation. Many of those participating in queer politics were younger gay men and lesbians, who did not share the experiences of the New Left, of Stonewall, of lesbian feminism, or the Golden Age of gay male sexuality of the 1970s with the baby boomers who were the architects of the gay identity movement. Queer politics succeeded at broadening the boundaries of the community to include bisexuals, transgenders, and others who identified as queer. It attempted to decenter privileged middle-class gay white men as "gay unmodified," while raising the status of those on the periphery of lesbian and gay worlds.

This domestication of queer politics can be seen in the way the term "queer" began to be treated interchangeably with "lesbian and gay." In the early 1990s gay identity organizations began incorporating "queer" into their names. For example, Digital Queers, founded in 1992, described itself as "a national group of computer professionals and technology aficionados who raise money for hardware and software for gay, lesbian, bisexual, and transgender community organizations."

The neutralization of the challenge posed by bisexuality and transgenderism is evidenced by the inclusion of "bisexual" and "transgender" within the gay identity movement. Many gay organizations changed their names and mission statements to include the terms "bisexual" and "transgender" beginning in the late 1980s. Bisexual and transgender activists targeted central community organizations, such as the lesbian/gay freedom day parade. Bisexual activist Autumn Courtney described her motivations for joining the parade committee as follows:

> I started working on the parade, the lesbian/gay freedom day parade, in 1983 after they so horribly discriminated against us. In 1982 they put the [bisexual] booth way, way, way out at the far edges of the grounds, in between NAMBLA, the North American Man/Boy Love Association, one of the most hated groups in existence,[24] and the Gay Republicans. And we were with the social deviants, within the lesbian/gay community we were considered social deviants, and that outraged me so much, that like two days after the parade I marched my butt into the office, and I said, I want to join your organization, because the way you run it stinks.[25]

A few years later, transgender activists followed the example of bisexuals, joining the parade committee. In 1994 their efforts succeeded in adding "bi-sexual" and "transgender" to the already unwieldy "San Francisco Lesbian/ Gay Freedom Day Parade and Celebration Committee."[26] By incorporating bisexuals and transgenders, the gay identity movement acknowledged the ambiguity, contradiction, and complexity of sexual categorization. Allowing for this ambiguity helped to forestall a more fundamental challenge to the logic of identity politics.

Thus, queer politics helped solidify gay identity politics instead of un-dermining it. Stryker and Van Buskirk's view that queer politics "represented an ideological and generational shift as profound as the transition from a ho-mophile mentality to gay liberation" overstated the case.[27]

The Obsolescence of Identity Politics?

The moment of effectiveness of [identity politics] may be waning, as every political strategy must.

Alexandra Chasin, *Selling Out:*
The Gay and Lesbian Movement Goes to Market (2000)

A tension between interest group, identity, and pleasure-seeking logics was built into the identity movement in the early 1970s. This section shows how field growth and a changing environment may be shifting the balance be-tween these logics. It also discusses the possible implications of an increasing dominance of the field by interest group politics and the likelihood of this trend being blocked or reversed.

Interest group, identity, and pleasure-seeking logics are fundamentally divergent notions of how gay people should act collectively. At the core of identity politics is the assumption that change happens from the bottom up, through the transformation of individual identities. It is local, individualistic, and expressive. Interest group politics is based on a top-down conception of change, through the transformation of public policy. Its logic is national, bureaucratic, and structured. In contrast to both, the pleasure-seeking logic is based on the notion that gay collective life should be primarily about the pursuit of pleasure through participation in purely social or commercial venues.

The gay identity movement privileged the identity logic. It framed the pursuit of gay rights (through interest group politics) and the pursuit of pleasure (through the commercialization of sex) as ways of achieving the larger goal of building and expressing a positive, unified, and diverse gay identity. Like other gay organizations, gay rights organizations marched in parades alongside organizations with diametrically opposed politics and reveled in the vitality of a community that could produce such diversity. This subordination of interest group and commercial logics to the logic of identity thus enabled the finessing of serious contradictions between these logics.

In the late 1990s, the growth and success of the movement may have begun to destabilize the balance between these logics. With gay identity firmly established, the cultivation and display of identity may be becoming less necessary. The gay identity movement nurtured the rise and growth of interest group organizations, with the result that interest group organizations are now large enough to attempt to successfully monopolize control of the movement. The lack of powerful interest group organizations earlier in the movement's history distinguishes it from women's and African American movements. In the 1970s, the gay movement had not produced a gay equivalent of NOW or the NAACP.[28]

Trends in the wider political environment may also be contributing to the destabilizing of the balance between identity and interest group politics. The political environment seems ever more hospitable to large interest group organizations, and the logic of the market seems to be penetrating more sectors of society, even arenas that have historically been able to resist it, such as medicine and education.[29] The focus on authenticity and self-expression that diffused through American culture in the wake of the movements of the 1960s may be receding, making the climate for a politics of identity display less nurturing.

The shifting balance between identity and interest group politics is evidenced by a growing unwillingness of interest group organizations to share decision-making power with other organizations. A few of these organizations seem to be trying to exert a top-down control of the field at odds with the more articulated form of field governance that has characterized the logic of identity politics. Interest group organizations seem to be pushing toward the "uniform and monolithic" movement that Jim Owles warned against in 1971.[30]

The Millennium March on Washington, which took place in April 2000, provides the most dramatic evidence to date of the growing domination of the movement by a few interest group organizations. This event was plagued with controversy both throughout the planning of the event and in the aftermath. Cultural critic Joshua Gamson referred to it as "the kind of diagnostic event that X-rays a movement at a particular historical moment."[31] What was most striking was the degree to which the Human Rights Campaign and the Metropolitan Community Church made decisions without taking into account the full range of community voices. The call for the march was virtually unilateral.[32] When activists from other organizations, even those from other interest group organizations, attempted to get involved in the planning, their efforts were frustrated. Kerry Lobel, executive director of the progressive National Gay and Lesbian Task Force (NGLTF),[33] resigned from the Board of Directors of the Millennium March Committee on April 25, 1999, a year before the march. In her resignation letter, she articulated many of the concerns of activists around the country. Lobel expressed "skeptic[ism about] the value of this event for the gay, lesbian, bisexual, and transgender (GLBT) movement at this time" and questioned whether there had been adequate input into crucial questions such as "whether to march at all, what agenda to march for, and how best to use the tremendous platform and visibility that such a march would provide." She noted that the march board had not succeeded at "win[ning] the involvement of the entire GLBT community." She, like other activists from around the country, worried about "the effectiveness of such an enormous commitment of time and resources at a moment when more and more energy is demanded of the GLBT movement at the state and local level" as well as about issues of financial accountability, saying that she could not "serve on a Board that will not open itself to greater input and scrutiny from the communities we claim to represent." She insisted that the march provide "full access to information about March management and finances."[34]

Lobel was far from the only critic of the march. A group of progressive activists formed an Ad Hoc Committee for an Open Process to critique the march.[35] These critics felt that the march was guarded about finances because it did not want it revealed that the event was "a profit-making business enterprise masquerading as a lesbian/gay/bisexual/transgender civil rights rally."[36] Critics of the march "were [also] turned off by the initial theme of the March, 'Faith and Family,' which seemed a capitulation to the credos of the Far Right."[37] The organizers initially defined the march as an opportunity to "celebrate our diversity as a community of family, spirituality, and equality," appealing to the resonance of the vision of diversity, while dramatically narrowing the parameters of this diversity.[38] The critiques of the march had little impact on how the march was ultimately run. While the march "went well enough," attended by anywhere from 125,000 to 800,000 people, the concerns about financial accountability proved to be on target when someone stole $750,000 of the revenue in the aftermath of the event.[39]

A recent conflict offers additional evidence of changes in the behavior of interest group organizations. In 1998, a group of conservative gay men in San Antonio, Texas, all affiliated with gay nonprofit or for-profit groups, successfully pressured the city council to cut the funding of another gay organization, the Esperanza Center.[40] They argued that the Esperanza Center was "damaging the cause of equal rights for gays and lesbians in San Antonio."[41] The Esperanza Center was an organization serving

> a diverse clientele, including immigrants, people of color, women, low-income people, and gay men and lesbians through programming that includes a cooperative art studio, a women's economic development project, and a video production training project for teenagers, and through fiscal sponsorship of the San Antonio Lesbian and Gay Media Project.[42]

The Esperanza Center endorsed the kind of multi-issue, multiracial politics utterly at odds with the single-issue, interest group politics endorsed by the center of the gay identity movement.

What is distinctive about the attack on the Esperanza Center is the center engaging in a hostile attack on the margins. A direct attack like this is in violation of the vision of unity through diversity that has defined the movement from the early 1970s. The belief that it is not possible or desirable to achieve complete ideological conformity has shaped the movement since the early 1970s. Gay groups at the margins have been encouraged to express themselves. By claiming that the activities of the Esperanza Center were damaging the cause, the attackers rejected the idea that progress results from all kinds of gay organizations simultaneously expressing their identities and political agendas. This policing of the margins was new. Historically, middle-class white gay men have been oblivious to and dismissive of issues of women and people of color, but they have not, until recently, engaged in campaigns to sabotage the efforts of these groups.

These changes in the behavior of interest group organizations have been accompanied by changes in the nature and extent of commercialism within the gay movement. In the 1970s and 1980s, gay commercialism was primarily about the survival, protection, and proliferation of gay bars, bathhouses, and other organizations such bookstores and newspapers that contributed to a subcultural sensibility. The success of the gay identity movement has contributed to the appeal of gays and lesbians as a target market of mainstream businesses. There is a meaningful difference between allowing gay bars to participate in the freedom day parade and allowing national beer distributors to sponsor freedom day parades. Alexandra Chasin argues that "the 1990s have seen the production, distribution, and consumption of commodities aimed at a gay and lesbian market" and that it was in the 1990s that "the idea of a gay niche market . . . became more elaborately formulated." Mainstream companies became interested in "gay and lesbian purchasing power, consumption habits, brand loyalty and other market behaviors."[43] Advertising targeted at lesbian and gay consumers has proliferated. While it would be naïve to think that all, or even most of, the money made by traditional subcultural establishments like gay bars primarily benefits the gay community, or even gay individuals, money made by Coors by advertising beer to gay men and lesbians quite clearly does not. And at least some of the businesses in gay neighborhoods founded in the 1970s and later were owned by gay individuals who plowed the proceeds back into the community. Gay businesses in the 1970s funded the careers of gay-friendly politicians.[44] Quite a few "for-profit" gay businesses, such as bookstores and newspapers, were only nominally so. The motivation of their owners was to serve the community while making enough money to avoid employment in the heterosexual world. The shift in the 1990s seems to have involved an increase in the sheer amount of money involved, the beneficiaries of the profit, and the content of the goods and services produced. In short, there seems to be more money to be made, the profit seems to be flowing increasingly to large multinational corporations, and the money seems to be being made off the production and sales of increasingly homogenized goods and services.

These changes could have major implications for the nature of the gay movement in the United States. The peculiar brilliance of the gay identity movement has been due to the way the identity, interest group, and commercialism have been held in balance. The notion of unity through diversity, which emerged out of the individualistic, expressive sentiments of the 1960s, produced an articulated structure of governance. The movement grew in many directions at the same time, but without having a center. It was not forced to homogenize around a narrow vision of goals, identities, and strategy.

If the Human Rights Campaign or organizations like it become too powerful and are able to silence other organizations, the peculiar strength of this movement may be lost. That is not to say that the movement will disappear. In all likelihood, it will simply become like other movements of the 1960s, which have become dominated by large, professionalized interest group organizations.[45] It may lose its connection to the grass roots. It may find it more difficult to organize events, like parades, that rely on an articulated structure. The movement may also become more racially exclusive. While the gay identity movement has never succeeded at responding to the critiques of people of color, the vision of unity through diversity at least provided a moral position from which to criticize the homogeneity of the movement. The decentralized and expressive nature of the movement allowed space for diverse ways of being gay. If the movement moves in the direction of ideological homogenization, these spaces may disappear. Without a vision of a unified but diverse movement, it may become much more difficult to defend the need for the movement to include lesbians and people of color.

The changing nature of the commercialization of gay communities may lead these communities to be more dependent on the whims and bottom-line calculations of large corporations. For instance, what happens when a major publishing group buys small gay newspapers but then discovers they are not profitable? Instead of maintaining them because of the community service they provide, large corporations may just shut down the businesses altogether. In addition, the interest of the mainstream in capturing the dollars of a gay market may produce cultural homogenization. Chasin argues that the commercialization of the movement also heightens exclusion along the lines of race, class, and gender.[46]

In spite of these signs of a shift in the relationship between interest group and identity politics within the gay movement, it is not yet possible to tell whether a fundamental transformation of the movement is under way. We have discussed a variety of indications that it is. However, evidence of the continued vitality of the gay identity-building project also exists. Organizations, events, and rituals continue to garner widespread participation and appreciation. The domination of the Millennium March by the Human Rights Campaign organizations was not taken for granted as an inevitable or desirable state of affairs. Lesbian/gay progressives, who might have been the gay power activists of yesteryear, continue to provide a consistent and vocal critique of the consolidation of power in the hands of a few mainstream interest group organizations and against the increasing commercialization of the movement.[47] Ironically, the preservation of the gay identity movement is not their primary agenda. Lesbian/gay progressives see their goal as transforming the gay movement into a "more inclusive and radical movement for social and economic justice."[48] While at this moment this seems an unlikely outcome, by continuing to fight for it lesbian and gay progressives might actually succeed at preserving the gay movement's synergistic balance. They may be able to prevent the movement from becoming more ideologically homogeneous, more dominated by a few large interest group organizations, less able to accommodate diversity, more tied to corporate interests, and more cut off from grassroots community.

In this chapter, I have shown how understanding the origins and nature of the gay identity movement provides a framework to understand contemporary conflicts within the movement. In the concluding chapter of the book, I review my central arguments, showing how each emerged out of a cultural-institutional approach to the study of social movements. I suggest how this approach might explain other cases and explore the implications of this study for American political culture, particularly for our understanding of other movements shaped by the New Left.

PART THREE

Conclusion

TEN

Institutions, Social Movements, and American Political Culture

The gay movement in San Francisco crystallized in the early 1970s. It took shape around the celebration of gay pride, the pursuit of gay rights, and a commercialized sexual subculture. A commitment to a vision of a unified but diverse movement held these three distinct agendas in dynamic tension. That the field crystallized in this form at this moment was not inevitable. It could have taken shape as the kind of multiracial, multi-issue movement gay power activists envisioned. It might have imploded completely, as did other parts of the New Left. Or it could have become more similar to the women's movement, in which the cultural and rights wings became almost entirely distinct projects. But it did not take any of those paths.

The movement crystallized in this form as a result of historically and culturally specific processes. Homophile organizing of the 1950s and 1960s established a precedent for single-issue interest group politics in pursuit of rights. But as homophile activists tried to pursue interest group politics, they found they were hampered by the impoverished state of the public identity of the group whose interests they advocated. The homophile encounter with the New Left solved this problem. The New Left provided a way of thinking about the goals and strategies of collective action that made the revelation of sexual identity meaningful to large numbers of people. The logic of identity politics highlighted authenticity, which made privacy about sexual identity seem both dishonest and personally unhealthy. The logic of identity viewed social change as resulting from the aggregation of the actions of individuals, making individual revelation of identity not only personally therapeutic but also politically effective.

The shift away from the more revolutionary politics of 1969 and 1970 was crucial to the crystallization of a gay identity movement. In 1969, the conflict between the identity-focused "gay pride" aspects of gay liberation and the social justice–focused "gay power" aspects of gay liberation threatened to paralyze the movement. The gay power view envisioned a movement of economic redistribution addressing class, race, gender, and sexuality issues simultaneously. The gay pride view defined commonalities primarily in terms of shared interest in same-gender sexual relations. The sudden and rapid decline of the New Left delegitimated revolutionary politics and the gay power strand of gay liberation.

The demise of gay power did not in and of itself ensure the survival of gay organizing or the creation of a gay identity movement. At this moment of crisis and opportunity, activists still faced contradictory ideas about how to organize around sexuality. The movement crystallized when activists stumbled upon a way to balance an individualistic, expressive identity politics, a top-down interest group politics seeking gay rights, and the appeal of the commercial sexual subculture. The balancing of these three agendas was made possible by the individualistic view of change characteristic of the identity logic of organizing. Interest group politics and commodified sex could be accommodated within a movement whose primary mission was expanding the variety of ways it was possible to be gay.

The crystallization of the gay identity movement in the early 1970s shaped later events. This consensus made possible the tremendous successes of gay organizing in the late 1970s and 1980s. The contradiction between movement claims to universality and diversity, in spite of actual racial and gender homogeneity, produced decades of challenges to the exclusivity of the political project. The gay identity movement shaped the cultural, organizational, and political resources available to respond to the AIDS epidemic. Initially, interpreting AIDS from within the categories of the gay identity movement contributed to denial of the seriousness of the epidemic. After the initial shock, the mature, highly organized movement in San Francisco produced an impressive response to AIDS, which, in turn, contributed to the growth of a separate AIDS field.

This book presented a novel description of the transformation of the gay movement, explained how the gay movement took the form that it did, and elaborated some implications of the movement. In the next sections I discuss how these arguments relied on a cultural-institutional perspective on movement transformation and the implications of this approach for the study of other contemporary movements. I then discuss the implications of the findings of the book for debates about the nature of American political culture.

Institutions, Fields, and Political Logics

A cultural-institutional approach to social movements structured my arguments about both the nature of the transformation of the gay movement and the causes and consequences of the transformation. A cultural-institutional perspective on social movements integrates the richest insights of a cultural approach to movements with concepts from organizational sociology. This approach is cultural, in that it sees meaning as structuring the possibilities for collective action at the bedrock level.[1] Culture constitutes what can be used as a resource, seen as an opportunity, or imagined as a possible way of acting collectively. Systems of meanings in which people are embedded are necessary not only to motivate people to take advantage of an objectively existing opportunity but also constitute an important part of the structure of opportunities. Available cultural materials limit what people can imagine doing and how they can imagine doing it. Gay identity is not treated as given or inevitable but as a historically specific political outcome. Gay activists debated at least three different ways to frame gay interests.

A cultural-institutional perspective extends established cultural approaches to social movements by incorporating the concept of the "field" from organizational sociology. The concept of the field shifts social movement scholarship away from privileging action targeting the state. Fields are institutionalized arenas of social action. Everyday action reproduces established fields. Social movements occur when actors engage in collective action geared toward carving out new arenas or redefining the rules of the game of existing arenas. Social movements can be directed toward establishing new fields, destroying or transforming existing fields, or blocking the efforts of other actors to transform arenas. Movements can occur within any arena of society (e.g., the state, the economy, or the religious sector).

The concept of the field directs attention to how actors define the boundaries of their collective projects. In this case, this led to an understanding that the gay movement included cultural and commercial organizations as well as those that are conventionally political. For example, some people attended freedom day parades with the primary intention of advocating for gay rights, while for others the political goal was merely a consequence of the affirmation of personal identity or an enjoyable social event. In contrast, a political process perspective on movements would have led me to concentrate on action that was conventionally political.

Incorporating sensitivity to processes of institutionalization into social movement analysis made it possible to see that a gay identity movement crystallized in the early 1970s. While acknowledging that movements are often highly organized, social movement scholars generally do not think of movements as susceptible to institutionalization in such early stages. They typically think of movement institutionalization in terms of movement incorporation into the established institutions of society, which often occurs late in the life cycle of a movement.

Defining social movement action as geared toward creating and transforming fields makes the community-building efforts of gay activists meaningful. The gay movement engaged in a field-building project both as an end in itself and to launch efforts to change the rules structuring other fields. Field formation in this case was both movement development and movement outcome. That movement development and outcome may be inseparable makes sense within a field perspective but is impossible to see when it is assumed that the primary goal of movements is to change social policy.

Explaining Field Formation

A cultural-institutional perspective assumes that outcomes are the result of political struggle. The way things work themselves out through time matters a great deal. Outcomes cannot be predicted simply by analyzing structural conditions. Instead, one must examine how political processes unfold through time. The order of events matters.

Homophile organizing in the 1950s was made possible by the attempt to extend an existing organizational logic, an interest group political logic, to a new constituency. Homophile organizing in the 1950s was both enabled and limited by the interest group model. The interest group model enabled homosexual organizing by making public homosexual organizations thinkable, but it also limited homosexual organizing by providing no viable way to appreciably enlarge the size of the group on whose behalf those organizations desired to speak. Simply realizing the need for a public collective identity did not solve the problem of how to bring that group into existence. Homophile activists were neither fully conscious of the assumptions structuring their organizations nor able to develop a new model more suitable for their needs. Reliance on the interest group model so structured the ways activists thought about what was politically possible and desirable that activists were initially unable to respond to a dramatic change in political opportunities.

The importance of the New Left for the gay movement has been treated as obvious, but we do not have a full understanding of how the New Left mattered for the explosive growth of gay organizing. A cultural-institutional approach provided the tools to develop a more precise understanding. The New Left and the political crisis on the 1960s unsettled taken-for-granted assumptions about the goals and means of collective action, producing a rare moment of cultural creativity.[2] Cultural streams usually isolated from each other were brought into dense interaction in the context of a systemwide crisis. The juxtaposition of multiple cultural traditions and the expansive feeling of possibility led activists to develop new cultural combinations. Within this context, activists, including gay activists, developed an identity political logic, which presented an understanding of the goals and strategies of organizing radically different from the existing interest group logic. This new political logic made possible the creation of new political strategies and new kinds of organizations. The focus on personal authenticity and the notion that change happens through the aggregation of individual actions made possible coming out, the zap, consciousness-raising groups, and new kinds of gay organizations. This logic was not invented out of whole cloth but rather translated long-standing American concerns about authenticity into an approach to political organizing. However, the generativity of this moment also led to the widespread availability of revolutionary socialist ideology. Gay power activists believed that sexual liberation was not possible without an overthrow of capitalism, while gay pride activists did not. Environmental uncertainty made it difficult to adjudicate between these positions, which produced paralyzing internal conflict.

The precipitous decline of the New Left in the early 1970s was as important to the crystallization of the gay identity movement as the emergence of the New Left in the first place. Had the New Left not receded as rapidly as it did and when it did, the conflict between gay power and gay pride might have led the movement to self-destruct. The rapid demise of the New Left eliminated the viability of the revolutionary socialist gay power vision, reducing destructive internal conflict. The presence of multiple political logics meant that the gay movement had available a fully formed "solution" to the problem presented by the demise of the New Left. Social movement scholarship tends to assume that actors shift goals in response to transformations in opportunities. But this does not always happen. For example, some parts of the New Left turned violent and went underground. The ability to survive and thrive after a moment of crisis depends both on the social skill of actors and the versatility of the cultural repertoire they have at their disposal at that moment.[3] The timing and pace of change in opportunity structure may matter a great deal, as the brevity of moments of opportunity may mean that only those who are culturally prepared will be able to exploit opportunities. The existence of gay pride and gay rights meant that gay activists were well situated to take advantage of the possibilities presented by the rapid demise of the New Left.

The demise of the New Left did not resolve the shape of the resulting gay movement. It was still unclear whether the gay movement would be an interest group movement pursuing rights, an identity movement focused on coming out, pride, and identity display, or simply about the collective pursuit of pleasure in the context of a sexualized commercial subculture. Initially, it seemed that these different approaches might be unable to coexist within the same movement. They have not been able to coexist within other movements. The individualistic, bottom-up nature of a politics of visibility was at odds with a top-down, policy-oriented interest group politics. Activists, as they struggled to bind together a movement, stumbled onto a way that the three approaches could be reconciled, or at least held in a synergistic tension. The individualism of the homophile and gay liberation movements led activists to be leery of top-down ideological homogenization. The identity logic provided activists with a way of framing the pursuit of these quite different projects as contributing to the larger goal of expanding the range of gay expression in society. Instead of highlighting the homogenizing, communitarian aspect of identity politics, the gay movement expressed a libertarian, individualist use of this logic. In this framework, the pursuit of gay rights and the participation in the sexual subculture could be seen as examples of gay people doing their own thing. Defining diversity as one of the core commonalities of the movement structured in a high tolerance for ambiguity. This balance proved to be highly synergistic. Fields may be particularly likely to consolidate around logics that tolerate ambiguity. Ambiguity may help to mobilize cooperation across diverse groups.

Implications of Field Formation

Field crystallization made possible enormous growth of the gay movement in the 1970s by providing the cultural tools necessary to exploit opportunities and to actively remake the environment. Field crystallization produced organizational proliferation.[4] The crystallization of the gay identity movement made new kinds of gay organizations thinkable and possible. Before field crystallization, the numbers of gay organizations were small. With field crystallization, new kinds of gay organizations suddenly appeared. These new gay identity organizations proliferated rapidly. Synergistic relationships between gay pride, gay rights, and the sexual subculture led all sectors of the movement to grow simultaneously.

The form of the resulting gay movement privileged the experiences and interests of gay white men. At this moment of time, historical processes had led many white lesbians, gay men of color, and lesbians of color to understand their interests and identities differently from many gay white men.

These interests were not reflected in the gay identity movement consensus. Nonetheless, the gay identity movement claimed to be universal and diverse, when, at least with respect to race, gender, and class, it was actually quite homogeneous. Successful fields usually claim to be in the general interest. Fields also usually advantage some groups and disadvantage others.[5] The deeper the institutionalization, the more difficult it is to locate the ways the rules of the game benefit some at the expense of others. Understanding that the interests of gay white men were built into the core assumptions of the gay identity movement helps explain why it has been so hard to integrate the movement. True integration means not just soliciting the participation of underrepresented groups, but changing the nature of core agreements defining the project. Changing these core agreements would transform the gay identity movement beyond recognition. Such a transformation of the political project is precisely what lesbian/gay progressives desire.

Field formation not only enables action but also makes other ways of interpreting reality unthinkable. When the AIDS epidemic emerged, the cultural categories available to gay men and lesbians to make sense of the disease were those provided by the gay identity movement. Initially, this produced skepticism about the existence of the disease and its possible route of transmission. As scientific evidence of the viral nature of the disease accumulated, gay San Francisco used this knowledge and the maturity of the field to launch an effective response to the epidemic. This led to the growth of an AIDS field distinguishable from the gay field and organized around a quite different logic. Most AIDS organizations, even those formed by gay men and lesbians, came to define themselves as AIDS organizations, not gay organizations. This new field competed with the gay field for resources, accounting for a decline in the numbers of gay identity organizations in the late 1980s.

Fields, even ones that are highly institutionalized, are dynamic. They must be in order to respond to changing environments. And fields can under certain circumstances become deinstitutionalized. Understanding the logic of a field, with its particular internal contradictions and its relationship with its environment, provides insight into which challenges might be accommodated and which might lead to field transformation. Queer politics emerged from the ways that field growth and environmental changes heightened contradictions between the field's claims to diversity and the reality of its homogeneity. Queer politics criticized the identity logic of the movement. To the extent that queer activists offered an alternative, it was a return to a redistributive politics, which required relinquishing core assumptions of the gay identity movement. This alternative was not very appealing to the most powerful members of the field. Not surprisingly, it was not successful. Instead, activists neutralized the most serious complaints of exclusion by extending the boundaries of the field and shuffling internal status hierarchies. In contrast, the growing dominance of interest group organizations in Washington may pose a more serious threat to the gay identity movement. While the growth of interest group politics is a logical consequence of the success of the gay identity movement, it threatens to shift the balance between the constitutive parts of the gay movement. This shift, while appearing inconsequential on the surface, could radically transform the nature of the entire endeavor. It may be inevitable, as it is endorsed by powerful segments of community and resonates with changes in the larger political and cultural environment.

Implications for Other Contemporary American Social Movements

A cultural-institutional analysis of the various movements coming from the New Left would start with an analysis of the New Left as a field. While ephemeral and unstable, the New Left created a strong sense of participation in a common enterprise. Analysis would describe the processes through which movements that were previously distinct were drawn into and transformed by the shared meanings of this field. Then, the analysis would trace the fate of various strands as the New Left declined. Starting from the hunch that other movements might have also consolidated in the early 1970s, the analysis would look carefully for evidence of field crystallization. Such a description would look closely at empirical materials to identify the boundaries of the various projects that did coalesce.

Movements that participated in the New Left were stamped with an identifiable set of cultural orientations. They were all influenced, to a greater or lesser extent, by the identity political logic that shaped the gay movement. In addition, most fields emerging from the New Left moved away from radical socialist perspectives toward interest group politics. Moderate, service-providing, and policy-oriented nonprofit organizations proliferated. Debra Minkoff refers to this sectorwide trend as an "advocacy explosion."[6] Given the shared participation in the New Left and exposure to the same general political context, these similarities are to be expected.

There were also clear differences in outcomes. A few of the most radical groups turned violent, fragmented, and went underground. Some parts of the New Left seemed to dissolve into thin air. The parts that survived varied considerably in terms of attachment to a politics of economic redistribution. For example, the women's movement remained more committed to a multi-issue, multiracial social justice politics than did the gay movement. And movements surviving the New Left varied in terms of the role played by identity politics, with the gay movement perhaps relying most heavily on it. The projects also varied in the extent of and rapidity of professionalization.

Scholars have assumed that these differences were the result of consequential differences in interests. It has been assumed that the level of commitment to a politics of economic redistribution explained differences in outcome, and that commitment to social justice politics flowed naturally out of interests. The less willing activists were to moderate, the less likely the movement strain was to survive. The decline of African American movements is attributed to the commitment of African American movements to redistributive politics, a commitment seen to emerge naturally from the social location of African Americans in the economic and political order. Conversely, the gay movement abandoned redistributive politics because its primary constituency was middle-class white men. In short, the successes of the various offshoots of the New Left has been explained by how well group interests meshed with the political possibilities provided by a political environment hostile to a politics of economic redistribution.

However, political views do not necessarily flow neatly from social location, nor is the construction of "interest" straightforward. Social base cannot account for the revolutionary views of white men from middle-class backgrounds. Gay men and lesbians battled over at least three distinct ways to interpret gay interests. Not only are interests subject to interpretation and reconstruction, but identities are as well. Before the 1950s, "homosexual" as an identity did not exist, meaning that it was quite difficult to talk in terms of homosexual interests. Similarly, Joane Nagel has shown that the numbers of those identifying as Native American increased in the 1960s and 1970s, as individuals converted to Native American identity.[7] Presumably, their interests shifted along with their identities.

Thus, to explain the differential outcomes of the New Left it is necessary to explain the evolution and reconstruction of interests and identities within the movements of the 1960s. Such an analysis would explain why some parts of the New Left were willing and able to moderate their goals to fit with a changing political environment while other parts were not. Before 1970, homosexual activists conceived of group interests narrowly in terms of rights, while after 1972 gay activists conceived of group interests in terms of both rights and collective visibility. It is likely that a similar reconstruction of identities and interests occurred within other movements that participated in the New Left.

A cultural-institutional perspective provides some insights into particular processes that may have been crucial to the reconstruction of interests and identities in other parts of the New Left. The argument developed in this book suggests that the way each strand of the New Left viewed its interests and identities can be accounted for by examining five factors. First, how were interests and identities understood before the emergence of the New Left? What was the history of organizing before this movement intersected with the New Left? Second, what specific cultural innovations did each branch of the New Left develop in the encounter with the New Left as a whole (e.g., coming out, consciousness-raising groups, "the personal is political," "black is beautiful," black power)? How novel and appealing were these innovations? Third, how debilitating was the conflict among political logics in this branch of the New Left? Did the sudden shift in political context occur early enough in the life cycle to prevent these conflicts from leading to movement faction-alization and implosion? Fourth, what did the sudden delegitimation of revo-lutionary politics mean for this branch of the New Left? Did viable alterna-tives exist? Fifth, how skilled were the political actors in their response to the crisis and opportunity presented by this rapid shift in political context? Did they respond by becoming more rigid, looking for a single correct political analysis? Or did they respond in a flexible fashion, searching for a way to unite people under a politically viable umbrella? Thus, a cultural-institutional ap-proach to social movements provides the theoretical tools that, combined with close empirical scholarship, could provide a comprehensive reinterpre-tation of the transformation of social movements influenced by the New Left.

Individualism, Authenticity, and American Political Culture

The findings of this study intersect with ongoing debates about the health and vitality of American political culture. The explosion of gay organizing I describe occurred when, according to political scientist Robert D. Putnam, the "fabric of American community life began to unravel."[8] The increase in social connectedness and organizational participation that has characterized gay communities in the past thirty years is at odds with how Putnam de-scribes the more general trends in society. According to Putnam, most forms of civic engagement have declined dramatically since the 1960s. Marshalling a vast quantity of data, Putnam documents declines in everything from presi-dential voting, membership rates in nonprofit organizations (such as the PTA), church attendance, union membership, social visiting, and bowling.[9]

Putnam acknowledges that the movements of the 1960s, including the lesbian/gay movement, may constitute an "important countertrend."[10] But after acknowledging this possibility he quickly rejects it. He does so through an analysis of the development of the environmental movement, which he treats as representative of the movements of the 1960s.[11] He claims that the environmental movement has become dominated by professionalized organizations that "provide neither connectedness among members nor direct engagement in civic give-and-take."[12] These organizations do not involve "real ties to real people," thus they do not build or reflect social capital.[13]

Putnam's analysis of the environmental movement does not describe the development of the lesbian/gay movement since the 1960s. As the analysis in this book has shown, with the possible exception of the very late 1990s, post-1960s gay organizing in San Francisco has not been dominated by professionalized interest group organizations. San Francisco saw a tremendous proliferation of lesbian/gay organizations in this time period. These organizations were cultural, hobby, religious, sexual, social, professional, service, and political organizations. Gay organizations involved the kinds of "real ties to real people" that Putnam sees as characteristic of organizations producing social capital. If the building of gay San Francisco had to be summed up, the development of social capital captures it very well. The social capital produced within gay communities in the 1970s was clearly exhibited in the gay response to AIDS in the late 1980s. Thus, the organizational and social development described in this book is a new form of connectedness arising from the 1960s.

While other movements may have become dominated by a few large bureaucratic interest group organizations, it is possible that Putnam has also glossed over forms of connectedness produced by these other movements. He certainly glossed over the possible relevance of the growth of self-help groups, by arguing that the "linkage of small groups to public life is sometimes tenuous and hard to detect."[14] In his haste to reduce the complexity of the changes in American civic and organizational life to one trend line, he has run roughshod over much variation.[15] While Putnam has indeed identified important changes in American civic life, he has too rapidly dismissed some important countertrends that might provide crucial clues to changes in our civic life.

The sources of the explosive growth of the gay movement also challenge Putnam's argument. Putnam sees the "free agent" mentality of baby boomers as the primary reason for the decline of social capital in the United States. He describes baby boomers as cynical about authority, nonreligious, antibureaucratic, and individualistic. According to Putnam, baby boomers value autonomy, have a high tolerance for diversity, and reject traditional roles. They are self-centered and materialistic. If there has been any group in society fitting this profile, it was the baby boomer men who birthed the gay identity movement. Gay identity politics was incubated within *precisely* the cultural milieu that Putnam sees as most antagonistic to civic connectedness. From within Putnam's framework, urban gay men should not have been able to produce the vibrant gay organizational worlds that exist now in American cities.

We have seen that the gay world in San Francisco exploded not in spite of, but because of, this individualistic orientation. Coming out, the central political strategy of the gay movement, is an act made meaningful by the valorization of individual expression and personal authenticity. Agreement about the centrality of freedom of expression, individual rights, and diversity generated an astonishing array of organizations and provided the glue that prevented the movement from fragmenting. The organizational generativity of individualism in this case suggests that the effects of individualism on American civic life may be more complex and contradictory than Putnam has suggested.[16]

The heightened preoccupation with the self that was particularly intense in the 1970s may have chilled some forms of connectedness while energizing others. Baby boomers may desire different results from their civic participation than earlier cohorts. An increased expectation of authentic self-expression within organizational involvement may have lowered satisfaction with organizational experiences experienced as inauthentic—perhaps leading to a decline in satisfaction with participation in the kind of civic associations Putnam valorizes. Participants in gay communities may be unusual in the extent to which they have found forms of commitment and participation that meet the needs of contemporary selves. Others seeking similar experiences of recognition and self-expression in organizational participation may not be finding them. The way the gay movement balances individual needs with the pursuit of collective interest could perhaps provide insights into the kinds of organizational experiences that could resuscitate civic engagement more broadly.

Thus, the ascendance of the gay movement in the post-1960s United States provides insight into general changes in the fabric of American cultural, political, and organizational life. By telling the story of the crystallization of the gay movement in the early 1970s, I have also told a story of the development of a sensibility that has shaped post-1960s life in the United States. Preoccupation with issues of identity transformed social movements, challenged the ability of social movement scholarship to account for them, and quite possibly contributed to a transformation of our civic landscape.

APPENDIX

Constructing a Database of San Francisco's Lesbian/Gay Organizations

A database of San Francisco's lesbian/gay organizations formed the evidentiary base for this book. I constructed this database by coding resource guides and directories. These provided a great source of data because they conveyed a rich picture of how actors within the field defined participation in the collective project. Institutional theorists have pointed out that guides are an indicator of field institutionalization because the very existence of guides suggests "the development of a mutual awareness among participants in a set of organizations that they are involved in a common enterprise."[1] John Mohr, in his work on poverty relief organizations in Progressive Era New York, argued that the New York City Charity's Directories revealed which organizations were "considered to fall within the bounds of the organizational field" which helped him discover "the meaning of poverty relief as an institutional activity."[2]

The quality of the database and the analysis based on it rests on the quality of the decisions made while identifying, locating, and coding the research guides. These decisions were necessary to translate the guides into a form amenable to systematic description and analysis.[3] However, this process of mediation introduces the possibility of misrepresentation. Would participants in this project have agreed that all the guides I used were indeed guides to their community? Would they have marveled at my omission of some crucial guide? Did the decisions I made violate the cognitive categories of actors in crucial ways? In this appendix, I discuss some of the crucial decisions made, highlighting those that I found to be particularly problematic so that the reader can assess the quality of the database.[4]

Locating and Selecting Lesbian/Gay Resource Guides

Acquiring resource guides and directories required identifying the full range of guides produced and locating physical copies of each guide. For contemporary resource guides, both steps were straightforward. Resource guides were sold in the gay sections of bookstores and published in every issue of a local gay newspaper. Locating guides of yesteryear was more difficult. Simply learning of the existence of some of the guides required scouring archives and periodical collections. Researching the archives of the Gay, Lesbian, Bisexual, Transgender Historical Society of Northern California, with the assistance of archivist Bill Walker, led me to ob-

scure guides from the 1960s and 1970s. Finding back issues of well-established contemporary guides was also surprisingly difficult. For the users of these guides and
therefore for the producers of these guides, old guides are useless. Thus, they tend
to be jettisoned once new, more accurate guides are published. I found back issues
in libraries, archives, and, in a couple of instances, through contacting the publish-
ers and printers of the guides.

After collecting guides, the next decision was which to code. Coding all guides
collected would have created uneven coverage. Often scholars just code every issue
of one hegemonic guide.[5] This was not an option, as no authoritative guide to
lesbian/gay organizations in San Francisco existed. The inchoate state of resource
guides is characteristic of a newly forming organizational field.

Guides found were of four general types—national guides, local guides, wom-
en's guides, and bar guides. National guides listed both nonprofit and commercial
organizations for every major city in the United States. Local guides listed only San
Francisco organizations. In addition to providing information on many of the same
organizations listed in the national guides, local guides listed smaller, more obscure
organizations. Women's guides included lesbian organizations that were sometimes
missed by national and local guides. Bar guides listed only commercial establishments, thus offering relatively little information on nonprofit organizations. In addition to using the guides as sources for organizational information, I also coded
every mention of a homosexual organization in the central publication of San
Francisco's homophile community, the *Vector,* from December 1964 through June
1971, to compensate for the lack of guides before 1972.

To the extent possible, I coded an example of each kind of guide for each year
of the time period, relying on guides published annually whenever possible. Table
A.1 lists the 104.5 guides of all types that were coded.

Coverage by national guides was consistent from 1972 through 1995. For virtually all years, I coded the *Gayellow Pages,* an annual listing of nonprofit and commercial organizations in the United States. In 1972 I coded the *Gay Insider,* a precursor
to the *Gayellow Pages.* Gaps in the coding of national guides coincide with gaps in
publication of the *Gayellow Pages.* Two national guides were coded in each of 1991
and 1995 to compensate for the missing 1990 *Gayellow Pages* and to ensure accurate
coding of the existence of organizations at the end of the time frame.

Before 1979, the publication of local resource guides was spotty. Listings for early
years were cobbled together through scouring archives for organizational lists. *Gaybook,* a local guide published since 1979, covered the rest of the time frame. Uncertainty about its quality, particularly fear that it underrepresented organizations existing after 1988, led me to code the *Bay Times,* another local resource guide, for the
years 1989 through 1994.

Figure A.1 shows the number of guides coded each year in a three-year moving
average that portrays the consistency of coverage because organizations remained
in the data set even if they fell out of the listings for one year. On average, more
resource guides were coded per year in the late 1980s and early 1990s. This was done

Table A.1 Resource Guides Coded by Type, 1963–94

	National[1]	Local	Women's	Bar	Vector[2]	Total
1963				1		1
1964						
1965				2	1	3
1966				2	1	3
1967				1	1	2
1968				1	1	2
1969		1[3]		1	1	3
1970		1[4]		1	1	3
1971		2[5]		1	0.5	3.5
1972	1			1		2
1973	1[6]	2[7]		2		5
1974	1[8]		1	1		3
1975	1			1		2
1976	1[8]	1[9]	1	1		4
1977	1		1	1		3
1978	1	1[10]		1		3
1979	1	1[11]		1		3
1980		1		1		2
1981	1	1	1	1		4
1982	1	1		1		3
1983		1	1	1		3
1984	1	1		1		3
1985		1	2	1		4
1986	1	1		1		3
1987	1	1	1	1		4
1988	1	1		1		3
1989	1	2[12]	1	1		5
1990		2		1		3
1991	2[13]	2	1	1		6
1992	1	2		1		4
1993	1	2	1	1		5
1994	1	2		1		4
1995	2[14]	1				3
Total	22	31	11	34	6.5	104.5

[1] *Gayellow Pages* was coded for each of the years for which a number appears here.

[2] For 1965–70, all twelve issues were coded and are counted in this table as one guide. Only six months were coded in 1971, and that is listed here as half a guide.

[3] Three versions of organization lists appeared in the *San Francisco Free Press* this year; they are counted here as one guide.

[4] Four versions of organization lists appeared in the *San Francisco Free Press* this year; they are counted here as one guide.

[5] *Bay Area Reporter* and *Carl Driver*.

[6] Three versions of *Gayellow Pages* appeared this year; they are counted here as one guide.

[7] The Emmaus House listings and the guide in the freedom day parade program.

[8] Two versions of *Gayellow Pages* appeared in each of these years; they are counted here as one guide for each year.

[9] *Bay Area Gay Social Services Guide*.

[10] *New Directions*.

[11] *Gaybook* is listed as a local guide for 1979 and thereafter.

[12] *Bay Times* is listed as a local guide for 1989 and thereafter.

[13] *Gayellow Pages* and *The Big Gay Book* were both coded to compensate for the missing 1990 *Gayellow Pages*.

[14] *Gayellow Pages* and *The Gay and Lesbian Address Book* were both coded to ensure accurate coding of the existence of organizations at the end of the time frame.

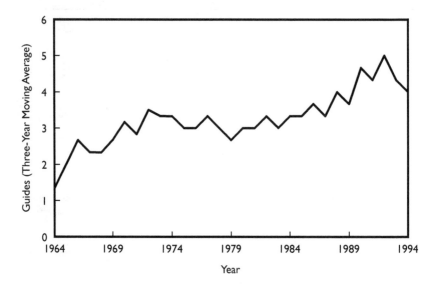

Figure A.1 Resource Guides Coded per Year

in order to see if a puzzling decline in organizational numbers in the late 1980s was simply an artifact of flawed data sources.

Inclusion and Exclusion of Organizations

After choosing which guides to code, I decided which organizations listed in the guides to include in the data set. Institutional theory suggested including all listed organizations in order to best reveal how actors understood the boundaries of the collective project. If I had followed this approach, my data set would have been quite unwieldy. I began in this fashion, but the database rapidly grew to twenty-five hundred organizations, with indications that it would grow substantially larger. Guides listed organizations and services that were clearly not gay (e.g., the city bus service), organizations located outside of San Francisco, and both commercial and nonprofit organizations.

Screening organizations before including them in the data set, while unfortunately imposing my own categories on the data, was necessary. I constructed inclusion rules with the intent of doing as little violence as possible to the construction of the world emerging through the guides.

To be included in the data set, the organization had to meet the following criteria:

• define in its name or mission statement that the organization was for or composed of sexual or gender minority individuals (including, but not limited to, those who defined themselves as homosexual, homophile, lesbian, gay, bisexual, queer, transvestite, transsexual, transgender, leather, BDSM, or sex workers)

• be nonprofit
• be in existence at some point from January 1, 1964, through December 31, 1994
• be located in the city of San Francisco
• have a name, be more formal than a friendship network, be publicly accessible, and have the intention of being permanent
• be clearly distinct from other organizations in the data set
• have a minimum amount of information available including, but not limited to, a name and some information on the purposes of the organization.

The decision to exclude commercial organizations was highly problematic as it was quite clear that actors saw both commercial and nonprofit organizations as full participants in their project. That actors made no distinction between commercial and nonprofit organizations became clear as I attempted to identify commercial organizations with the intention of excluding them. Many for-profit organizations, such as newspapers, magazines, and bookstores, engaged in gay identity building activities in ways indistinguishable with nonprofit organizations. Dennis Altman points out that many gay merchants see their businesses in terms of community building. He observes:

> What is striking is the profusion of services and institutions, many of which straddle both movement and commercial activities. . . . Starting a business is often a way of integrating one's working and one's social life, and to start a gay hotel or a women's restaurant can be a way of expressing commitment to the gay community.[6]

In spite of these compelling reasons to include commercial organizations in the core data set, I felt that I had to separate the for-profit and not-for-profit organizations. With commercial organizations moved to a related dataset, it was possible to make sense out of what looked like pure organizational chaos. The identity political logic was more purely in evidence in the nonprofit organizations, which were not simultaneously shaped by the logic of profit seeking. I incorporated the second data set into the analysis at crucial moments in the book.

The decision to exclude nongay organizations was also problematic. Given my contention throughout the book that the gay/nongay divide was central to the way actors defined their world, excluding these organizations potentially eliminated evidence contrary to my claim. But after analyzing the kinds of nongay organizations listed in the guides and how they were listed, I decided that excluding these organizations could be done with integrity. Usually the guides listed nongay organizations under separate headings such as "Emergency Numbers" or "Financial Assistance" as opposed to "Gay/Lesbian Publications and Media," clearly indicating that the makers of the guides did not think of these organizations as gay. The cognitive divide between gay and nongay that made construction of these guides relevant and possible was reproduced within the guides. Nongay organizations included in the guides tended to be of a certain type: crisis services, such as suicide

Table A.2 Organizational Information Collected

Organization name	
Address	
Phone	
Year of first mention	year organization first mentioned in a resource guide
Founding date	date (month and year) organization founded, if available
Year of last mention	year organization last mentioned in a resource guide
Disbanding date	date (month and year) organization disbanded, if available
Source	all issues of all resource guides that listed organization
Description	how organization described itself in resource guides or organization flyer
Function	organizational goal or function, from information in resource guide or organization flyer
Gender	gender of participants (men, women, men and women, or transgender)

lines, available to all; city or state services available to all; organizations providing general information or services; inclusive community centers; organizations geared to other constituencies (such as youth, runaways, older people, Jewish people) that might include gay people; or inclusive mainstream churches. The inclusion of these organizations asserted that gays in San Francisco were entitled to the full range of public services available to heterosexuals. This revealed a view of gay San Francisco as embedded within and connected to the mainstream institutions of the city.

In addition to general service organizations, guides also listed two other groups of nongay organizations: AIDS and feminist organizations. That these organizations were seen to be of particular interest to lesbians and gay men was not surprising, given the numbers of gay men with AIDS and the connections between lesbianism and feminism. However, it was clear that many of these organizations did not define themselves as lesbian or gay organizations. I included organizations that identified as gay or lesbian while excluding those that indicated that they did not. For example, AIDS organizations that served all constituencies were excluded, while gay AIDS organizations were included.

Information Collected about Each Organization

Information collected from resource guides on each organization is described in table A.2.

Note that I collected both the actual founding and disbanding dates and the dates of listing in the resource guides. Ultimately, I was able to find actual founding and disbanding dates for only 150 of the 958 organizations in the core data set. For the sake of consistency, all analysis is done based on dates of listing rather than on actual founding and disbanding dates. In order to make sure the dates of listing in the guides map onto actual founding dates in a meaningful fashion, I compared dates of first mention in resource guides with actual founding dates. The 150 organizations for which I had an actual founding date were listed in the guides, on average, 2.8 years after they were founded. Some 71 percent (107/150) were listed in guides within two years of founding.

It would have been useful to collect systematic data on changes in organizational names and missions, organizational size and membership, organizational structure, and the fit between organizational presentation and reality (whether the actual composition of the membership matched the claims that the organization made about its membership). At the time these data were collected, this information could have been collected only through intensive archival investigation. Preliminary efforts suggested that it might have taken several hours to research each of the 958 organizations in the data set. Given the revolution in internet usage that has taken place in the intervening years, the barriers to obtaining much of this information have been substantially reduced. However, even now, some of this information, particularly the highly interesting information on membership rates, may simply not be available.

Data Cleaning

The three biggest problems with data quality were duplicate organizational listings (guides were often inconsistent in the exact wording of organizational names, producing multiple entries in the database), entry of organizations that did not meet the inclusion rules (this problem was exacerbated by the slow process of accumulating information about each organization), and insufficient information about organization goals and purposes. Looking for similarities in names and duplication of addresses and phone numbers gradually eliminated duplicate listings. I used temporary codes to identify organizations that failed to meet the criteria for inclusion, culling through the database again and again to check organizations along every dimension. I used a variety of sources to discover more information about elusive organizations, removing 75 organizations from the data set as a last recourse. This left a data set of 958 organizations.

Calculating Organizational Density

Figures in the text presented changes over time in the numbers of various kinds of organizations in existence over time. An organization was coded as being "alive" in a year if it was listed in a resource guide published in that year (or if it was listed in resource guides in either proceeding or subsequent years). For example, 1986 organizations were those whose first listing in a guide ("founding date") was any year before 1987 *and* whose last listing ("disbanding date") was any year after 1985.

NOTES

Chapter One

1. Numbers derived from an exhaustive database of San Francisco's lesbian/gay organizations. See the appendix for details on the construction of this database.

2. Marotta developed an even more complex categorization of the strains of gay liberation ideology in *The Politics of Homosexuality* (Boston: Houghton Mifflin, 1981).

3. "Marching in the Pride Parade? Here's How to Find Your Contingent . . . ," *San Francisco Bay Times*, June 15, 1995, 8.

4. Mary Bernstein, "Celebration and Suppression: The Strategic Uses of Identity by the Lesbian and Gay Movement," *American Journal of Sociology* 103 (1997); Alberto Melucci, *Nomads of the Present: Social Movements and Individual Needs in Contemporary Society* (Philadelphia: Temple University Press, 1989).

5. Some might argue that instead of a case study of San Francisco, I should have focused on the dynamics of the movement at the national level. To this critique I would respond that during the 1950s through the late 1970s a national-level gay movement existed only in an extremely attenuated form. The political activism that would ultimately produce a national movement occurred in a few core cities. San Francisco was not the only site of these processes, but it was a very important one. It is through understanding what happened in San Francisco, and other major urban areas, that the birth of a national gay movement can be understood. The crystallization of the movement on the national level in the late 1970s, which was marked by the first gay march on Washington in 1979, built on the city-level organizing of the 1950s, 1960s, and 1970s.

Others could also argue that the focus on San Francisco is misplaced given that New York was the site of the famous Stonewall uprising. Movement legend implies that all gay political and cultural accomplishments since 1969 can be traced back to this event. However, even a cursory examination of the history challenges this view. Gay liberation developed in San Francisco before the Stonewall uprising in New York, suggesting that the view of Stonewall as the one and only "ground zero" is incorrect. A focus on San Francisco provides a corrective to the assumption that the gay movement diffused from one point. The movement appeared simultaneously in several different cities. While there were multiple origin points, they were not independent. Particularly in late 1969 and 1970, ideological battles spanned the continent, with gay liberation groups in New York critiquing the agendas and plans of gay liberation groups in San Francisco. The spread of goals and strategies of organizing seemed to be virtually instantaneous. For example, the idea for a gay takeover of Alpine County in California in 1969 was debated not only by West Coast gay liberationists, but also by New York groups (see chapter 4). Given the intensity of this interaction and feedback, I do not treat San Francisco as a completely independent case. Particularly in my analysis of the years 1969 and 1970, I reference movement events on both coasts.

6. For reviews of various cultural approaches to movements see Robert D. Benford and David A. Snow, "Framing Processes and Social Movements: An Overview and Assessment," *Annual Review of Sociology* 26 (2000); Kelly Moore and Michael P. Young, "Social Movements and Organizations" (unpublished paper, Barnard College, Department of Sociology, 2000); Nelson A. Pichardo, "New Social Movements: A Critical Review," *Annual Review of Sociology* 23 (1997); Francesca Polletta and James M. Jasper, "Collective Identity and Social Movements," *Annual Review of Sociology* 27 (2001).

7. John D. McCarthy and Mayer N. Zald, "Resource Mobilization and Social Movements: A Partial Theory," *American Journal of Sociology* 82 (1977); Doug McAdam, *Political Process and the Development of Black Insurgency, 1930–1970* (Chicago: University of Chicago Press, 1982); and William Gamson, *The Strategy of Social Protest,* 2d ed. (Belmont, Calif.: Wadsworth, 1990), are key foundational pieces for these traditions. I borrow the designation "resource-rationalist" from Moore and Young, "Social Movements and Organizations."

8. Moore and Young, "Social Movements and Organizations," 1.

9. Both Doug McAdam and J. Craig Jenkins made this point. See McAdam, *Political Process;* J. Craig Jenkins, *The Politics of Insurgency: The Farm Worker Movement in the 1960s* (New York: Columbia University Press, 1985).

10. See chaps. 2 and 3 of McAdam, *Political Process,* and chap. 1 of Jenkins, *The Politics of Insurgency.*

11. Steven M. Buechler, "Beyond Resource Mobilization? Emerging Trends in Social Movement Theory," *Sociological Quarterly* 34, no. 2 (1993): 218.

12. Ibid.

13. Bernstein, "Celebration and Suppression," 534.

14. For discussions of the normative consequences of a heightened focus on identity in post-1960s movements see Jenny Bourne, "Homelands of the Mind: Jewish Feminism and Identity Politics," *Race and Class* 29, no. 1 (summer 1987); Alexandra Chasin, *Selling Out: The Gay and Lesbian Movement Goes to Market* (New York: St. Martin's, 2000); Charles Fernández, "Undocumented Aliens in the Queer Nation," *Out/Look: National Lesbian and Gay Quarterly,* spring 1991; Joshua Gamson, "Must Identity Movements Self-Destruct? A Queer Dilemma," in *Social Perspectives in Lesbian and Gay Studies: A Reader,* ed. Peter M. Nardi and Beth E. Schneider (London: Routledge, [1995] 1998); Todd Gitlin, *The Twilight of Common Dreams: Why America Is Wracked by Culture Wars* (New York: Holt, 1995); Liz A. Highleyman, "Identity and Ideas: Strategies for Bisexuals," in *Bisexual Politics: Theories, Queries, and Visions,* ed. Naomi Tucker (New York: Haworth, 1995); L. A. Kauffman, "The Anti-politics of Identity," *Socialist Review* 70, no. 1 (1990); Bernice Johnson Reagon, "Coalition Politics: Turning the Century," in *Home Girls: A Black Feminist Anthology,* ed. Barbara Smith (New York: Kitchen Table/Women of Color, [1981] 1983); Arlene Stein, *Sex and Sensibility: Stories of a Lesbian Generation* (Berkeley and Los Angeles: University of California Press, 1997); Arlene Stein, "Sisters and Queers: The Decentering of Lesbian Feminism," *Socialist Review* 22, no. 1 (1992).

15. Mancur Olson, *The Logic of Collective Action* (Cambridge: Harvard University Press, 1965).

16. Debra Friedman and Doug McAdam, "Collective Identity and Activism: Networks, Choices, and the Life of a Social Movement," in *Frontiers in Social Movement Theory,* ed. Aldon D. Morris and Carol McClurg Mueller (New Haven: Yale University Press, 1992).

17. Polletta and Jasper, "Collective Identity and Social Movements," 290. See also James M. Jasper, *The Art of Moral Protest* (Chicago: University of Chicago Press, 1997), 23–29.

18. For examples of work in this tradition, see Jean L. Cohen, "Strategy or Identity? New Theoretical Paradigms and Contemporary Social Movements," *Social Research* 52 (1985); Ronald Inglehart, *The Silent Revolution: Changing Values and Political Styles among Western Publics* (Princeton: Princeton University Press, 1977); Herbert Kitschelt, "New Social Movements in West Germany and the United States," *Political Power and Social Theory* 5 (1985); Melucci, *Nomads of the Present;* Alberto Melucci, "The Symbolic Challenge of Contemporary Movements," *Social Research* 52 (1985); Alan Touraine, *The Voice and the Eye: An Analysis of Social Movements* (Cambridge: Cambridge University Press, 1981).

19. Pichardo, "New Social Movements," 414. This highly critical 1997 review of NSM theory represents current American views on this line of theorizing.

20. Ibid., 412. American social movement scholars saw NSM theorists as exaggerating the disjuncture between "old" and "new" movements, minimizing variation among "new movements," and exaggerating changes in the fundamental nature of society. Overgeneralizations by NSM scholars left them open to attack by PP/RM theorists, whose theoretical paradigms encouraged them to dismiss the idea that there was anything fundamentally new about post-1960s social movements. See also Polletta and Jasper, "Collective Identity and Social Movements."

21. Craig Calhoun, " 'New Social Movements' of the Early Nineteenth Century," in *Repertoires and Cycles of Collective Action,* ed. M. Traugott (Durham: Duke University Press, 1995).

22. William H. Sewell Jr., "A Theory of Structure: Duality, Agency, and Transformation," *American Journal of Sociology* 98 (1992); William H. Sewell Jr., "Historical Events as Transformations of Structures: Inventing Revolution at the Bastille," *Theory and Society* 25 (1996); William H. Sewell Jr., *Work and Revolution in France: The Language of Labour from the Old Regime to 1848* (New York: Cambridge University Press, 1980); Roger V. Gould, *Insurgent Identities: Class, Community, and Protest in Paris from 1848 to the Commune* (Chicago: University of Chicago Press, 1995).

23. See Moore and Young, "Social Movements and Organizations" for a review of this scholarship.

24. Benford and Snow, "Framing Processes and Social Movements: An Overview and Assessment," 612. See also David A. Snow and Robert D. Benford, "Ideology, Frame Resonance, and Participant Mobilization," *International Social Movement Research* 1 (1988); David A. Snow and Robert D. Benford, "Master Frames and Cycles of Protest," in *Frontiers in Social Movement Theory,* ed. Aldon Morris and Carol McClurg Mueller (New Haven: Yale University Press, 1992); David A. Snow et al., "Frame Alignment Processes, Micromobilization, and Movement Participation," *American Sociological Review* 51 (1986).

25. Polletta and Jasper, "Collective Identity and Social Movements."

26. In the late 1990s, key American social movements scholars proposed an "emerging synthesis." This synthesis was outlined in Doug McAdam, John D. McCarthy, and Mayer N. Zald, eds., *Comparative Perspectives on Social Movements: Political Opportunities, Mobilizing Structures, and Cultural Framings* (Cambridge: Cambridge University Press, 1996), and is represented by Sidney Tarrow, *Power in Movement: Social Movements, Collective Action, and Politics* (Cambridge: Cambridge University Press, 1994). It integrates the insights of the resource mobilization and political process approaches with work on framing processes and some insights from NSM theory. However, the framework is still primarily based on resource-rationalist assumptions. (See the introduction to McAdam, McCarthy, and Zald, *Comparative Perspectives.*)

27. Rob Kleidman, Dan Cress, and Ann Mische, "CBSM Workshop Proposal," *Critical Mass Bulletin: Newsletter of the Section on Collective Behavior and Social Movements, American Sociological Association,* spring 2001.

28. Ibid.; Nicole Raeburn, "The Rise of Lesbian, Gay, and Bisexual Rights in the Corporate Workplace: The Impact of Employee Mobilization" (paper presented at the Pacific Sociological Association meeting, San Francisco, 1998); Laura Anne Schmidt, *The Corporate Transformation of American Health Care: A Study in Institution Building* (Princeton: Princeton University Press, forthcoming).

29. Frank R. Dobbin reviews the development of organizational theory critical of the assumptions of a resource-rationalistic model in "Cultural Models of Organization: The Social Construction of Rational Organizing Principles," in *The Sociology of Culture: Emerging Theoretical Perspectives,* ed. Diana Crane (Oxford: Blackwell, 1994).

30. Michael T. Hannan and John Freeman, *Organizational Ecology* (Cambridge: Harvard University Press, 1989); Michael T. Hannan and John Freeman, "The Population Ecology of Organizations," *American Journal of Sociology* 82 (1977).

31. John W. Meyer and Brian Rowan, "Institutionalized Organizations: Formal Structure as Myth and Ceremony," in *The New Institutionalism in Organizational Analysis,* ed. Walter W. Powell and Paul J. DiMaggio (Chicago: University of Chicago Press, [1977] 1991).

32. Paul J. DiMaggio and Walter W. Powell, "The Iron Cage Revisited: Institutional Isomorphism and Collective Rationality," in *The New Institutionalism in Organizational Analysis,* ed. Walter W. Powell and Paul J. DiMaggio (Chicago: University of Chicago Press, [1983] 1991).

33. For definitions and discussions of fields see Pierre Bourdieu, *Outline of a Theory of Practice* (Cambridge: Cambridge University Press, 1977); Paul DiMaggio, "State Expansion and Organizational Fields," in *Organizational Theory and Public Policy,* ed. Richard H. Hall and Robert E. Quinn (Beverly Hills: Sage, 1983); DiMaggio and Powell, "The Iron Cage Revisited"; Neil Fligstein, "Markets as Politics: A Political Cultural Approach to Market Institutions," *American Sociological Review* 61 (1996); Neil Fligstein, "Social Skill and the Theory of Fields" (Department of Sociology, University of California, Berkeley, 2001); Neil Fligstein, *The Transformation of Corporate Control* (Cambridge: Harvard University Press, 1990); Neil Fligstein and Doug McAdam, "A Political-Cultural Approach to the Problem of Strategic Action" (Department of Sociology, University of California, Berkeley, 1995); John W. Meyer and W. Richard Scott, *Organizational Environments: Ritual and Rationality* (Beverly Hills: Sage, 1983); John Mohr, "Community, Bureaucracy, and Social Relief: An Institutional Analysis of Organizational Forms in New York City, 1888–1917" (Ph.D. diss., Department of Sociology, Yale University, 1992); Schmidt, *The Corporate Transformation;* W. Richard Scott, "Conceptualizing Organizational Fields: Linking Organizations and Societal Systems," in *Systemrationalität und Partialinteresse,* ed. Hans-Ulrich Derlien, Uta Gerhardt, and Fritz W. Scharph (Baden-Baden: Nomos, 1994); W. Richard Scott, *Institutions and Organizations* (Thousand Oaks, Calif.: Sage, 1995).

34. Ann Swidler, *Talk of Love: How Culture Matters* (Chicago: University of Chicago Press, 2001), 202. See also Elisabeth Clemens and James Cook, "Politics and Institutionalism: Explaining Durability and Change," *Annual Review of Sociology* 25 (1999); Roger Friedland and Robert R. Alford, "Bringing Society Back In: Symbols, Practices, and Institutional Contradictions," in *The New Institutionalism in Organizational Analysis,* ed. Walter W. Powell and Paul J. DiMaggio (Chicago: University of Chicago Press, 1991); Ronald L. Jepperson, "Institutions, Institutional Effects, and Institutionalism," in *The New Institutionalism in Organizational Analysis,* ed. Walter W. Powell and Paul J. DiMaggio (Chicago: University of Chicago Press, 1991), 145; Scott, *Institutions and Organizations;* W. Richard Scott and John W. Meyer, eds., *Institutional Environments and Organizations: Structural Complexity and Individualism* (Thousand Oaks, Calif.: Sage, 1994).

35. DiMaggio and Powell, "The Iron Cage Revisited."

36. Walter W. Powell and Paul J. DiMaggio, eds., *The New Institutionalism in Organizational Analysis* (Chicago: University of Chicago Press, 1991). Various essays in the collection point to the need for institutional theory to address change. See also Paul DiMaggio, "Interest and Agency in Institutional Theory," in *Institutional Patterns and Organizations: Culture and Environment,* ed. Lynne Zucker (Cambridge: Ballinger, 1988).

37. This interest among organizational scholars in social movement theory occurred about twenty years after Mayer N. Zald and Michael A. Berger advocated such a cross-fertilization in 1978. Zald and Berger, "Social Movements in Organizations: Coup d'Etat, Insurgency, and Mass Movements," *American Journal of Sociology* 83 (1978). In spring 2001, Zald noted that, in sharp contrast to the 1977 paper outlining resource mobilization theory, "the 1978 paper with Berger did not appear to have much of an impact except in my own memory of it. . . . It seemed to have sunk in the scholarly ocean of unread papers." Zald, "Taking It to the Streets in the Office: Collective Actions and Protest in Organizations," *LSAmagazine,* spring 2001, 18. It appears that Zald and Berger's 1978 paper may now be on its way to being rescued from the scholarly ocean of unread papers and established as a foundational piece for this new area of scholarship.

38. Fligstein and McAdam, "A Political-Cultural Approach"; Hayagreeva Rao, Calvin Morrill, and Mayer N. Zald, "Power Plays: How Social Movements and Collective Action Create New Organizational Forms," *Research in Organizational Behaviour* 22 (2000); Anand Swaminathan and James B. Wade, "Social Movement Theory and the Evolution of New Organization Forms," in *The Entrepreneurship Dynamic in Industry Evolution,* ed. C. B. Schoonhoven and E. Romanelli (Stanford: Stanford University Press, forthcoming).

39. Moore and Young, "Social Movements and Organizations," 24, 28.

40. Dobbin, "Cultural Models of Organization."

41. Michael Lounsbury and Marc J. Ventresca, introduction to *Social Structure and Organizations Revisited,* ed. Michael Lounsbury and Marc J. Ventresca (Oxford: JAI, forthcoming).

42. Elisabeth Clemens, "Organizational Repertoires and Institutional Change: Women's Groups and the Transformation of U.S. Politics, 1890–1920," *American Journal of Sociology* 98 (1993); Fligstein and McAdam, "A Political-Cultural Approach"; Doug McAdam and W. Richard Scott, "Organizations and Movements" (Department of Sociology, Stanford University, 2001), 12; Debra Minkoff, *Organizing for Equality: The Evolution of Women's and Racial-Ethnic Organizations in America, 1955–1985* (New Brunswick: Rutgers University Press, 1995).

43. Jepperson, "Institutions, Institutional Effects, and Institutionalism."

44. McAdam and Scott, "Organizations and Movements," 11.

45. Leila J. Rupp and Verta Taylor, *Survival in the Doldrums: The American Women's Rights Movement, 1945 to the 1960s* (Columbus: Ohio State University Press, 1990). See also Verta Taylor and Nancy Whittier, "Collective Identity in Social Movement Communities: Lesbian Feminist Mobilization," in *Frontiers in Social Movement Theory,* ed. Aldon D. Morris and Carol McClurg Mueller (New Haven: Yale University Press, 1992).

46. Neil Fligstein, "The Cultural Construction of Political Action: The Case of the European Community's Single Unitary Market Program" (paper presented at the American Sociological Association annual meeting, Miami, 1993).

47. Kim Voss and Rachel Sherman, "Breaking the Iron Law of Oligarchy: Union Revitalization in the American Labor Movement," *American Journal of Sociology* 106 (2000).

48. Friedland and Alford, "Bringing Society Back In"; Snow and Benford, "Master Frames and Cycles of Protest." See also Patricia H. Thornton and William Ocasio, "Institutional Logics and the Historical Contingency of Power in Organizations: Executive Succession in the

Higher Education Publishing Industry, 1958–1990," *American Journal of Sociology* 105 (1999), and
Heather A. Haveman and Hayagreeva Rao, "Structuring a Theory of Moral Sentiments: In-
stitutional and Organizational Coevolution in the Early Thrift Industry," *American Journal of
Sociology* 102 (1997).

49. Snow and Benford, "Master Frames and Cycles of Protest," 138.

50. Haveman and Rao, "Structuring a Theory of Moral Sentiments."

51. See the appendix for details on construction of the data set.

52. Clemens begins her study of the rise of interest group politics in the United States
explaining that interest group politics has not always been a part of our political and organizational repertoire. Clemens, *The People's Lobby: Organizational Innovation and the Rise of Interest Group
Politics in the United States, 1890–1925* (Chicago: University of Chicago Press, 1997). Schmidt's
study of the transformation of American medicine begins by establishing that the market-
ization of American health care was not inevitable but the result of a historically contingent processes of institution building. Schmidt, *The Corporate Transformation of American Health
Care.*

53. Readers familiar with population ecology theory will observe that the density of
lesbian/gay organizations follows the expected pattern of "initially low rates of growth,
which accelerate over time, reach a maximum rate, and then slowly decline." David J.
Tucker et al., "Ecological and Institutional Sources of Change in Organizational Populations," in *Ecological Models of Organizations,* ed. Glenn R. Carroll (Cambridge: Ballinger, 1988),
127. Initially, founding increases the legitimacy of a particular organizational form. Eventually, as the population approaches the environment's carrying capacity, competitive processes kick in, halting the expansion of the size of the population. See Glenn R. Carroll, ed.,
Ecological Models of Organization (Cambridge: Ballinger, 1988); Glenn R. Carroll and Michael T.
Hannan, "Density Dependence in the Evolution of Populations of Newspaper Organizations," *American Sociological Review* 54 (1989); Michael T. Hannan and John Freeman, "Density
Dependence in the Growth of Organizational Populations," in *Ecological Models of Organizations,*
ed. Glenn R. Carroll (Cambridge: Ballinger, 1988); Michael T. Hannan and John Freeman,
"The Ecology of Organizational Mortality: American Labor Unions, 1836–1985," *American Jour-
nal of Sociology* 94 (1988); Hannan and Freeman, *Organizational Ecology;* Hannan and Freeman,
"The Population Ecology of Organizations." This perspective was of limited usefulness for
several reasons. It does not provide a theory of the source of organizational innovations.
Its measurement of institutionalization is circular and it assumes a static carrying capacity.
Fundamentally, this perspective is not a theory that can do justice to the complex processes
of the construction of meaning systems. See Lynne G. Zucker, "Combining Institutional
Theory and Population Ecology: No Legitimacy, No History," *American Sociological Review* 54
(1989), for a critique of this approach.

54. The desire for public recognition distinguished these homosexual organizations from
those classified as "other." Homosexual organizations founded before 1969 with the desire
for public recognition can be classified as homophile organizations. In addition to bars, restaurants, bathhouses, and cafes, there were also private homosexual social groups, organized
as motorcycle clubs, which I do not consider to be homophile organizations. These organizations are discussed in more detail in chapter 2.

55. Clemens, *The People's Lobby;* McAdam, *Political Process.*

56. Wini Breines, *Community and Organization in the New Left, 1962–1968: The Great Refusal* (New
Brunswick: Rutgers University Press, 1989); Doug Rossinow, *The Politics of Authenticity* (New
York: Columbia University Press, 1998).

57. Rossinow, *The Politics of Authenticity,* 343.

58. Kauffman, "The Anti-politics of Identity," 67.

59. Breines, *Community and Organization.*

60. Pamela Allen, *Free Space: A Perspective on the Small Group in Women's Liberation* (Washington, N.J.: Times Change, 1970), 14.

61. This discussion oversimplifies homophile politics. In chapter 2 I show that homosexual activists had limited success in applying an interest group political logic given that homosexuals barely constituted a group that could be said to have interests. In addition, agreement about the desirability of creating a homosexual group identity was far from universal among those invested in improving the circumstances of homosexuals. Activists advocating interest group politics were in conflict with a preexisting understanding of how homosexuals ought to act collectively. Some felt that building a public identity and pursuing rights was misguided. They were primarily interested in participating in a private social-sexual world and thought that this world could be best protected and expanded by keeping mainstream society as innocent as possible of its existence. This purely private orientation, centered around a commercialized social-sexual subculture, can be seen as a competing logic. I discuss this conflict between "legitimacy seeking" and "pleasure seeking" in chapter 2.

62. All organizational dates in this chapter, unless specifically mentioned otherwise, refer to the dates the organization was listed in resource guides, not to precise founding and disbanding dates. There was sometimes a lag after organizational founding before the organization was listed, and sometimes a lag after disbanding before resource guides registered the demise of an organization. In spite of this limitation, it seemed best to use these proxy dates since I have actual founding and disbanding data on only a minority of the organizations. Organizations listed in 1995 resource guides, the last guides coded, are indicated as still alive by the convention of omitting the closing year of the life span.

63. Functional diversification also strengthened the claim that gay identity was like ethnic identity by showing the self-sufficiency of the lesbian/gay community. Sociologists have referred to the ability of a community to "perform all the services required by its members" as evidence of "institutional completeness." R. Breton, "Institutional Completeness of Ethnic Communities and the Personal Relations of Immigrants," *American Journal of Sociology* 70 (1964). See also Stephen O. Murray, *American Gay* (Chicago: University of Chicago Press, 1996), 73; Claude Fischer, "20th-Year Assessment of the Subcultural Theory of Urbanism," *American Journal of Sociology* 101 (1995); Susan Olzak and Elizabeth West, "Ethnic Conflict and the Rise and Fall of Ethnic Newspapers," *American Sociological Review* 56 (1991); Arthur Stinchcombe, "Social Structure and Organizations," in *Handbook of Organizations,* ed. J. G. March (Chicago: Rand McNally, 1965); Peter J. Venturelli, "Institutions in an Ethnic District," *Human Organization* 41, no. 1 (1982).

64. For a discussion of the role of internal contradictions in field transformation, see Schmidt, *The Corporate Transformation,* and Clemens and Cook, "Politics and Institutionalism."

65. Scholars are beginning to trace the diffusion of American-style gay identity around the globe. In a book chapter entitled "The Globalization of Sexual Identities," Dennis Altman notes that "the United States remains the dominant cultural model for the rest of the world." Dennis Altman, *Global Sex* (Chicago: University of Chicago Press, 2001), 87. He describes some ways that American/"modern" ways of understanding same-gender sexuality clash with "traditional"/indigenous meaning systems and suggests that the diffusion of American-style gay identity poses a threat to these traditional meaning systems.

Chapter Two

1. Wini Breines, *Community and Organization in the New Left, 1962–1968: The Great Refusal* (New Brunswick: Rutgers University Press, 1989); Todd Gitlin, *The Sixties: Years of Hope, Days of Rage*

(New York: Bantam, 1987); Anthony Oberschall, "The Decline of the 1960s Social Movements," *Research in Social Movements, Conflicts and Change* 1 (1978).

2. Historians of sexuality have been aware of the homophile roots of the contemporary gay movement at least since the important work of historian John D'Emilio, who wrote the definitive account of homophile politics in the United States, *Sexual Politics, Sexual Communities: The Making of a Homosexual Minority in the United States, 1940–1970* (Chicago: University of Chicago Press, 1983).

3. The central primary source was the *Vector*, a magazine published by the Society for Individual Rights from December 1964 through July 1976. The *Vector* was one of only three San Francisco homosexual periodicals spanning the crucial years from 1964 through 1970. The other two were publications of the lesbian organization the Daughters of Bilitis.

4. I found, as Elisabeth Clemens did, that radical innovation emerges through new combinations of organizational forms, actors and goals. Clemens, *The People's Lobby: Organizational Innovation and the Rise of Interest Group Politics in the United States, 1890–1925* (Chicago: University of Chicago Press, 1997), 6.

5. Ibid. See also Elizabeth Clemens and James Cook, "Politics and Institutionalism: Explaining Durability and Change," *Annual Review of Sociology* 25 (1999).

6. Leila J. Rupp and Verta Taylor, *Survival in the Doldrums: The American Women's Rights Movement, 1945 to the 1960s* (Columbus: Ohio State University Press, 1990), 139.

7. For detailed accounts of anticommunist attacks on homosexuals in the 1950s see D'Emilio, *Sexual Politics*, and David K. Johnson, "'Homosexual Citizens': Washington's Gay Community Confronts the Civil Service," *Washington History*, fall/winter 1994–95.

8. Historians of sexuality have written extensively on the processes through which homosexual identity developed to the point where I begin the story. Some of this scholarship identifies the late nineteenth century as when "the homosexual" became a kind of person. Before that, homosexuality had been viewed as a practice in which any individual might engage. See Michel Foucault, *The History of Sexuality*, vol. 1, *An Introduction*, trans. Robert Hurley (New York: Vintage, 1978), and Jeffrey Weeks, *Coming Out: Homosexual Politics in Britain from the Nineteenth Century to the Present* (London: Quartet, 1977). Other scholarship traces the impact of capitalism, wage labor, and World War II on developing group consciousness. See Allan Bérubé, *Coming Out under Fire: The History of Gay Men and Women in World War II* (New York: Macmillan, 1990); George Chauncey, *Gay New York: Gender, Urban Culture, and the Making of the Gay Male World, 1890–1940* (New York: HarperCollins, 1994); D'Emilio, *Sexual Politics*; Lillian Faderman, *Odd Girls and Twilight Lovers: A History of Lesbian Life in Twentieth-Century America* (New York: Columbia University Press, 1991); Elizabeth Lapovsky Kennedy and Madeline D. Davis, *Boots of Leather, Slippers of Gold: The History of a Lesbian Community* (New York: Routledge, 1993).

9. Allan Bérubé, "The First Stonewall," *Lesbian and Gay Freedom Parade and Celebration Magazine*, June 1983, 27; D'Emilio, *Sexual Politics*; Eric Garber, *A Historical Directory of Lesbian and Gay Establishments in the San Francisco Bay Area* (San Francisco: San Francisco Lesbian and Gay History Project, 1986); Ellen Klages, "When the Bar Was the Only Place in Town," *San Francisco Lesbian and Gay Freedom Parade and Celebration Magazine*, 1984; Susan Stryker and Jim Van Buskirk, *Gay by the Bay: A History of Queer Culture in the San Francisco Bay Area* (San Francisco: Chronicle, 1996).

10. Gayle Rubin, "Valley of the Kings," *Sentinel*, September 13, 1984, 11.

11. Stryker and Van Buskirk, *Gay by the Bay*, 44.

12. Documenting the existence of motorcycle clubs is difficult, as these organizations intentionally obscured evidence of their existence. Motorcycle clubs never published organiza-

tional mailing addresses or contact telephone numbers, even in homosexual publications ("SIR Awards Motorcycle Trophies," *Vector*, November 1966).

13. Klages, "When the Bar Was the Only Place in Town."

14. Kennedy and Davis, *Boots of Leather*, 29.

15. For more on the role of the Alcoholic Beverage Control Department see Rubin, "Valley of the Kings," and Stryker and Van Buskirk, *Gay by the Bay*, 30.

16. Bérubé, "The First Stonewall"; D'Emilio, *Sexual Politics*, 112; Klages, "When the Bar Was the Only Place in Town"; Stryker and Van Buskirk, *Gay by the Bay*, 30.

17. Bérubé, "The First Stonewall"; Klages, "When the Bar Was the Only Place in Town."

18. Bérubé, "The First Stonewall."

19. Ibid.; D'Emilio, *Sexual Politics*, 187.

20. D'Emilio, *Sexual Politics*, 187.

21. Clemens, *The People's Lobby*, 2.

22. Rupp and Taylor, *Survival in the Doldrums*, 24.

23. Ibid., 27.

24. D'Emilio, *Sexual Politics*, 63–64.

25. While drawing heavily on the work of historians of sexuality, I place more emphasis on processes of organizational imitation than they do. They tend to give the biographies of the remarkable individuals who founded these first organizations a more central place in their accounts. This discussion of Harry Hay's role in the founding of the Mattachine Society is based on ibid., 58–60.

26. Ibid., 58.

27. Marvin Cutler, *Homosexuals Today: A Handbook of Organizations and Publications* (Los Angeles: ONE, 1956), 10.

28. D'Emilio, *Sexual Politics*, 73.

29. Ibid., 72.

30. Ibid.

31. Del Martin and Phyllis Lyon, *Lesbian/Woman*, Twentieth Anniversary ed. (Volcano, Calif.: Volcano, 1991).

32. Martin and Lyon, *Lesbian/Woman*, x.

33. Ibid., 227.

34. Ibid.

35. Paul J. DiMaggio and Walter W. Powell, "The Iron Cage Revisited: Institutional Isomorphism and Collective Rationality," in *The New Institutionalism in Organizational Analysis*, ed. Walter W. Powell and Paul J. DiMaggio (Chicago: University of Chicago Press, [1983] 1991).

36. D'Emilio, *Sexual Politics*, 119.

37. Robert Walker, letter, *Vector*, August 1967, 15.

38. This supports Clemens's point that even when particular organizational forms are not novel, putting them in service of new groups can be. Clemens, *The People's Lobby*, 11.

39. This also supports Laura Schmidt's points that field transformation occurs through actors attempting to remake the environment. Schmidt, *The Corporate Transformation of American Health Care: A Study in Institution Building* (Princeton: Princeton University Press, forthcoming).

40. Cutler, *Homosexuals Today*, 9.

41. D'Emilio, *Sexual Politics*, 62.

42. "State Fair Booth Cancelled," *Vector*, September 1966, 1.

43. Ibid., 1.

44. Ibid., 9.

45. "State Fair Booth Cancelled: Loss or Gain to Homophile Movement," *Vector*, October 1966, 4.

46. D. C. and R. S., "Ma Bell Gets Yellow Suit!!!," *Vector*, October 1968.

47. Ibid., 29.

48. Cutler, *Homosexuals Today*, 13.

49. "S.I.R.'s Statement of Policy," *Vector*, December 1964, 1.

50. D'Emilio, *Sexual Politics*, 67.

51. Ibid., 65.

52. Ibid., 79. Marilyn Rieger said this in a speech made in May 1953 to a Mattachine convention.

53. D'Emilio, *Sexual Politics*, 79.

54. Cutler, *Homosexuals Today*, 10. See also D'Emilio, *Sexual Politics*, 67.

55. Martin and Lyon, *Lesbian/Woman*, 219; D'Emilio, *Sexual Politics*, 102.

56. Martin and Lyon, *Lesbian/Woman*, 231. Martin and Lyon insist that Daughters of Bilitis never denied that it was an organization composed of lesbians. This suggests that homophile organizations disagreed about how much distance to place between the organization and the identity of its members.

57. Ibid.

58. Toby Marotta, *The Politics of Homosexuality* (Boston: Houghton Mifflin, 1981), 17.

59. Ibid., 15.

60. Martin and Lyon, *Lesbian/Woman*, 251.

61. While it may seem contradictory that the privacy-oriented pleasure seekers had sex in public places, a discussion of the differing ways pleasure and legitimacy seekers sought to relate to the public realm clarifies this. Pleasure seekers wanted to be able to have sex on beaches and in public parks without threat of arrest, but they did not want to have to create a *political public* sexual identity to attain this right. They wanted privacy to engage in public sex. In contrast, legitimacy seekers were willing to forgo the practice of public sex in return for legitimate public political recognition.

62. Marotta, *The Politics of Homosexuality*, 18.

63. Jaye Bell, "DOB Anniversary Message from the President," *Ladder*, October 1961, 5, quoted in D'Emilio, *Sexual Politics*, 186.

64. D'Emilio, *Sexual Politics*, chap. 10, esp. 186.

65. Eric Marcus, *Making History: The Struggle for Gay and Lesbian Equal Rights, 1945–1990, An Oral History* (New York: HarperCollins, 1992).

66. For more on the role of the Alcoholic Beverage Control Department see Rubin, "Valley of the Kings," and Stryker and Van Buskirk, *Gay by the Bay*, 30.

67. Historians of lesbian/gay life have devoted book-length studies to homophile organizations, while largely ignoring motorcycle clubs and bars. Kennedy and Davis, *Boots of Leather*, is a notable exception, with its detailed description of lesbian bar culture of the 1950s. Because motorcycle clubs and other private clubs did not seek to engage with mainstream society, the role they may have played in birthing the contemporary gay world has been largely unexplored. Gayle Rubin, *The San Francisco Leather Community* [tentative title] (Chicago: University of Chicago Press, forthcoming), promises to provide a wealth of detail about this relatively invisible aspect of homosexual life.

68. Martin and Lyon, *Lesbian/Woman*, 228.

69. Marcus, *Making History*, 68.

70. Bill Beardemphl, "On Leadership," *Vector,* January 1965, 2.

71. "Special Report: C.R.H. Needs Donations," *Vector,* March 1965, 3.

72. Bill Beardemphl, "President's Column," *Vector,* August 1966, 2.

73. "ORH 'A Brief of Injustices' Published," *Vector,* September 1965, 9.

74. I considered the League for Civil Education (LCE), Citizen's News, and Strait and Associates to be the same organization, as all were projects of homophile activist Guy Strait.

75. "State Fair Booth Cancelled: Loss or Gain to the Homophile Movement," *Vector,* October 1966, 5.

76. Bill Beardemphl, "Conference Trip a Bummer," *Vector,* September 1968, 28.

77. Laud Humphreys, *Out of the Closets: The Sociology of Homosexual Liberation* (Englewood Cliffs, N.J.: Prentice-Hall, 1972), 110.

78. D'Emilio, *Sexual Politics,* 121.

79. Ibid.

80. Ibid., 122.

81. Ibid., 182.

82. Ibid., 184.

83. Klages, "When the Bar was the Only Place in Town."

84. Susan Olzak and Elizabeth West, "Ethnic Conflict and Dynamics of Ethnic Newspapers," chap. 10 of Susan Olzak, *The Dynamics of Ethnic Competition and Conflict* (Stanford: Stanford University Press, 1992), 182. They refer to Doug McAdam, *Political Process and the Development of Black Insurgency, 1930–1970* (Chicago: University of Chicago Press, 1982), and Charles Tilly, *From Mobilization to Revolution* (Reading, Mass.: Addison-Wesley, 1978), to support their point.

85. D'Emilio, *Sexual Politics,* 183.

86. Ibid., 189.

87. Bérubé, "The First Stonewall."

88. D'Emilio, *Sexual Politics,* 202. My coding of bar guides supported D'Emilio's claim that the number of homosexual bars in San Francisco increased rapidly in the 1960s. However, in my coding of the bar guides, I found only 37 bars operating in 1968.

89. Ibid., 191; Beardemphl, untitled article, January 1965, 2.

90. Stryker and Van Buskirk, *Gay by the Bay,* 41.

91. D'Emilio, *Sexual Politics,* 194.

92. Ibid.

93. D'Emilio, *Sexual Politics,* and Marotta, *The Politics of Homosexuality,* chronicle this tension in homophile politics.

94. Franklinlin Kameny, "Civil Liberties: A Progress Report," *New York Mattachine Newsletter,* January 1965, quoted in Marotta, *The Politics of Homosexuality,* 24.

95. Shirley Willer, "The Lesbian, the Homosexual, and the Homophile Movement," *Vector,* October 1966, 8.

96. L. A. Kauffman, "The Anti-politics of Identity," *Socialist Review* 20, no. 1 (1990): 70.

97. Quoted in Marotta, *The Politics of Homosexuality,* 63.

98. Craig Rodwell, *New York Hymnal I,* August–September 1968, quoted in Marotta, *The Politics of Homosexuality,* 66.

99. Gary Teller, "I Give You My Word as a Homosexual . . . ," *Vector,* January 1966, 1.

100. Cecil Williams, untitled article, *Vector,* November 1968, 5.

101. Don Collins, editorial, *Vector,* October 1969, 10.

102. Larry Littlejohn, untitled article, *Vector,* November 1968, 9.

Chapter Three

1. It is beyond the scope of this book to attempt a definitive account of the New Left. A vast literature exists on the movements of the 1960s. On the New Left, see Wini Breines, *Community and Organization in the New Left, 1962–1968: The Great Refusal* (New Brunswick: Rutgers University Press, 1989); Todd Gitlin, *The Sixties: Years of Hope, Days of Rage* (New York: Bantam, 1987); Maurice Isserman, *If I Had a Hammer: The Death of the Old Left and the Birth of the New Left* (New York: Basic, 1987); James Miller, *Democracy Is in the Streets: From Port Huron to the Siege of Chicago* (New York: Simon and Schuster, 1987). On the civil rights movement see Mary King, *Freedom Song: A Personal Story of the 1960s Civil Rights Movement* (New York: Morrow, 1987); Doug McAdam, *Freedom Summer* (New York: Oxford University Press, 1988); Doug McAdam, *Political Process and the Development of Black Insurgency, 1930–1970* (Chicago: University of Chicago Press, 1982); Aldon Morris, *The Origins of the Civil Rights Movement: Black Communities Organizing for Change* (New York: Free Press, 1984). On women's liberation see Sara Margaret Evans, *Personal Politics: The Roots of Women's Liberation in the Civil Rights Movement and the New Left* (New York: Knopf, 1979); Jo Freeman, *The Politics of Women's Liberation* (New York: McKay, 1975). On black power see Clayborne Carson, *In Struggle: SNCC and the Black Awakening of the 1960s* (Cambridge: Harvard University Press, 1981); Howard Zinn, *SNCC: The New Abolitionists* (Boston: Beacon, 1965). On the counterculture see Breines, *Community and Organization;* John Case and Rosemary C. R. Taylor, eds., *Co-ops, Communes, and Collectives: Experiments in Social Change in the 1960s and 1970s* (New York: Pantheon, 1979); Rosabeth Moss Kanter, *Commitment and Community: Communes and Utopias in Sociological Perspective* (Cambridge: Harvard University Press, 1972); Doug Rossinow, *The Politics of Authenticity* (New York: Columbia University Press, 1998); Theodore Roszak, *The Making of a Counter-culture: Reflections on the Technocratic Society and Its Youthful Opposition* (New York: Doubleday, 1969).

2. Rossinow, *The Politics of Authenticity.* Paul Lichterman refers to this focus on personal authenticity as "personalism," which he describes as "the individualism women and men practice when they seek self-fulfillment and individualized expression, 'growth' in personal development." Lichterman also notes the "growing personalism in the U.S. cultural mainstream in the last thirty years." Lichterman, *The Search for Political Community: American Activists Reinventing Commitment* (Cambridge: Cambridge University Press, 1996), 6, 7.

3. Miller, *Democracy Is in the Streets,* 332.

4. Breines, *Community and Organization,* 24.

5. Ibid., 25.

6. Ibid.

7. Ibid., 23.

8. Ibid., 29.

9. Toby Marotta, *The Politics of Homosexuality* (Boston: Houghton Mifflin, 1981), 92.

10. Pamela Allen, *Free Space: A Perspective on the Small Group in Women's Liberation* (Washington, N.J.: Times Change, 1970), 8.

11. Ibid., 14.

12. Alice Echols, *Daring to Be BAD: Radical Feminism in America, 1967–1975* (Minneapolis: University of Minnesota Press, 1989), 16–17. See also Evans, *Personal Politics.*

13. For a nuanced account, see Terrence Kissack, "Freaking Fag Revolutionaries: New York's Gay Liberation Front, 1969–1971," *Radical History Review* 62 (1995).

14. Susan Stryker and Jim Van Buskirk, *Gay by the Bay: A History of Queer Culture in the San Francisco Bay Area* (San Francisco: Chronicle, 1996), 49. See also Susan Stryker, "Anatomy of a

Riot: The Compton's Cafeteria Disturbance of 1966" (paper presented at American Historical Association meetings, San Francisco, 2002); Stephen O. Murray, *American Gay* (Chicago: University of Chicago Press, 1996), 59.

15. From a Vanguard publication [August 1966?], quoted in Edward Sagarin, *Odd Man In: Societies of Deviants in America* (Chicago: Quadrangle, 1969), 94–95.

16. Personal conversation, February 25, 2002.

17. Leo Laurence, "My Boss Knows: Gay-Is-Good at Work, Too!," *Vector,* January 1969, 13.

18. John D'Emilio, *Sexual Politics, Sexual Communities: The Making of a Homosexual Minority in the United States, 1940–1970* (Chicago: University of Chicago Press, 1983), 230–31; Donn Teal, *The Gay Militants: How Gay Liberation Began in America, 1969–1971,* 2d ed., ed. Keith Kahla (New York: St. Martin's, 1995), 30.

19. Leo Laurence, "Gay Revolution," *Vector,* April 1969, 11.

20. Teal, *The Gay Militants,* 30.

21. Ibid.

22. Stryker and Van Buskirk, *Gay by the Bay,* 53; Teal, *The Gay Militants,* 30.

23. Stevens, "Sir?," *San Francisco Free Press,* November 1, 1969.

24. Ibid., 7.

25. Kissack, "Freaking Fag Revolutionaries."

26. Laud Humphreys claims that this acrimony also had a "personal dynamic," in which the older homophile men resented their declining sexual appeal and rejection by young, attractive gayrevs. Humphreys, *Out of the Closets: The Sociology of Homosexual Liberation* (Englewood Cliffs, N.J.: Prentice-Hall, 1972), 115–20.

27. Dennis Altman, *Homosexual Oppression and Liberation,* 2d ed. (New York: New York University Press, 1993), 237; John D'Emilio, foreword to *Out of the Closets: Voices of Gay Liberation,* ed. Karla Jay and Allen Young (New York: New York University Press, [1972] 1992), xxviii.

28. George Chauncey, *Gay New York: Gender, Urban Culture, and the Making of the Gay Male World, 1890–1940* (New York: HarperCollins, 1994), 7.

29. Mel Warner, "Anxious Ingenues Await 4th Annual Coitillion," *Vector,* June 1970, 10.

30. Sociological and psychological studies of homosexual identity of the late 1960s and early 1970s defined "coming out" as self-labeling as homosexual, as beginning to participate in the homosexual subculture, or as the first homosexual sexual experience. Barry M. Dank, "Coming Out in the Gay World," *Psychiatry* 34 (May 1971); John H. Gagnon and William Simon, "Homosexuality: The Formulation of a Sociological Perspective," in *Social Perspectives in Lesbian and Gay Studies: A Reader,* ed. Peter M. Nardi and Beth E. Schneider (London: Routledge, [1967] 1998); Evelyn Hooker, "Male Homosexuals and Their Worlds," in *Sexual Inversion: The Multiple Roots of Homosexuality,* ed. Judd Marmor (New York: Basic, 1965).

31. Quoted in Marotta, *The Politics of Homosexuality,* 187.

32. The first issue of Gay Liberation Front's *Come Out!* was published in New York on November 14, 1969 (Marotta, *The Politics of Homosexuality,* 101). The *San Francisco Free Press* reported that picket signs at the October 24, 1969, protest of the annual Halloween Beaux Arts drag ball read "Out of the closets, into the streets, wear your gown all year around!" ("Gay 'Guerillas' Picket Drag Ball," *San Francisco Free Press,* November 1, 1969, 1).

33. Gale Whittington, letter, *Vector,* April 1970, 27.

34. *Come Out!,* November 14, 1969, 2, quoted in Marotta, *The Politics of Homosexuality,* 102.

35. Humphreys, *Out of the Closets,* 142.

36. Nancy Adair and Casey Adair, eds., *Word Is Out: Stories of Our Lives* (New York: Dell, 1978); W. Curtis, ed., *Revelations: A Collection of Gay Male Coming Out Stories* (Boston: Alyson, 1988);

Julia Penelope and Susan Wolfe, eds., *The Original Coming Out Stories* (Freedom, Calif.: Crossing, 1989).

37. Martha Shelley, "Gay Is Good," in *Out of the Closets: Voices of Gay Liberation,* ed. Karla Jay and Allen Young (New York: New York University Press, [1972] 1992), 32.

38. Carl Wittman, "A Gay Manifesto," in *Out of the Closets: Voices of Gay Liberation,* ed. Karla Jay and Allen Young (New York: New York University Press, [1972] 1992), 334.

39. "The Life Style of the Homosexual Succeeds," *Vector,* December 1968, 40.

40. Charles P. Thorp, "I.D., Leadership, and Violence," in *Out of the Closets: Voices of Gay Liberation,* ed. Karla Jay and Allen Young (New York: New York University Press, [1972] 1992).

41. Tim Edwards, *Erotics and Politics: Gay Male Sexuality, Masculinity, and Feminism* (London: Routledge, 1994), 26.

42. Gary Alinder, article in *Gay Sunshine,* September 1970, quoted in Teal, *The Gay Militants,* 155.

43. *Gay Liberation Front,* November 1970, quoted ibid., 145.

44. Marotta, *The Politics of Homosexuality,* 115; Teal, *The Gay Militants,* 70.

45. Teal, *The Gay Militants,* 63.

46. Humphreys, *Out of the Closets,* 110.

47. Ibid., 111.

48. John D'Emilio, "Gay Politics, Gay Community: San Francisco's Experience," in *Making Trouble: Essays on Gay History, Politics, and the University,* ed. John D'Emilio (New York: Routledge, 1992), 85–86.

49. Ibid.

50. Marotta, *The Politics of Homosexuality,* 163.

51. Ibid., 185.

52. Ibid., 186.

53. This description of the *Harper's* zap is based on Marotta, *The Politics of Homosexuality,* 181–85.

54. Marotta, *The Politics of Homosexuality,* 182.

55. Ibid., 183–84.

56. Michael Brown, Lois Hart, and Ron Ballard, "Gay Revolution Comes Out," *Rat,* August 12, 7, quoted in Marotta, *The Politics of Homosexuality,* 88.

57. Allen Young, "Out of the Closets, into the Streets," in *Out of the Closets: Voices of Gay Liberation,* ed. Karla Jay and Allen Young (New York: New York University Press, [1972] 1992), 26.

58. Kissack, "Freaking Fag Revolutionaries"; Marotta, *The Politics of Homosexuality;* Teal, *The Gay Militants.*

59. Kissack, "Freaking Fag Revolutionaries," 108.

60. See, e.g., Don Collins, "Interview with Dorr Jones." *Vector,* September 1969, in which Jones, a militant homophile activist, comments on gay liberation and summarizes the differences between homophile and gay liberation views.

61. Larry Littlejohn, president's column, *Vector,* January 1970, 10.

62. Marotta, *The Politics of Homosexuality,* 139.

63. Teal, *The Gay Militants,* 73.

64. Perry A. George, "The Gay Revolution (?) and S.I.R.?," *Vector,* January 1970, 28.

65. Ibid., 11.

66. "S.F. to Host National Conference," *Vector,* August 1966.

67. For analysis of this conference, see Rob Cole, "Collision in San Francisco, 1, Old, New

Ideas Tangle at NACHO Convention," *Advocate,* September 30, 1970; Rob Cole, "Collision in San Francisco, 2, NACHO 'Liberated' on Final Day," *Advocate,* October 14, 1970; Humphreys, *Out of the Closets,* 103–9; Teal, *The Gay Militants,* 288–89.

68. Cole, "Collision in San Francisco, 1," 1.

69. Teal, *The Gay Militants,* 289–90.

Chapter Four

1. Donn Teal, *The Gay Militants: How Gay Liberation Began in America, 1969–1971,* 2d ed. (New York: St. Martin's, 1995), 53.

2. Ibid.

3. At the last minute, Humphreys changed his mind and speculated that rather than disappearing, gay organizing might adopt a new form. He accurately predicted that the "divisions of the movement may provide the advantages of diversification." Humphreys, "New Styles in Homosexual Manliness," *Trans-Action* 8 (March–April 1971): 66.

In 1978, Joseph Harry and William DeVall noted that the expectations of those who had predicted in 1972–73 that the gay movement would die out or factionalize had not been borne out. This observation provides additional evidence that at the time some had expected the gay movement to be irreparably damaged by the decline of the New Left. Joseph and DeVall, *The Social Organization of Gay Males* (New York: Praeger, 1978), 171.

4. Todd Gitlin, *The Sixties: Years of Hope, Days of Rage* (New York: Bantam, 1987).

5. Debra Minkoff, *Organizing for Equality: The Evolution of Women's and Racial-Ethnic Organizations in America, 1955–1985* (New Brunswick: Rutgers University Press, 1995), 65.

6. Alice Echols, " 'We Gotta Get Out of This Place': Notes toward a Remapping of the Sixties," *Socialist Review* 22, no. 2 (1992): 22. The causes (and salience for the Movement as a whole) of the implosion of SDS are a topic of debate in literature on the New Left. For example, one of the central goals of Wini Breines's work is to counter the argument, promoted by Todd Gitlin, James Miller, and Maurice Isserman, that "the new left was responsible for its own demise primarily because the leadership did not build an adequately responsible, disciplined, democratic, and centralized organization that would have enabled the movement to function realistically in the world of American politics." Breines, *Community and Organization in the New Left, 1962–1968: The Great Refusal* (New Brunswick: Rutgers University Press, 1989), xii. See Gitlin, *The Sixties;* Maurice Isserman, *If I Had a Hammer: The Death of the Old Left and the Birth of the New Left* (New York: Basic, 1987); James Miller, *Democracy Is in the Streets: From Port Huron to the Siege of Chicago* (New York: Simon and Schuster, 1987). Gitlin and Sean Stryker also point to the shift to an armed revolutionary strategy as a central factor in the New Left's demise. Gitlin, *The Sixties;* Sean D. Stryker, "Knowledge and Power in the Students for a Democratic Society, 1960–1970," *Berkeley Journal of Sociology* 38 (1993–94): 89.

7. Books by white male Movement leaders include Gitlin, *The Sixties;* Tom Hayden, *Reunion: A Memoir* (New York: Random House, 1988); Miller, *Democracy Is in the Streets.*

8. Echols, "We Gotta Get Out," 23.

9. The largest antiwar demonstratation occurred on May 9, 1970, five days after the Kent State killings (Gitlin, *The Sixties,* 410). Gitlin describes this mobilization as the "student movement's last hurrah." In his assessment, "activism never recovered from the summer vacation of 1970" (Gitlin, *The Sixties,* 411). See also Laud Humphreys, *Out of the Closets: The Sociology of Homosexual Liberation* (Englewood Cliffs, N.J.: Prentice-Hall, 1972), 160.

10. Breines, *Community and Organization,* xv; Echols, "We Gotta Get Out."

11. Breines claims that the gay movement was born in the late 1960s, presumably out of the New Left (ibid.). However, chapters 2 and 3 showed that the gay movement was not born out of the New Left, but rather out of the New Left's encounter with the homophile movement.

12. Echols, "We Gotta Get Out," 13.

13. Minkoff, *Organizing for Equality*, 74.

14. Minkoff cites Herbert H. Haines, "Black Radicalization and the Funding of Civil Rights: 1957–1970," *Social Problems* 32 (1984); Doug McAdam, *Political Process and the Development of Black Insurgency, 1930–1970* (Chicago: University of Chicago Press, 1982); and J. Craig Jenkins and Craig M. Ekert, "Channeling Black Insurgency," *American Sociological Review* 51 (1986). See also David S. Meyer and Douglas R. Imig, "Political Opportunity and the Rise and Decline of Interest Group Sectors," *Social Science Journal* 30, no. 3 (1993), and John D. McCarthy, David W. Britt, and Mark Wolfson, "The Institutional Channeling of Social Movements by the State in the United States," *Research in Social Movements, Conflicts, and Change* 13 (1991).

15. J. Craig Jenkins, "Foundation Funding of Progressive Social Movements," in *The Grant Seekers Guide*, ed. Jill Shellow (Nyack, N.Y.: Glenmeade, 1985); J. Craig Jenkins, "Nonprofit Organizations and Policy Advocacy," in *The Nonprofit Sector: A Research Handbook*, ed. Walter Powell (New Haven: Yale University Press, 1987).

16. Jack Walker, "The Origins and Maintenance of Interest Groups in America," *American Political Science Review* 77 (1983).

17. Minkoff, *Organizing for Equality*, 55.

18. Jenkins, "Nonprofit Organizations and Policy Advocacy," 301.

19. Ibid.

20. McCarthy, Britt, and Wolfson, "The Institutional Channeling."

21. John D'Emilio, foreword to *Out of the Closets: Voices of Gay Liberation*, ed. Karla Jay and Allen Young (New York: New York University Press, [1972] 1992), xxvii; Steven Epstein, "Gay Politics, Ethnic Identity: The Limits of Social Constructionism," *Socialist Review* 17, no. 2 (1987): 2; Joshua Gamson, "Must Identity Movements Self-Destruct? A Queer Dilemma," in *Social Perspectives in Lesbian and Gay Studies: A Reader*, ed. Peter M. Nardi and Beth E. Schneider (London: Routledge, [1995] 1998), 20.

22. Epstein, "Gay Politics," 2.

23. Marotta developed an even more complex categorization of the strains of gay liberation ideology in *The Politics of Homosexuality* (Boston: Houghton Mifflin, 1981). I borrow the distinction between gay power and gay pride from Teal, *The Gay Militants*, 68.

24. This concern manifested itself in a debate within gay liberation about the quality of gay life in Cuba. Karla Jay and Allen Young, eds., *Out of the Closets: Voices of Gay Liberation*, 20th-anniversary ed. (New York: New York University Press, [1972] 1992); Teal, *The Gay Militants*, 77.

25. Dennis Altman, *Homosexual Oppression and Liberation*, 2d ed. (New York: New York University Press, 1993), 239.

26. Ibid., 246.

27. Allen Young, "Out of the Closets, Into the Streets," in *Out of the Closets: Voices of Gay Liberation*, ed. Karla Jay and Allen Young (New York: New York University Press, [1972] 1992), 28.

28. Altman, *Homosexual Oppression*, 242.

29. Steve Dansky, "Hey Man," *Come Out!*, June–July 1970, 6, quoted in Marotta, *The Politics of Homosexuality*, 121.

30. Marotta, *The Politics of Homosexuality*, 142. For details on east coast divisions around support of the Black Panthers see Arthur Dong (director), *The Question of Equality*, pt. 1, *Out Rage '69* (television program) (New York: Testing the Limits, 1995); Teal, *The Gay Militants*, 78.

31. Teal, *The Gay Militants*, 89.

32. Terrence Kissack, "Freaking Fag Revolutionaries: New York's Gay Liberation Front, 1969–1971," *Radical History Review* 62 (1995): 117; Teal, *The Gay Militants*, 8.

33. Teal, *The Gay Militants*, 110.

34. Marotta, *The Politics of Homosexuality*, 145.

35. Ibid., 144.

36. Michael Francis Irkin, "The Homosexual Liberation Movement: What Direction?," *San Francisco Free Press*, December 7, 1969, 8.

37. Ibid., 9.

38. Ibid., 8.

39. On the role of organizations in traditional ethnic communities, see R. Breton, "Institutional Completeness of Ethnic Communities and the Personal Relations of Immigrants," *American Journal of Sociology* 70 (1964); Susan Olzak and Elizabeth West, "Ethnic Conflict and the Rise and Fall of Ethnic Newspapers," *American Sociological Review* 56 (1991); Arthur Stinchcombe, "Social Structure and Organizations," in *Handbook of Organizations*, ed. J. G. March (Chicago: Rand McNally, 1965).

40. Teal, *The Gay Militants*, 294.

41. Ibid.

42. Ibid., 297–98.

43. Ibid., 39.

44. Marcus Overseth, "Grows Rapidly: What Kind of People?" *San Francisco Free Press*, December 7, 1969, 6.

45. Young, "Out of the Closets," 11.

46. Ibid., 12.

47. Marotta, *The Politics of Homosexuality*, 147.

48. Humphreys, *Out of the Closets*, 161. On the decline of gay liberation, also see D'Emilio, foreword; Marotta, *The Politics of Homosexuality*; Jeffrey Weeks, *Coming Out: Homosexual Politics in Britain from the Nineteenth Century to the Present* (London: Quartet, 1977).

49. Kissack, "Freaking Fag Revolutionaries," 128.

50. Information about gay liberation organizations is from my data set, described in the appendix. Information about gay liberation periodicals was located in the Gay Liberation Press Collection, part of the San Francisco Bay Area Serials collection organized by Bill Walker ("San Francisco Bay Area Gay and Lesbian Serials: A Guide to the Microfilm Collection" [University of California, Berkeley, and the Gay, Lesbian, Bisexual, Transgender Historical Society of Northern California, 1991]). The collection includes thirty-one titles. The number of periodicals declines to zero, even though *Gay Sunshine* survived. Later issues of *Gay Sunshine* are not included in the collection because permission to microfilm was denied.

51. John D'Emilio, *Making Trouble: Essays on Gay History, Politics, and the University* (New York: Routledge, 1992), 245. In this 1991 essay, "After Stonewall," D'Emilio dates the decline of "radical gay liberation" to the mid-1970s. He admitted that his effort at constructing a history of post-Stonewall activism was "still in the early stages" and suggested that "more research" into the issue be done. The primary materials I have located strongly support a much earlier demise of gay power.

52. Marotta, *The Politics of Homosexuality*, 146.

53. Humphreys, *Out of the Closets,* 160.

54. *Vector,* untitled editorial, June 1971, 4.

55. Ray Broshears, "S.I.R., the Society for Individual Rights[,] Conducts Fantastic 'Work-In' at Federal Building," *Gay Activists Alliance Lifeline,* June 1971, 1.

56. *San Francisco Chronicle,* June 8, 1971, 17, quoted in Broshears, "S.I.R., the Society for Individual Rights[,] Conducts Fantastic 'Work-In,'" 1.

57. Teal, *The Gay Militants,* 297–98.

58. John D'Emilio, *Sexual Politics, Sexual Communities: The Making of a Homosexual Minority in the United States, 1940–1970* (Chicago: University of Chicago Press, 1983), chap. 10; Kissack, "Freaking Fag Revolutionaries," 108.

59. Dong, *The Question of Equality.*

60. Teal, *The Gay Militants,* 76.

61. Marotta, *The Politics of Homosexuality,* 145.

62. Jewelle Gomez, "Out of the Past," in *The Question of Equality: Lesbian and Gay Politics in America since Stonewall,* ed. David Deitcher (New York: Scribner, 1995), 33.

Chapter Five

1. Laud Humphreys, *Out of the Closets: The Sociology of Homosexual Liberation* (Englewood Cliffs, N.J.: Prentice-Hall, 1972), 123.

2. Dennis Altman, *The Homosexualization of America* (Boston: Beacon, 1982); Mary Bernstein, "Celebration and Suppression: The Strategic Uses of Identity by the Lesbian and Gay Movement," *American Journal of Sociology* 103 (1997): 532; John D'Emilio, "After Stonewall," in *Making Trouble: Essays on Gay History, Politics, and the University,* ed. John D'Emilio (New York: Routledge, 1992); John D'Emilio, "Gay Politics, Gay Community: San Francisco's Experience," in *Making Trouble: Essays on Gay History, Politics, and the University,* ed. John D'Emilio (New York: Routledge, 1992); Steven Epstein, "Gay Politics, Ethnic Identity: The Limits of Social Constructionism," *Socialist Review* 17, no. 2 (1987); Jeffrey Escoffier, "Sexual Revolution and the Politics of Gay Identity," *Socialist Review,* no. 82/83 (July–October 1985); Joshua Gamson, "Must Identity Movements Self-Destruct? A Queer Dilemma," in *Social Perspectives in Lesbian and Gay Studies: A Reader,* ed. Peter M. Nardi and Beth E. Schneider (London: Routledge, [1995] 1998); William Paul, "Minority Status for Gay People: Majority Reaction and Social Context," in *Homosexuality: Social, Psychological, and Biological Issues,* ed. William Paul, et al. (Beverly Hills: Sage, 1982); Steven Seidman, "Identity and Politics in a 'Postmodern' Gay Culture: Some Historical and Conceptual Notes," in *Fear of a Queer Planet: Queer Politics and Social Theory,* ed. Michael Warner (Minneapolis: University of Minnesota Press, 1993); Urvashi Vaid, *Virtual Equality: The Mainstreaming of Gay and Lesbian Liberation* (New York: Anchor, 1995).

3. Seidman, "Identity and Politics," 117.

4. Ibid.

5. Ibid.

6. D'Emilio, "After Stonewall," 246.

7. Bernstein, "Celebration and Suppression," 532.

8. Dudley Clendinen and Adam Nagourney acknowledge the unprecedented feat of arriving at a gay rights agenda. However, they emphasize that the conference was quite contentious and that the participants disagreed about more issues than they could agree upon. They also suggest that this event planted seeds for future conflict within the gay movement. Clendinen and Nagourney, *Out for Good: The Struggle to Build a Gay Rights Movement in America* (New York: Simon and Schuster, 1999), 136–38. See also Humphreys, *Out of the Closets,* 168.

9. Humphreys, *Out of the Closets,* 165.

10. John D'Emilio, *Sexual Politics, Sexual Communities: The Making of a Homosexual Minority in the United States, 1940–1970* (Chicago: University of Chicago Press, 1983).

11. Paul J. DiMaggio and Walter W. Powell, "The Iron Cage Revisited: Institutional Isomorphism and Collective Rationality," in *The New Institutionalism in Organizational Analysis,* ed. Walter W. Powell and Paul J. DiMaggio (Chicago: University of Chicago Press, [1983] 1991); John Mohr, "Community, Bureaucracy, and Social Relief: An Institutional Analysis of Organizational Forms in New York City, 1888–1917" (Ph.D. diss., Department of Sociology, Yale University, 1992), 42.

12. See Toby Marotta, *The Politics of Homosexuality* (Boston: Houghton Mifflin, 1981), chap. 7, "Conflicts between Political and Cultural Leaders," esp. 191.

13. Quoted in ibid.

14. *New Left Notes,* November 26, 1966, quoted in Wini Breines, *Community and Organization in the New Left, 1962–1968: The Great Refusal* (New Brunswick: Rutgers University Press, 1989), 48.

15. Marotta, *The Politics of Homosexuality,* 173.

16. The way a lesbian bar community in the 1950s socialized newcomers is beautifully described in Elizabeth Lapovsky Kennedy and Madeline D. Davis, *Boots of Leather, Slippers of Gold: The History of a Lesbian Community* (New York: Routledge, 1993), 80.

17. A marginalized minority continued to espouse the gay power vision, representing a fourth logic of organizing.

18. Humphreys, *Out of the Closets,* 126.

19. Ibid.

20. Ibid., 127.

21. Ibid.

22. Ibid.

23. Ibid.

24. Ibid.

25. Ibid.

26. Clendinen and Nagourney, *Out for Good,* 62; Marotta, *The Politics of Homosexuality,* 164.

27. Marotta, *The Politics of Homosexuality,* 164.

28. Ibid., 167.

29. Ibid.

30. Ibid.

31. Ibid., 169.

32. Humphreys, *Out of the Closets,* 5.

33. "Christopher Street West S.F. Gay Parade," *Advocate,* July 19, 1972, 3; Susan Stryker and Jim Van Buskirk, *Gay by the Bay: A History of Queer Culture in the San Francisco Bay Area* (San Francisco: Chronicle, 1996); Greg L. Pennington, "A Parade Almanac," *San Francisco Lesbian/Gay Freedom Parade and Celebration Magazine,* June 25, 1989, 15. The 1972 event was the first sizeable commemoration of Stonewall to take place in San Francisco. In 1970, "20 to 30 people marched down Polk Street from Aquatic Park to City Hall." Stryker and Van Buskirk, *Gay by the Bay,* 67. See also Pennington, "A Parade Almanac," 8. In 1971 there was no event at all. Stryker and Van Buskirk, *Gay by the Bay,* 67; Pennington, "A Parade Almanac," 8.

34. "Christopher Street West S.F. Gay Parade," 3.

35. Ibid.

36. Ibid.

37. Ibid., 10.

38. For a discussion of Chicago's lesbian/gay freedom day parade, see Richard K. Herrell, "The Symbolic Strategies of Chicago's Gay and Lesbian Pride Day Parade," in *Gay Culture in America: Essays from the Field,* ed. Gilbert Herdt (Boston: Beacon, 1992).

Chapter Six

1. Dudley Clendinen and Adam Nagourney, *Out for Good: The Struggle to Build a Gay Rights Movement in America* (New York: Simon and Schuster, 1999), 348.

2. John D'Emilio, "A Generation of Progress," in *Making Trouble: Essays on Gay History, Politics, and the University,* ed. John D'Emilio (New York: Routledge, 1992), 228.

3. George Chauncey, *Gay New York: Gender, Urban Culture, and the Making of the Gay Male World, 1890–1940* (New York: HarperCollins, 1994); John D'Emilio, *Sexual Politics, Sexual Communities: The Making of a Homosexual Minority in the United States, 1940–1970* (Chicago: University of Chicago Press, 1983); Elizabeth Lapovsky Kennedy and Madeline D. Davis, *Boots of Leather, Slippers of Gold: The History of a Lesbian Community* (New York: Routledge, 1993); Susan Stryker and Jim Van Buskirk, *Gay by the Bay: A History of Queer Culture in the San Francisco Bay Area* (San Francisco: Chronicle, 1996).

4. Randy Shilts, "Castro Street: Mecca or Ghetto?," in *Long Road to Freedom: The Advocate History of the Gay and Lesbian Movement,* ed. Mark Thompson (New York: St. Martin's, 1994), 156. On the novelty of a gay neighborhood see also Clendinen and Nagourney, *Out for Good,* 332.

5. Carl Wittman, "A Gay Manifesto," in *Out of the Closets: Voices of Gay Liberation,* ed. Karla Jay and Allen Young (New York: New York University Press, [1972] 1992), 339.

6. Shilts, "Castro Street," 156.

7. Clendinen and Nagourney, *Out for Good,* 332; Frances FitzGerald, *Cities on a Hill: A Journey through Contemporary American Cultures* (New York: Simon and Schuster, [1981] 1986), 43; Randy Shilts, *The Mayor of Castro Street: The Life and Times of Harvey Milk* (New York: St. Martin's, 1982).

8. A few scholars are beginning the fascinating process of documenting and analyzing this migration. Martin Meeker, " 'I Wanted to Be at the Gay Center of the Universe': Exploring Motivations among Gay and Lesbian Migrants: 1945–1992" (unpublished paper, Department of History, University of Southern California, 1995); Stephen O. Murray, *American Gay* (Chicago: University of Chicago Press, 1996); Gayle Rubin, "Thinking Sex: Notes for a Radical Theory of the Politics of Sexuality," in *Pleasure and Danger: Exploring Female Sexuality,* ed. Carole S. Vance (Boston: Routledge, 1984).

9. Doug McAdam, *Freedom Summer* (New York: Oxford University Press, 1988), 44. See Armistead Maupin's *Tales of the City* for a flavor of the lifestyles of young migrants to San Francisco in the 1970s (New York: HarperPerennial, 1978).

10. FitzGerald, *Cities on a Hill,* 27.

11. Karen S. Heller, "Silence Equals Death: Discourses on AIDS and Identity in the Gay Press, 1981–1986" (Ph.D. diss., Department of Medical Anthropology, University of California, San Francisco, 1993), 46.

12. FitzGerald, *Cities on a Hill,* 55.

13. See chapter 4 for a more detailed discussion of gay liberation debates about the subculture.

14. Clendinen and Nagourney, *Out for Good,* 150.

15. Myra Marx Ferree and Frederick D. Miller, "Winning Hearts and Minds: Some Psychological Contributions to the Resource Mobilization Perspective of Social Movements" (unpublished paper, 1977), 34; Doug McAdam, John D. McCarthy, and Mayer N. Zald, eds.,

Comparative Perspectives on Social Movements: Political Opportunities, Mobilizing Structures, and Cultural Framings (Cambridge: Cambridge University Press, 1996), 9.

16. Shilts, *The Mayor of Castro Street*, 63.

17. See also Jay P. Paul, Robert B. Hayes, and Thomas J. Coates, "The Impact of the HIV Epidemic on U.S. Gay Male Communities," in *Lesbian, Gay, and Bisexual Identities over the Lifespan: Psychological Perspectives*, ed. Anthony R. D'Augelli and Charlotte J. Patterson (New York: Oxford University Press, 1995).

18. Heller, "Silence Equals Death," 154.

19. Clendinen and Nagourney, *Out for Good*, 334.

20. Dennis Altman, *The Homosexualization of America* (Boston: Beacon, 1982), 21; see also John D'Emilio, "After Stonewall," in *Making Trouble: Essays on Gay History, Politics, and the University*, ed. John D'Emilio (New York: Routledge, 1992), 251.

21. Harvey Milk's life and political career have been well documented. See Robert Epstein (director), *The Times of Harvey Milk* (Beverly Hills: Pacific Arts Video, 1984); Clendinen and Nagourney, *Out for Good*; John D'Emilio, "Gay Politics, Gay Community: San Francisco's Experience," in *Making Trouble: Essays on Gay History, Politics, and the University*, ed. John D'Emilio (New York: Routledge, 1992); FitzGerald, *Cities on a Hill*; Shilts, *The Mayor of Castro Street*.

22. The discussion of the changes in San Francisco's economy is based on FitzGerald, *Cities on a Hill*, 44.

23. Ibid., 45.

24. Clendinen and Nagourney, *Out for Good*, 155.

25. Ibid.

26. Ibid., 343.

27. Ibid., 157.

28. Ibid., 335.

29. Ibid., 159. See also FitzGerald, *Cities on a Hill*, 45.

30. Quoted in Clendinen and Nagourney, *Out for Good*, 159.

31. Clendinen and Nagourney, *Out for Good*, 340.

32. Quoted in Clendinen and Nagourney, *Out for Good*, 340.

33. Clendinen and Nagourney, *Out for Good*, 161.

34. Ibid., 343.

35. D'Emilio, "Gay Politics," 88.

36. Clendinen and Nagourney, *Out for Good*, 344.

37. Ibid., 345.

38. Ibid.

39. Ibid.

40. Shilts, *The Mayor of Castro Street*, 152.

41. D'Emilio, "Gay Politics," 88.

42. For an analysis of the relationship between the gay movement and the countermovement in the 1990s, see Chris Bull and John Gallagher, *Perfect Enemies: The Religious Right, the Gay Movement, and the Politics of the 1990s* (New York: Crown, 1996).

43. For a discussion of the conditions under which repression stimulates organizing and the conditions under which repression suppresses organizing, see Susan Olzak and Elizabeth West, "Ethnic Conflict and the Rise and Fall of Ethnic Newspapers," *American Sociological Review* 56 (1991); Susan Olzak, *The Dynamics of Ethnic Competition and Conflict* (Stanford: Stanford University Press, 1992).

44. Mark Thompson, ed., *Long Road to Freedom: The Advocate History of the Gay and Lesbian Movement* (New York: St. Martin's, 1994), 147.

45. Clendinen and Nagourney, *Out for Good,* 292; Robert Dawidoff, "Kill a Queer for Christ," in *Long Road to Freedom: The Advocate History of the Gay and Lesbian Movement,* ed. Mark Thompson (New York: St. Martin's, 1994), 146.

46. D'Emilio, "Gay Politics," 88.

47. Ibid.

48. Thompson, *Long Road to Freedom,* 147.

49. Shilts, *The Mayor of Castro Street,* 360.

50. Clendinen and Nagourney, *Out for Good,* 300.

51. Ibid., 310.

52. Ibid., 336; D'Emilio, "Gay Politics," 88.

53. Shilts, *The Mayor of Castro Street,* 160.

54. D'Emilio, "Gay Politics," 89.

55. Clendinen and Nagourney, *Out for Good,* chap. 27.

56. Shilts, *The Mayor of Castro Street,* 364.

57. The speech appears in ibid., 364–71.

58. Clendinen and Nagourney, *Out for Good,* 389.

59. Ibid.

60. Ibid., 403.

61. Shilts, *The Mayor of Castro Street,* chap. 18, vividly describes these events.

62. Clendinen and Nagourney, *Out for Good,* 404.

63. Louis Freedberg and Christopher Heredia, "Mixed Feelings about Gay March," *San Francisco Chronicle,* April 10, 2000, A2.

64. John-Manuel Andriote, *Victory Deferred: How AIDS Changed Gay Life in America* (Chicago: The University of Chicago Press, 1999), 14.

Chapter Seven

1. Paris Poirier (director), *Pride Divide* (film) (New York: Filmakers Library, 1997); Barry D. Adam, *The Rise of a Gay and Lesbian Movement* (Boston: Twayne, 1987), 92; Lillian Faderman, *Odd Girls and Twilight Lovers: A History of Lesbian Life in Twentieth-Century America* (New York: Columbia University Press, 1991), 211.

2. Joe DeMarco, "Gay Racism," in *Black Men/White Men,* ed. Michael J. Smith (San Francisco: Gay Sunshine, 1983), 110; Poirier, *Pride Divide.*

3. Poirier, *Pride Divide.*

4. Arthur Dong (director), *The Question of Equality,* pt. 1, *Out Rage '69* (television program) (New York: Testing the Limits, 1995); Poirier, *Pride Divide.*

5. Steven Seidman, "Identity and Politics in a 'Postmodern' Gay Culture: Some Historical and Conceptual Notes," in *Fear of a Queer Planet: Queer Politics and Social Theory,* ed. Michael Warner (Minneapolis: University of Minnesota Press, 1993), 120.

6. Tomás Almaguer, "Chicano Men: A Cartography of Homosexual Identity and Behavior," in *Social Perspectives in Lesbian and Gay Studies: A Reader,* ed. Peter M. Nardi and Beth E. Schneider (London and New York: Routledge, 1993); Steven Epstein, "Gay Politics, Ethnic Identity: The Limits of Social Constructionism," *Socialist Review* 17, no. 2 (1987); Seidman, "Identity and Politics."

7. Isaac Julien and Kobena Mercer, "True Confessions: A Discourse on Images of Black Male Sexuality," in *Brother to Brother,* ed. Essex Hemphill (Boston: Alyson, 1991), 168.

8. Almaguer, "Chicano Men," 544–45.

9. Adam, *The Rise of a Gay and Lesbian Movement,* 92; Jewelle Gomez, "Out of the Past," in *The Question of Equality: Lesbian and Gay Politics in America since Stonewall,* ed. David Deitcher (New York: Scribner, 1995), 49.

10. Thom Beame, "Racism from a Black Perspective," in *Black Men/White Men,* ed. Michael J. Smith (San Francisco: Gay Sunshine, 1983).

11. Poirier, *Pride Divide.*

12. Faderman, *Odd Girls and Twilight Lovers,* 211; Toby Marotta, *The Politics of Homosexuality* (Boston: Houghton Mifflin, 1981), 239.

13. Robin Ruth Linden et al., eds., *Against Sadomasochism: A Radical Feminist Analysis* (San Francisco: Frog in the Well, 1982).

14. Julien and Mercer, "True Confessions," 169.

15. Ibid.

16. Adam, *The Rise of a Gay and Lesbian Movement,* 94; Mary Daly, *Gyn/Ecology* (Boston: Beacon, 1978); Jill Johnston, "Are Lesbians 'Gay'?," *Ms.* 1975, 85.

17. Marotta, *The Politics of Homosexuality;* Radicalesbians, "The Woman-Identified Woman," in *Out of the Closets: Voices of Gay Liberation,* ed. Karla Jay and Allen Young (New York: New York University Press, [1972] 1992).

18. On the emergence of Radicalesbians and the authoring of "The Woman-Identified Woman," see also Alice Echols, *Daring to Be BAD: Radical Feminism in America, 1967–1975* (Minneapolis: University of Minnesota Press, 1989), 213–20; Marotta, *The Politics of Homosexuality,* chap. 4; and Gomez, "Out of the Past."

19. Marotta, *The Politics of Homosexuality,* 231.

20. On the relationship between lesbianism and feminism, see Radicalesbians, "The Woman-Identified Woman"; Adrienne Rich, "Compulsory Heterosexuality and Lesbian Existence," in *Powers of Desire: The Politics of Sexuality,* ed. Ann Snitow, Christine Stansell, and Sharon Thompson (New York: Monthly Review, 1983); Alice Echols, "The Taming of the Id: Feminist Sexual Politics, 1968–83," in *Pleasure and Danger: Exploring Female Sexuality,* ed. Carole S. Vance (Boston: Routledge, 1984); and Ti-Grace Atkinson, *Amazon Odyssey: The First Collection of Writings by the Political Pioneer of the Women's Movement* (New York: Link, 1974).

21. Faderman, *Odd Girls and Twilight Lovers,* 207.

22. Gay Revolution Party Women's Caucus, "Realesbians and Politicalesbians," in *Out of the Closets: Voices of Gay Liberation,* ed. Karla Jay and Allen Young (New York: New York University Press, [1972]) 1992); Arlene Stein, *Sex and Sensibility: Stories of a Lesbian Generation* (Berkeley and Los Angeles: University of California Press, 1997).

23. Del Martin, "Columnist Resigns, Blasts Male Chauvinism," *Vector,* October 1970. Del Martin's farewell was also published in the *Advocate* in the fall of 1970 and reprinted in Mark Thompson, ed., *Long Road to Freedom: The Advocate History of the Gay and Lesbian Movement* (New York: St. Martin's, 1994), 41–42.

24. Dong, *The Question of Equality: Part One, Out Rage '69;* Poirier, *Pride Divide.*

25. John D'Emilio, "After Stonewall," in *Making Trouble: Essays on Gay History, Politics, and the University,* ed. John D'Emilio (New York: Routledge, 1992), 254. On lesbian feminism, see also D'Emilio, "After Stonewall," 251–56; Stein, *Sex and Sensibility;* Arlene Stein, "Sisters and Queers: The Decentering of Lesbian Feminism," *Socialist Review* 22, no. 1 (1992); Faderman, *Odd Girls and Twilight Lovers;* Dennis Altman, *Homosexual Oppression and Liberation,* 2d ed. (New York: New York University Press, 1993); Susan Stryker and Jim Van Buskirk, *Gay by the Bay: A History of Queer Culture in the San Francisco Bay Area* (San Francisco: Chronicle, 1996); Del Martin and

Phyllis Lyon, *Lesbian/Woman,* 20th-anniversary ed. (Volcano, Calif.: Volcano, 1991); Deborah Goleman Wolf, *The Lesbian Community* (Berkeley and Los Angeles: University of California Press, 1979); and Verta Taylor and Nancy Whittier, "Collective Identity in Social Movement Communities: Lesbian Feminist Mobilization," in *Frontiers in Social Movement Theory,* ed. Aldon D. Morris and Carol McClurg Mueller (New Haven: Yale University Press, 1992).

26. Examples of this lesbian feminist theorizing include Rich, "Compulsory Heterosexuality"; Sidney Abbott and Barbara Love, *Sappho Was a Right-On Woman* (New York: Stein and Day, 1972); Sarah H. Hoagland and Julia Penelope, eds., *For Lesbians Only: A Separatist Anthology* (London: Onlywomen, 1988); Jill Johnston, *Lesbian Nation: The Feminist Solution* (New York: Simon and Schuster, 1973); and Julia Penelope and Susan Wolfe, eds., *Lesbian Culture: An Anthology* (Freedom, Calif.: Crossing, 1993).

27. Adam, *The Rise of a Gay and Lesbian Movement,* 91.

28. For this analysis, I include *all* women-only organizations I found. Some of these organizations involve nonlesbians, including heterosexual feminists, bisexual women, prostitutes, prostitute's rights advocates, and women engaged in S/M sexual practices with men.

29. Wolf, *The Lesbian Community,* 80.

30. Taylor and Whittier, "Collective Identity," 107; Alberto Melucci, *Nomads of the Present: Social Movements and Individual Needs in Contemporary Society* (Philadelphia: Temple University Press, 1989).

31. Taylor and Whittier, "Collective Identity," 107.

32. Bill Walker, "San Francisco Bay Area Gay and Lesbian Serials: A Guide to the Microfilm Collection" (University of California, Berkeley, and Gay, Lesbian, Bisexual, Transgender Historical Society of Northern California, 1991).

33. Poirier, *Pride Divide;* Faderman, *Odd Girls and Twilight Lovers,* 211.

34. D'Emilio, "After Stonewall," esp. 251–52.

35. Chris Bearchell, "Why I Am a Gay Liberationist," *Resources for Feminist Research* 12, no. 1 (1983): 59, quoted in Adam, *The Rise of a Gay and Lesbian Movement,* 95.

36. Carole FitzGibbon, "Gay Day Official Responds to Dissidents," *Bay Area Reporter,* June 5, 1980, 1.

37. Konstantin Berlandt, "Gay Parade: Last Meetings," *Bay Area Reporter,* June 5, 1980, 5.

38. Konstantin Berlandt, "Parade Dissidents Meet and Challenge Structure," *Bay Area Reporter,* August 28, 1980, 8.

39. Konstantin Berlandt, "Parade Committees to Fuse: No Funds for Audit," *Bay Area Reporter,* December 4, 1980, 10.

40. Konstantin Berlandt, "Gay Parade Unity Ratified: Theme Debated," *Bay Area Reporter,* February 26, 1981, 11.

41. Fred R. Methered, "I Love a Parade," *Bay Area Reporter,* June 18, 1981, 6.

42. "Gay Freedom Week: 1981," June 18, 1981, 8.

43. Margaret Cruikshank, *The Gay and Lesbian Liberation Movement* (New York: Routledge, 1992), 183.

44. Ruth L. Schartz, "New Alliances, Strange Bedfellows: Lesbians, Gay Men, and AIDS," in *Sisters, Sexperts, Queers: Beyond the Lesbian Nation,* ed. Arlene Stein (New York: Penguin, 1993), 232.

45. Cruikshank, *The Gay and Lesbian Liberation Movement,* 183.

46. Poirier, *Pride Divide.*

47. Lesbians of color also experienced exclusion. However, they complained of exclusion from lesbian feminist communities. See Audre Lorde, *Sister Outsider: Essays and Speeches by Audre*

Lorde (Freedom, Calif.: Crossing, 1984); Cherríe Moraga and Gloria Anzaldúa, eds., *This Bridge Called My Back: Writings by Radical Women of Color* (New York: Kitchen Table/Women of Color, 1983); and Barbara Smith, ed., *Home Girls: A Black Feminist Anthology* (New York: Kitchen Table/Women of Color, 1983).

48. DeMarco, "Gay Racism," 110.

49. Beame, "Racism from a Black Perspective," 59, also 58.

50. Ibid., 58.

51. Charles Fernández, "Undocumented Aliens in the Queer Nation," *Out/Look: National Lesbian and Gay Quarterly,* spring 1991.

52. Dong, *The Question of Equality: Part One, Out Rage '69.*

53. Yong Lee, "A Question of Political Styles: A Comparison of Gays and Lesbians of Color in Inclusive and Ethnic Organizations" (senior thesis, Department of Sociology, University of California, Berkeley, 1994), 26.

54. Ibid.

55. Martin Duberman, Michelangelo Signorile, and Urvashi Vaid, "A Roundtable with Betsy Billard: State of the Struggle," *Harvard Gay and Lesbian Review* 6, no. 3 (1999).

56. Beverly Greene, ed., *Ethnic and Cultural Diversity among Lesbians and Gay Men,* vol. 3, *Psychological Perspectives on Lesbian and Gay Issues* (Thousand Oaks, Calif.: Sage, 1997).

57. Barbara Smith and Beverly Smith, "Across the Kitchen Table: A Sister-to-Sister Dialogue," in *This Bridge Called My Back: Writings by Radical Women of Color,* ed. Cherríe Moraga and Gloria Anzaldúa (New York: Kitchen Table/Women of Color, 1983), 121.

58. Seidman, "Identity and Politics," 119.

59. Gloria Anzaldúa, "Bridge, Drawbridge, Sandbar, or Island," in *We Are Everywhere: A Historical Sourcebook of Gay and Lesbian Politics,* ed. Mark Blasius and Shane Phelan (New York: Routledge, [1988] 1997), 713.

60. Bernice Johnson Reagon, "Coalition Politics: Turning the Century," in *Home Girls: A Black Feminist Anthology,* ed. Barbara Smith (New York: Kitchen Table/Women of Color, [1981] 1983).

61. Ibid., 356.

62. Seidman, "Identity and Politics."

Chapter Eight

1. Quoted in Frances FitzGerald, *Cities on a Hill: A Journey through Contemporary American Cultures* (New York: Simon and Schuster, [1981] 1986), 54.

2. I discovered this as a result of coding lists of San Francisco's gay bars for the years 1963 though 1994.

3. Ronald Bayer and David L. Kirp, "The United States: At the Center of the Storm," in *AIDS in the Industrialized Democracies: Passions, Politics, and Policies,* ed. David L. Kirp and Ronald Bayer (New Brunswick: Rutgers University Press, 1992), 11. In December 1994, the San Francisco Department of Public Health AIDS Office reported that thirteen AIDS cases had been diagnosed in the first half of 1981. San Francisco Department of Public Health AIDS Office, *AIDS Surveillance Report: AIDS Cases Reported through December 1994* (San Francisco: San Francisco Department of Public Health, 1994). See also Gerald J. Stine, *AIDS Update 1998: An Annual Overview of Acquired Immune Deficiency Syndrome* (Upper Saddle River, N.J.: Prentice-Hall, 1998).

4. The naming of the disease is discussed in Randy Shilts, *And the Band Played On: People, Politics, and the AIDS Epidemic* (New York: Penguin, 1987), 171. These numbers include all San

Franciscans who had been diagnosed and died of AIDS, not only gay men. San Francisco Department of Public Health, *AIDS Surveillance Report*.

5. Stine, *AIDS Update 1998*, 29.

6. Karen S. Heller, "Silence Equals Death: Discourses on AIDS and Identity in the Gay Press, 1981–1986" (Ph.D. diss., Department of Medical Anthropology, University of California, San Francisco, 1993), 293.

7. Stine, *AIDS Update 1998*.

8. Sabin Russell, "S.F. AIDS Summit Will Shift Focus as Death Rate Drops," *San Francisco Chronicle*, January 27, 1998, 1.

9. See, e.g., Dennis Altman, *AIDS in the Mind of America* (New York: Doubleday, 1986); John-Manuel Andriote, *Victory Deferred: How AIDS Changed Gay Life in America* (Chicago: University of Chicago Press, 1999); Ronald Bayer, *Private Acts, Social Consequences: AIDS and the Politics of Public Health* (New York: Free Press, 1989); Michael Callen, *Surviving AIDS* (New York: HarperCollins, 1990); Steven Epstein, *Impure Science: AIDS, Activism, and the Politics of Knowledge* (Berkeley and Los Angeles: University of California Press, 1996); John Fortunato, *AIDS: The Spiritual Dilemma* (New York: Harper and Row, 1987); Charles Garfield, *Sometimes My Heart Goes Numb: Love and Caregiving in a Time of AIDS* (San Francisco: Jossey-Bass, 1995); Albert R. Jonsen and Jeff Stryker, eds., *The Social Impact of AIDS in the United States* (Washington: National Academy, 1993); Stephen C. Joseph, *Dragon within the Gates: The Once and Future AIDS Epidemic* (New York: Carrol and Graf, 1992); Philip M. Kayal, *Bearing Witness: Gay Men's Health Crisis and the Politics of AIDS* (Boulder: Westview, 1993); James Kinsella, *Covering the Plague: AIDS and the American Media* (New Brunswick: Rutgers University Press, 1989); Lon G. Nungesser, *Epidemic of Courage: Facing AIDS in America* (New York: St. Martin's, 1986); Charles Perrow and Maurio F. Guillen, *The AIDS Disaster* (New Haven: Yale University Press, 1990); Gabriel Rotello, *Sexual Ecology: AIDS and the Destiny of Gay Men* (New York: Dutton, 1997); Benjamin Heim Shepard, *White Nights and Ascending Shadows* (London: Cassell, 1997); Shilts, *And the Band Played On*.

10. Some still do not believe HIV causes AIDS. Peter Duesberg, a molecular biologist at the University of California, Berkeley, is perhaps the most visible scientist advocating this position. Stine and Epstein discuss Duesberg's theory and the surrounding controversy. Epstein analyzes this controversy in depth, referring to it in a chapter title as "the debate that wouldn't die." Epstein, *Impure Science*; Stine, *AIDS Update 1998*, 36–40.

11. Epstein, *Impure Science*; Shilts, *And the Band Played On*.

12. Andriote, *Victory Deferred*, 67. Andriote documents similar comments by Moral Majority founder Jerry Falwell and Senator Jesse Helms. Ibid., 68, 122.

13. See ibid., 55–60, for a comparison of the responses to the epidemic of San Francisco and New York.

14. Shilts, *And the Band Played On*, 311.

15. Andriote, *Victory Deferred*, 58.

16. Ibid.

17. Deborah Gould, "Sex, Death, and the Politics of Anger: Emotions and Reason in ACT UP's Fight against AIDS" (Ph.D. diss., Department of Political Science, University of Chicago, 2000), 143.

18. Andriote, *Victory Deferred*, 145.

19. Callen, *Surviving AIDS*, 4.

20. Lawrence D. Mass, "Early Warnings," in *Long Road to Freedom: The Advocate History of the Gay and Lesbian Movement*, ed. Mark Thompson (New York: St. Martin's, 1994), 211.

21. Shilts, *And the Band Played On*, 122.

22. Andriote, *Victory Deferred,* 76.

23. Dennis Altman quoted in ibid., 51. See also Shepard, *White Nights,* 62.

24. Andriote, *Victory Deferred,* 69.

25. Ibid.

26. Andriote, Gould, and Shepard all discuss ways gay men initially distanced themselves from the epidemic. Andriote, *Victory Deferred,* 71; Gould, "Sex, Death," chap. 3; Shepard, *White Nights.*

27. Andriote, *Victory Deferred,* 78.

28. Bayer, *Private Acts,* 31.

29. For more detailed accounts of the controversy over the bathhouses, see ibid.; Fitz-Gerald, *Cities on a Hill;* Perrow and Guillen, *The AIDS Disaster;* Shilts, *And the Band Played On.*

30. Bayer, *Private Acts,* 31.

31. Ibid.

32. Ibid., 36.

33. Nathan Fain, writing in the *Advocate,* quoted in Bayer, *Private Acts,* 40.

34. Andriote, *Victory Deferred,* 73; FitzGerald, *Cities on a Hill,* 107; Gould, "Sex, Death."

35. M. Michael, "Alternate Prophylaxis" (letter), *New York Native,* October 21, 1985, 5.

36. Bayer, *Private Acts,* 27.

37. See, e.g., Richard Berkowitz and Michael Callen, "How to Have Sex in an Epidemic," in *We Are Everywhere: A Historical Sourcebook of Gay and Lesbian Politics,* ed. Mark Blasius and Shane Phelan (New York: Routledge, [1988] 1997).

38. Jay P. Paul, Robert B. Hayes, and Thomas J. Coates, "The Impact of the HIV Epidemic on U.S. Gay Male Communities," in *Lesbian, Gay, and Bisexual Identities over the Lifespan: Psychological Perspectives,* ed. Anthony R. D'Augelli and Charlotte J. Patterson (New York: Oxford University Press, 1995), 348.

39. This view is implicit in Gould's study of the origins of ACT UP. She puzzles over why ACT UP (AIDS Coalition to Unleash Power), a movement shaped by outrage at government neglect, did not emerge until 1987, five years into the epidemic. See Gould, "Sex, Death," chap. 3.

40. Cathy Jean Cohen compares lesbian and gay response to the epidemic to that of the African American community. Cohen, "Power, Resistance, and the Construction of Crisis: Marginalized Communities Respond to AIDS" (Ph.D. diss., Department of Political Science, University of Michigan, 1993).

41. Andriote, *Victory Deferred,* 87.

42. Ibid.; Shepard, *White Nights;* Shilts, *And the Band Played On,* chap. 10, esp. 161.

43. Shilts, *And the Band Played On,* 161.

44. Ibid.

45. Andriote, *Victory Deferred,* 83–84.

46. Ibid., 58–59.

47. Epstein, *Impure Science,* 11.

48. Paul Lorch, "Gay Men Dying: Shifting Gears, Part 1," *Bay Area Reporter,* March 31, 1983, 6. See also Andriote, *Victory Deferred,* 53.

49. Andriote, *Victory Deferred,* 88–89. See also Gould, "Sex, Death." 213.

50. Gould, "Sex, Death," chap. 3.

51. Quoted in Andriote, *Victory Deferred,* 89.

52. Andriote, *Victory Deferred,* 83–92.

53. Ibid., 84.

54. Epstein, *Impure Science*, 12.

55. Andriote, *Victory Deferred*.

56. Ibid., 90. See also Shepard, *White Nights*.

57. Andriote, *Victory Deferred*, 85.

58. A description and analysis of this important form of activism are, unfortunately, beyond the scope of this book. See Joshua Gamson, "Silence, Death, and the Invisible Enemy: AIDS Activism and Social Movement 'Newness,'" *Social Problems* 36 (1989); Gould, "Sex, Death."

59. See Stephen O. Murray, *American Gay* (Chicago: University of Chicago Press, 1996), 112, for data on the rapid decline in San Francisco cases of rectal gonorrhea from 1981 to 1985.

60. Stine, *AIDS Update 1998*, 243. Similarly, Quam and Ford report that "evidence from epidemiological studies in San Francisco suggests that by 1988 less than 2 percent of seronegative homosexual men were being infected annually." Michael Quam and Nancy Ford, "AIDS Policies and Practices in the United States," in *Action on AIDS: National Policies in Comparative Perspective*, ed. Barbara A. Misztal and David Moss (New York: Greenwood, 1990), 26.

61. Andriote, *Victory Deferred*, 136; Kathleen McAuliffe et al., "AIDS: At the Dawn of Fear," *U.S. News and World Report*, January 12, 1987.

62. Andriote, *Victory Deferred*, chap. 4.

63. Ibid.

64. Shepard, *White Nights*, 105.

65. Ibid.

66. Amy Weiss, "The AIDS Bereaved: Counseling Strategies," in *Face to Face: A Guide to AIDS Counseling*, ed. James W. Dilley, Cheri Pies, and Michael Helquist (San Francisco: AIDS Health Project, 1989), 273.

67. Larry Gross (flg@asc.upenn.edu), "AIDS and the Creation of LGB Communities" (e-mail message to the Gay/Lesbian/Queer Social Sciences List), November 16, 1996.

68. For an example of this argument, see Heller, "Silence Equals Death," viii. In contrast, Steven Seidman rejects the "silver lining" framing of the epidemic. Steven Seidman, "AIDS and the Discursive Construction of Homosexuality," in *The New American Cultural Sociology*, ed. Philip Smith (Cambridge: Cambridge University Press, 1998), 56. See also Robert N. Bellah et al., *Habits of the Heart: Individualism and Commitment in American Life* (New York: Harper and Row, 1985), for a discussion of the difference between life-style enclave and community.

69. Murray, *American Gay*, 197.

70. Jean Latz Griffin, "The Pain and Gain of Being Gay: Reflections on a Cause That Came Out of the Closet 20 Years Ago," *Chicago Tribune*, June 26, 1989, 1.

71. Gould, "Sex, Death," 169.

72. Ibid., 14.

73. When I first noticed the decline in numbers, I questioned my data sources. To compensate for the possibility of deterioration of *Gaybook*, my primary data source, I coded additional resource guides for these years. Even with this overrepresentation, the decline in numbers is a distinct pattern. I coded resource guides from 1995 to ensure that all organizations extant in 1994 were included. See the appendix for more details on the construction of the organizational data set.

74. Other scholars have remarked on AIDS as an impetus to building gay identity in other U.S. cities and other countries, particularly developing countries. See Dennis Altman, "Political Sexualities: Meanings and Identities in the Time of AIDS," in *Conceiving Sexualities: Approaches to Sex Research in a Postmodern World*, ed. Richard G. Parker and John H. Gagnon

(Routledge: New York, 1995), 102, and Matthew Roberts, "Gay Identities and Social Movement Formation in the Developing World: The AIDS Crisis as Catalyst," *Alternatives* 20 (1995). AIDS may have had different effects in different places; my claim should not be generalized beyond highly developed urban centers in the United States.

75. Paul J. DiMaggio and Walter W. Powell, "The Iron Cage Revisited: Institutional Isomorphism and Collective Rationality," in *The New Institutionalism in Organizational Analysis,* ed. Walter W. Powell and Paul J. DiMaggio (Chicago: The University of Chicago Press, [1983] 1991).

76. Robert A. Padgug and Gerald M. Oppenheimer, "Riding the Tiger: AIDS and the Gay Community," in *AIDS: The Making of a Chronic Disease,* ed. Elizabeth Fee and Daniel M. Fox (Berkeley and Los Angeles: University of California Press, 1992), 269.

77. Shepard, *White Nights,* 234.

78. Ibid.

79. Given the powerful groups involved in the epidemic, the extent to which gay communities were able to retain control over AIDS organizations, influence the directions and interpretation of research, and insist on making decisions regarding treatment is surprising. Padgug and Oppenheimer attribute this to the combination of the gay community's early claim staking and high degree of prior community organization. Padgug and Oppenheimer, "Riding the Tiger." Epstein explains how social movement activism enabled AIDS activists to become included in the production of scientific knowledge about AIDS. Epstein, *Impure Science.*

80. Quam and Ford, "AIDS Policies," 26, citing *Confronting AIDS: Update 1988* (Washington: National Academy Press, 1988); Stine, *AIDS Update 1998,* 213, reports that approximately 60 percent of homosexual men in San Francisco were infected in 1998.

81. San Francisco AIDS Foundation, brochure, 1995.

82. Ibid.

83. P. S. Arno, "The Non-profit Sector's Response to the AIDS Epidemic: Community-Based Services in San Francisco," *American Journal of Public Health* 76 (1986).

84. Eric E. Rofes, "Gay Groups vs. AIDS Groups: Averting Civil War in the 1990s," *Out/Look: National Lesbian and Gay Quarterly* 8 (spring 1990). See also Darrell Yates Rist, "AIDS as Obsession: The Deadly Cost of an Obsession," *Nation,* February 13, 1989.

85. Rofes, "Gay Groups," 9.

86. Ibid., 10.

87. Ibid.

88. Ibid.

89. Ibid. In one of the ironies of the epidemic, the loss of gay male leadership to death, burnout, and AIDS activism created a leadership vacuum in gay identity organizations into which lesbians stepped. Paris Poirier (director), *Pride Divide* (film) (New York: Filmakers Library, 1997).

90. Shepard, *White Nights,* 242.

91. This explanation is consistent with an ecological explanation. Ecologists would argue that the carrying capacity of the niche was reduced because of competition for resources with an emerging field drawing on an overlapping resource pool. Michael T. Hannan and John Freeman, "The Population Ecology of Organizations," *American Journal of Sociology* 82 (1977).

In developing this explanation, I evaluated three other explanations of the decline of gay identity organizations in San Francisco in the late 1980s. First: Perhaps gay organizing in the

1970s and 1980s so thoroughly affirmed gay identity that people no longer felt the need to participate in gay organizations. While the notion that cultural success might lead to movement failure is provocative, the fact that the AIDS epidemic provoked a resurgence of stigma associated with homosexuality makes this explanation implausible. If obsolescence of identity politics is a factor, it seems that it would only start becoming relevant in the late 1990s. Thanks to David Frank (personal communication, November 17, 1996) and Paul Halsall ("Re: The End of AIDS," e-mail messages to Gay/Lesbian/Queer Social Sciences List, November 11–12, 1996) for proposing this explanation. See also Debra Friedman and Doug McAdam, "Collective Identity and Activism: Networks, Choices, and the Life of a Social Movement," in *Frontiers in Social Movement Theory*, ed. Aldon D. Morris and Carol McClurg Mueller (New Haven: Yale University Press, 1992). Second: Consolidation of gay identity organizations might present another explanation for the decline in gay identity organizations. However, there is little evidence of an increase in the size of gay identity organizations. If gay identity organizations increased in size, this would likely have increased gradually. But the decline in numbers of organizations happened suddenly. Thanks to David Frank for this hypothesis. Some evidence suggests that in the late 1970s and the early 1980s, the lesbian/gay movement reached a new level of crystallization at the national level. A small fraction of the decline in numbers of San Francisco's gay identity organizations in the late 1980s may have been due to the relocation of local San Francisco organizations to Washington to establish a presence in the national arena. Third: The AIDS epidemic may have led to a decline in the numbers of gay identity organizations by reducing the numbers of individuals available for organizational participation. Illness, care taking, death, or abandonment of gay identity might all have reduced the population of gay men. This explanation would not contradict the general argument that the AIDS epidemic had negative consequences for the gay identity movement. However, evidence suggests that gay men responded to the epidemic by increasing civic involvement. In addition, new individuals growing up, coming out, and migrating to San Francisco have continually replenished the population of gay men. And there seems to have been relatively little movement out of gay identity. Given the costs associated with developing gay identity in the contemporary United States, it is unlikely that men who experienced themselves as having other options would have developed a gay identity in the first place.

92. Paul, Hayes, and Coates, "The Impact of the HIV Epidemic," 347–48.

Chapter Nine

1. For a discussion of the dynamics of stable fields, see Laura Anne Schmidt, *The Corporate Transformation of American Health Care: A Study in Institution Building* (Princeton: Princeton University Press, forthcoming).

2. Gayle Rubin, "Thinking Sex: Notes for a Radical Theory of the Politics of Sexuality," in *Pleasure and Danger: Exploring Female Sexuality*, ed. Carole S. Vance (Boston: Routledge, 1984).

3. See David Gelman, "A Perilous Double Love Life," *Newsweek*, July 13, 1987; Katie Leishman, "Heterosexuals and AIDS," *Atlantic*, February 1987.

4. Joshua Gamson, "Must Identity Movements Self-Destruct? A Queer Dilemma," in *Social Perspectives in Lesbian and Gay Studies: A Reader*, ed. Peter M. Nardi and Beth E. Schneider (London: Routledge, [1995] 1998); Steven Seidman, "Identity and Politics in a 'Postmodern' Gay Culture: Some Historical and Conceptual Notes," in *Fear of a Queer Planet: Queer Politics and Social Theory*, ed. Michael Warner (Minneapolis: University of Minnesota Press, 1993).

5. Gamson, "Must Identity Movements Self-Destruct?"; Seidman, "Identity and Politics."

6. Gamson, "Must Identity Movements Self-Destruct?"; Seidman, "Identity and Politics," 123.

7. This perspective is captured in a series of anthologies of writings on bisexuality published in the early 1990s. Loraine Hutchins and Lani Kaahumanu, eds., *Bi Any Other Name: Bisexual People Speak Out* (Boston: Alyson, 1991); Naomi Tucker, ed., *Bisexual Politics: Theories, Queries, and Visions* (New York: Haworth, 1995); Elizabeth Reba Weise, ed., *Closer to Home: Bisexuality and Feminism* (Seattle: Seal, 1992).

8. Jenny Bourne, "Homelands of the Mind: Jewish Feminism and Identity Politics," *Race and Class* 29, no. 1 (summer 1987): 1.

9. Charles Fernández, "Undocumented Aliens in the Queer Nation," *Out/Look: National Lesbian and Gay Quarterly*, spring 1991, 21–23.

10. Liz A. Highleyman, "Identity and Ideas: Strategies for Bisexuals," in *Bisexual Politics: Theories, Queries, and Visions*, ed. Naomi Tucker (New York: Haworth, 1995), 75.

11. Ibid. Other sources of this critique of identity politics include Todd Gitlin, *The Twilight of Common Dreams: Why America Is Wracked by Culture Wars* (New York: Holt, 1995); L. A. Kauffman, "The Anti-politics of Identity," *Socialist Review* 20, no. 1 (1990): 76; Doug Rossinow, *The Politics of Authenticity* (New York: Columbia University Press, 1998); Seidman, "Identity and Politics."

12. Alexandra Chasin, *Selling Out: The Gay and Lesbian Movement Goes to Market* (New York: St. Martin's, 2000), 224; Seidman, "Identity and Politics in a 'Postmodern' Gay Culture: Some Historical and Conceptual Notes."

13. Allan Bérubé and Jeffrey Escoffier, "Queer/Nation," *Out/Look: National Lesbian and Gay Quarterly* 11 (winter 1991). The confrontational mobilization against AIDS embodied by ACT UP was a precursor to Queer Nation. Stryker and Van Buskirk claim that a group in San Francisco, Arms Akimbo, also foreshadowed queer politics. Stryker and Van Buskirk, *Gay by the Bay*, 121.

14. Stryker and Van Buskirk, *Gay by the Bay*, 121.

15. Bérubé and Escoffier, "Queer/Nation," 14.

16. Seidman, "Identity and Politics," 133.

17. Stryker and Van Buskirk, *Gay by the Bay*, 124.

18. Dan Levy, "Queer Nation in S.F. Suspends Activities," *San Francisco Chronicle*, December 27, 1991.

19. Seidman, "Identity and Politics," 135.

20. Gamson, "Must Identity Movements Self-Destruct?," 594.

21. Chasin, *Selling Out*, 229.

22. Ibid. For a discussion of the marginalization of race and gender issues within queer politics see Bérubé and Escoffier, "Queer/Nation."

23. Chasin, *Selling Out*, 240.

24. The North American Man/Boy Love Association, a group that strives "to educate society about the positive and beneficial nature of man/boy love, and support men and boys involved in consensual sexual and emotional relationships with each other" was founded in Boston in 1978. North American Man/Boy Love Association, *An Introduction to The North American Man/Boy Love Association* (San Francisco: North American Man/Boy Love Association, 1995). The San Francisco chapter, to which she is referring, was listed in guides from 1982–94.

25. Personal interview with Autumn Courtney, October 30, 1990.

26. I attended a meeting of the San Francisco parade committee in February 1994 precisely because one of the agenda items was "voting on possible organization name change." In my field notes, I recorded that five of the slightly more than thirty people in attendance were wearing "Transgender Nation" T-shirts. This provides additional evidence of the highly active role of those who had once been excluded in the renaming of central community organizations.

27. Stryker and Van Buskirk, Gay by the Bay, 118.

28. Scholars and activists have found Robert Michels's "iron law of oligarchy" to be confirmed in case after case since the publication of Political Parties in 1911 (Glencoe: Free Press [1911] 1962). Current patterns in the gay movement seem to be confirming the iron law yet again. This in itself is not particularly interesting or surprising. What is interesting is how the identity logic managed to forestall this process for many years, leading the gay movement to be less oligarchic than parallel movements.

29. Eyal Press and Jennifer Washburn, "The Kept University," Atlantic, March 2000; Schmidt, The Corporate Transformation.

30. Quoted in Laud Humphreys, Out of the Closets: The Sociology of Homosexual Liberation (Englewood Cliffs, N.J.: Prentice-Hall, 1972), 127.

31. Joshua Gamson, "The Gay Movement's Long-Simmering Tensions Erupt in a High-Stakes Mud Fight: Whose Millennium March?," Nation, April 17, 2000. Thanks to Amin Panjwani for alerting me to the importance of the Millennium March, the Human Rights Campaign, and Joshua Gamson's analysis.

32. Ibid.

33. NGLTF identifies itself as "one of the few explicitly progressive national GLBT groups." Kerry Lobel, "Fuzzy Goals, Rising Costs Plague Millennium March," Harvard Gay and Lesbian Review 6, no. 3 (1999).

34. Ibid., 4. See also Phoung Ly, "March Shows Gays Taking Different Roads," Washington Post, March 29, 2000.

35. Kim Diehl, "Here's the Movement, Let's Start Building: An Interview with Barbara Smith," ColorLines 3, no. 3 (2000); Paul Harris, "New Leadership Needed at the HRC," Harvard Gay and Lesbian Review 6, no. 2 (1999); Victoria Stanhope, "NOW Lesbian Rights Summit: More Mayhem about the Millennium, March," Off Our Backs 29, no. 6 (1999).

36. Gamson, "The Gay Movement's Long-Simmering Tensions."

37. Richard Schneider Jr., "Stonewall Hits the Big 3-0," Harvard Gay and Lesbian Review 6, no. 3 (1999), 4. The official slogan of the march was ultimately the less controversial "For Lesbian, Gay and Bisexual Equal Rights and Liberation." David Tuller, "Gays, Lesbians Head for Capital," San Francisco Chronicle, April 17, 1993.

38. Gamson, "The Gay Movement's Long-Simmering Tensions."

39. Crowd estimates from Donald Hammonds, "Where Do We Go from Here?," Post-Gazette, May 10, 2000, A15. For a report on the missing funds, see Darryl Fears and Patrice Gaines, "FBI Probing Gay Festival Funds," Washington Post, May 10, 2000, and Stacy Finz and Dan Levy, "$750,000 Reported Stolen at Gay March in D.C.," San Francisco Chronicle, May 11, 2000. A San Francisco Chronicle editorial suggests that "the clear message of the event was that San Francisco is no longer the center of gay politics." "A Message about Gay Power," San Francisco Chronicle, May 2, 2000, A20. Perhaps a discussion of the Millennium March is indeed a bookend of this study, marking the end of a distinct era in which San Francisco played a pivotal role in shaping the nation's gay culture and gay movement.

40. Chasin, *Selling Out*, 230.

41. Ibid.

42. Ibid.

43. Ibid., 23, 24.

44. Dudley Clendinen and Adam Nagourney, *Out for Good: The Struggle to Build a Gay Rights Movement in America* (New York: Simon and Schuster, 1999), 151.

45. Robert D. Putnam, *Bowling Alone: The Collapse and Revival of American Community* (New York: Simon and Schuster, 2000).

46. Chasin, *Selling Out*.

47. Mandy Carter, "Our LesbiGayTrans Movement at a Crossroads," *Sojourner: The Women's Forum* 23, no. 10 (1998).

48. Diehl, "Here's the Movement," 28.

Chapter Ten

1. Mitchell Stevens, "Kingdom of Children: Culture and Controversy in the Home-schooling Movement" (presentation, Department of Sociology, Indiana University, February 16, 2001).

2. Ann Swidler, "Culture in Action: Symbols and Strategies," *American Sociological Review* 51 (1986); Ann Swidler, *Talk of Love: How Culture Matters* (Chicago: University of Chicago Press, 2001).

3. Neil Fligstein, "Social Skill and the Theory of Fields" (unpublished paper, Department of Sociology, University of California, Berkeley, 2001).

4. Elisabeth S. Clemens, *The People's Lobby: Organizational Innovation and the Rise of Interest Group Politics in the United States, 1890–1925* (Chicago: University of Chicago Press, 1997); Arthur Stinchcombe, "Social Structure and Organizations," in *Handbook of Organizations*, ed. J. G. March (Chicago: Rand McNally, 1965).

5. Fligstein, "Social Skill"; Neil Fligstein and Doug McAdam, "A Political-Cultural Approach to the Problem of Strategic Action" (unpublished paper, Department of Sociology, University of California, Berkeley, 1995).

6. Debra Minkoff, *Organizing for Equality: The Evolution of Women's and Racial-Ethnic Organizations in America, 1955–1985* (New Brunswick: Rutgers University Press, 1995), 1.

7. Joane Nagel, "American Indian Ethnic Renewal: Politics and the Resurgence of Identity," *American Sociological Review* 60 (1995).

8. Robert D. Putnam, *Bowling Alone: The Collapse and Revival of American Community* (New York: Simon and Schuster, 2000), 184.

9. Ibid., 32, 57.

10. Ibid., 148.

11. Ibid., 155.

12. Ibid., 160.

13. Ibid., 158.

14. Ibid., 152.

15. The work of Pamela Paxton supports the view that Putnam has oversimplified. Paxton, "Is Social Capital Declining in the United States? A Multiple Indicator Assessment," *American Journal of Sociology* 105 (1999).

16. Lichterman found that individualism could also, under some conditions, motivate movement participation. Lichterman, *The Search for Political Community: American Activists Reinventing Commitment* (Cambridge: Cambridge University Press, 1996).

Appendix

1. Paul J. DiMaggio and Walter W. Powell, "The Iron Cage Revisited: Institutional Isomorphism and Collective Rationality," in *The New Institutionalism in Organizational Analysis*, ed. Walter W. Powell and Paul J. DiMaggio (Chicago: University of Chicago Press, [1983] 1991), 65.

2. John Mohr, "Community, Bureaucracy, and Social Relief: An Institutional Analysis of Organizational Forms in New York City, 1888–1917" (Ph.D. diss., Department of Sociology, Yale University, 1992), 40, 42.

3. Scholarship participates in affirming the reality of the objects it turns its gaze upon, even when the gaze is purportedly neutral. According to Steven Seidman, "Social constructionism, at least the historical scholarship of the late 1970s through the 1980s, often served as a kind of celebration of the coming of age of a gay ethnic minority." Seidman, "Identity and Politics in a 'Postmodern' Gay Culture: Some Historical and Conceptual Notes," in *Fear of a Queer Planet: Queer Politics and Social Theory*, ed. Michael Warner (Minneapolis: University of Minnesota Press, 1993), 127. By studying the formation of the lesbian/gay field I inevitably participate in solidifying the field. The enthusiasm for this project expressed by community members encountered in doing this research suggests both that they recognized that this research advanced their agenda of identity solidification and that they felt (or assumed) that my understanding of the boundaries and nature of the project matched their own views.

4. For more details on the construction of the database, see also the dissertation on which this book is based, Elizabeth Ann Armstrong, "Multiplying Identities: Identity Elaboration in San Francisco's Lesbian/Gay Organizations, 1964–1994" (Ph.D. diss., Department of Sociology, University of California, Berkeley, 1998).

5. For examples, see Mohr, "Community, Bureaucracy," and Debra Minkoff, *Organizing for Equality: The Evolution of Women's and Racial-Ethnic Organizations in America, 1955–1985* (New Brunswick: Rutgers University Press, 1995).

6. Dennis Altman, *The Homosexualization of America* (Boston: Beacon, 1982), 19.

WORKS CITED

Abbott, Sidney, and Barbara Love. *Sappho Was a Right-On Woman.* New York: Stein and Day, 1972.

Adair, Nancy, and Casey Adair, eds. *Word Is Out: Stories of Our Lives.* New York: Dell, 1978.

Adam, Barry D. *The Rise of a Gay and Lesbian Movement.* Boston: Twayne, 1987.

Advocate. Editorials. September 29, 1971, 22.

Allen, Pamela. *Free Space: A Perspective on the Small Group in Women's Liberation.* Washington, N.J.: Times Change, 1970.

Almaguer, Tomás. "Chicano Men: A Cartography of Homosexual Identity and Behavior." In *Social Perspectives in Lesbian and Gay Studies: A Reader,* edited by Peter M. Nardi and Beth E. Schneider, 537–52 (London: Routledge, 1993).

Altman, Dennis. *AIDS in the Mind of America.* New York: Doubleday, 1986.

———. *Global Sex.* Chicago: University of Chicago Press, 2001.

———. *Homosexual Oppression and Liberation.* 2d ed. New York: New York University Press, 1993.

———. *The Homosexualization of America.* Boston: Beacon, 1982.

———. "Political Sexualities: Meanings and Identities in the Time of AIDS." In *Conceiving Sexualities: Approaches to Sex Research in a Postmodern World,* edited by Richard G. Parker and John H. Gagnon, 97–106. (New York: Routledge, 1995).

Andriote, John-Manuel. *Victory Deferred: How AIDS Changed Gay Life in America.* Chicago: University of Chicago Press, 1999.

Anzaldúa, Gloria. "Bridge, Drawbridge, Sandbar, or Island." In *We Are Everywhere: A Historical Sourcebook of Gay and Lesbian Politics,* edited by Mark Blasius and Shane Phelan, 712–23. (New York: Routledge, [1988] 1997).

Armstrong, Elizabeth Ann. "Multiplying Identities: Identity Elaboration in San Francisco's Lesbian/Gay Organizations, 1964–1994." Ph.D. diss., Department of Sociology, University of California, 1998.

Arno, P. S. "The Non-profit Sector's Response to the AIDS Epidemic: Community-Based Services in San Francisco." *American Journal of Public Health* 76 (1986): 1325–30.

Atkinson, Ti-Grace. *Amazon Odyssey: The First Collection of Writings by the Political Pioneer of the Women's Movement.* New York: Link, 1974.

Bayer, Ronald. *Private Acts, Social Consequences: AIDS and the Politics of Public Health.* New York: Free Press, 1989.

Bayer, Ronald, and David L. Kirp. "The United States: At the Center of the Storm." In *AIDS in the Industrialized Democracies: Passions, Politics, and Policies,* edited by David L. Kirp and Ronald Bayer, 7–48. (New Brunswick: Rutgers University Press, 1992).

Beame, Thom. "Racism from a Black Perspective." In *Black Men/White Men,* edited by Michael J. Smith, 57–63 (San Francisco: Gay Sunshine, 1983).

Beardemphl, Bill. "Conference Trip a Bummer." *Vector,* September 1968, 5, 28.

———. "On Leadership." *Vector,* January 1965, 2.

———. "President's Column." *Vector,* August 1966, 2.

Bellah, Robert N., Richard Madsen, William M. Sullivan, Ann Swidler, and Steven M. Tip-ton. *Habits of the Heart: Individualism and Commitment in American Life.* New York: Harper and Row, 1985.

Benford, Robert D., and David A. Snow. "Framing Processes and Social Movements: An Overview and Assessment." *Annual Review of Sociology* 26 (2000): 611–39.

Berkowitz, Richard, and Michael Callen. "How to Have Sex in an Epidemic." In *We Are Ev-erywhere: A Historical Sourcebook of Gay and Lesbian Politics,* edited by Mark Blasius and Shane Phelan, 571–74 (New York: Routledge, [1988] 1997).

Berlandt, Konstantin. "Gay Parade: Last Meetings." *Bay Area Reporter,* June 5, 1980, 5.

———. "Gay Parade Unity Ratified: Theme Debated." *Bay Area Reporter,* February 26, 1981, 11.

———. "Parade Committees to Fuse: No Funds for Audit." *Bay Area Reporter,* December 4, 1980, 10.

———. "Parade Dissidents Meet and Challenge Structure." *Bay Area Reporter,* August 28, 1980, 8.

Bernstein, Mary. "Celebration and Suppression: The Strategic Uses of Identity by the Les-bian and Gay Movement." *American Journal of Sociology* 103 (1997): 531–65.

Bérubé, Allan. *Coming Out under Fire: The History of Gay Men and Women in World War II.* New York: Macmillan, 1990.

———. "The First Stonewall." *Lesbian and Gay Freedom Parade and Celebration Magazine,* June 1983, 27.

Bérubé, Allan, and Jeffrey Escoffier. "Queer/Nation." *Out/Look: National Lesbian and Gay Quar-terly* 11 (winter 1991): 14–23.

Bourdieu, Pierre. *Outline of a Theory of Practice.* Cambridge: Cambridge University Press, 1977.

Bourne, Jenny. "Homelands of the Mind: Jewish Feminism and Identity Politics." *Race and Class* 29, no. 1 (summer 1987): 1–24.

Breines, Wini. *Community and Organization in the New Left, 1962–1968: The Great Refusal.* New Brunswick: Rutgers University Press, 1989.

Breton, R. "Institutional Completeness of Ethnic Communities and the Personal Relations of Immigrants." *American Journal of Sociology* 70 (1964): 293–318.

Broshears, Ray. "S.I.R., the Society for Individual Rights[,] Conducts Fantastic 'Work-In' at Federal Building." *Gay Activists Alliance Lifeline,* June 1971, 1.

Buechler, Steven M. "Beyond Resource Mobilization? Emerging Trends in Social Move-ment Theory." *Sociological Quarterly* 34, no. 2 (1993): 217–35.

Bull, Chris, and John Gallagher. *Perfect Enemies: The Religious Right, the Gay Movement, and the Poli-tics of the 1990s.* New York: Crown, 1996.

Calhoun, Craig. " 'New Social Movements' of the Early Nineteenth Century." In *Repertoires and Cycles of Collective Action,* edited by M. Traugott, 173–215 (Durham: Duke University Press, 1995).

Callen, Michael. *Surviving AIDS.* New York: HarperCollins, 1990.

Carroll, Glenn R., ed. *Ecological Models of Organization.* Cambridge: Ballinger, 1988.

Carroll, Glenn R., and Michael T. Hannan. "Density Dependence in the Evolution of Popu-lations of Newspaper Organizations." *American Sociological Review* 54 (1989): 524–41.

Carson, Clayborne. *In Struggle: SNCC and the Black Awakening of the 1960s.* Cambridge: Harvard University Press, 1981.

Carter, Mandy. "Our LesbiGayTrans Movement at a Crossroads." *Sojourner: The Women's Forum* 23, no. 10 (1998): 6.

Case, John, and Rosemary C. R. Taylor, eds. *Co-ops, Communes, and Collectives: Experiments in Social Change in the 1960s and 1970s.* New York: Pantheon, 1979.

Chasin, Alexandra. *Selling Out: The Gay and Lesbian Movement Goes to Market.* New York: St. Martin's, 2000.

Chauncey, George. *Gay New York: Gender, Urban Culture, and the Making of the Gay Male World, 1890–1940.* New York: HarperCollins, 1994.

"Christopher Street West S.F. Gay Parade." *Advocate,* July 19, 1972, 3, 30.

Clemens, Elisabeth. "Organizational Repertoires and Institutional Change: Women's Groups and the Transformation of U.S. Politics, 1890–1920." *American Journal of Sociology* 98 (1993): 775–98.

———. *The People's Lobby: Organizational Innovation and the Rise of Interest Group Politics in the United States, 1890–1925.* Chicago: University of Chicago Press, 1997.

Clemens, Elisabeth, and James Cook. "Politics and Institutionalism: Explaining Durability and Change." *Annual Review of Sociology* 25 (1999): 441–66.

Clendinen, Dudley, and Adam Nagourney. *Out for Good: The Struggle to Build a Gay Rights Movement in America.* New York: Simon and Schuster, 1999.

Cohen, Cathy Jean. "Power, Resistance, and the Construction of Crisis: Marginalized Communities Respond to AIDS." Ph.D. diss., Department of Political Science, University of Michigan, 1993.

Cohen, Jean L. "Strategy or Identity? New Theoretical Paradigms and Contemporary Social Movements." *Social Research* 52 (1985): 663–716.

Cole, Rob. "Collision in San Francisco. 1. Old, New Ideas Tangle at NACHO Convention." *Advocate,* September 30, 1970, 1–2, 6–7, 12, 23.

———. "Collision in San Francisco. 2. NACHO 'Liberated' on Final Day." *Advocate,* October 14, 1970, 8, 11.

Collins, Don. Editorial. *Vector,* October 1969, 10.

———. "Interview with Dorr Jones." *Vector,* September 1969, 20–21, 30–31.

"CRH 'A Brief of Injustices' Published." *Vector,* September 1965, 2.

Cruikshank, Margaret. *The Gay and Lesbian Liberation Movement.* New York: Routledge, 1992.

Curtis, W., ed. *Revelations: A Collection of Gay Male Coming Out Stories.* Boston: Alyson, 1988.

Cutler, Marvin. *Homosexuals Today: A Handbook of Organizations and Publications.* Los Angeles: ONE, 1956.

D. C. and R. S. "Ma Bell Gets Yellow Suit!!!" *Vector,* October 1968, 5, 29.

Daly, Mary. *Gyn/Ecology.* Boston: Beacon, 1978.

Dank, Barry M. "Coming Out in the Gay World." *Psychiatry* 34 (May 1971): 180–97.

Dawidoff, Robert. "Kill a Queer for Christ." In *Long Road to Freedom: The Advocate History of the Gay and Lesbian Movement,* ed. Mark Thompson, 145–46 (New York: St. Martin's, 1994).

DeMarco, Joe. "Gay Racism." In *Black Men/White Men,* edited by Michael J. Smith, 109–18 (San Francisco: Gay Sunshine, 1983).

D'Emilio, John. "After Stonewall." In *Making Trouble: Essays on Gay History, Politics, and the University,* edited by John D'Emilio, 234–74 (New York: Routledge, 1992).

———. Foreword to *Out of the Closets: Voices of Gay Liberation,* edited by Karla Jay and Allen Young, xi–xxix (New York: New York University Press, [1972] 1992).

———. "Gay Politics, Gay Community: San Francisco's Experience." In *Making Trouble: Essays on Gay History, Politics, and the University,* edited by John D'Emilio, 74–95 (New York: Routledge, 1992).

————. "A Generation of Progress." In *Making Trouble: Essays on Gay History, Politics, and the University*, edited by John D'Emilio, 224–33 (New York: Routledge, 1992).

————. *Making Trouble: Essays on Gay History, Politics, and the University*. New York: Routledge, 1992.

————. *Sexual Politics, Sexual Communities: The Making of a Homosexual Minority in the United States, 1940–1970*. Chicago: University of Chicago Press, 1983.

Diehl, Kim. "Here's the Movement, Let's Start Building: An Interview with Barbara Smith." *ColorLines* 3, no. 3 (2000): 28.

DiMaggio, Paul J. "Interest and Agency in Institutional Theory." In *Institutional Patterns and Organizations: Culture and Environment*, edited by Lynne Zucker, 3–22 (Cambridge: Ballinger, 1988).

————. "State Expansion and Organizational Fields." In *Organizational Theory and Public Policy*, edited by Richard H. Hall and Robert E. Quinn, 147–61 (Beverly Hills: Sage, 1983).

DiMaggio, Paul J., and Walter W. Powell. "The Iron Cage Revisited: Institutional Isomorphism and Collective Rationality." In *The New Institutionalism in Organizational Analysis*, edited by Walter W. Powell and Paul J. DiMaggio, 63–82 (Chicago: University of Chicago Press, [1983] 1991).

Dobbin, Franklin R. "Cultural Models of Organization: The Social Construction of Rational Organizing Principles." In *The Sociology of Culture: Emerging Theoretical Perspectives*, edited by Diana Crane, 117–41 (Oxford: Blackwell, 1994).

Dong, Arthur (director). *The Question of Equality*. Part 1: *Out Rage '69* (television program). New York: Testing the Limits, 1995.

Duberman, Martin, Michelangelo Signorile, and Urvashi Vaid. "A Roundtable with Betsy Billard: State of the Struggle." *Harvard Gay and Lesbian Review* 6, no. 3 (1999): 17.

Echols, Alice. *Daring to Be BAD: Radical Feminism in America, 1967–1975*. Minneapolis: University of Minnesota Press, 1989.

————. "The Taming of the Id: Feminist Sexual Politics, 1968–83." In *Pleasure and Danger: Exploring Female Sexuality*, edited by Carole S. Vance, 50–72 (Boston: Routledge, 1984).

————. " 'We Gotta Get Out of This Place': Notes toward a Remapping of the Sixties." *Socialist Review* 22, no. 2 (1992): 9–33.

Edwards, Tim. *Erotics and Politics: Gay Male Sexuality, Masculinity, and Feminism*. London: Routledge, 1994.

Epstein, Robert (director). *The Times of Harvey Milk*. Beverly Hills: Pacific Arts Video, 1984.

Epstein, Steven. "Gay Politics, Ethnic Identity: The Limits of Social Constructionism." *Socialist Review* 17, no. 2 (1987): 10–54.

————. *Impure Science: AIDS, Activism, and the Politics of Knowledge*. Berkeley and Los Angeles: University of California Press, 1996.

Escoffier, Jeffrey. "Sexual Revolution and the Politics of Gay Identity." *Socialist Review* 15, no. 3 (1985): 119–53.

Evans, Sara Margaret. *Personal Politics: The Roots of Women's Liberation in the Civil Rights Movement and the New Left*. New York: Knopf, 1979.

Faderman, Lillian. *Odd Girls and Twilight Lovers: A History of Lesbian Life in Twentieth-Century America*. New York: Columbia University Press, 1991.

Fears, Darryl, and Patrice Gaines. "FBI Probing Gay Festival Funds." *Washington Post*, May 10, 2000, B04.

Fernández, Charles. "Undocumented Aliens in the Queer Nation." *Out/Look: National Lesbian and Gay Quarterly* 12 (spring 1991): 20–23.

Ferree, Myra Marx, and Frederick D. Miller. "Winning Hearts and Minds: Some Psychological Contributions to the Resource Mobilization Perspective of Social Movements." Unpublished paper, 1977.

Finz, Stacy, and Dan Levy. "$750,000 Reported Stolen at Gay March in D.C." *San Francisco Chronicle,* May 11, 2000, A6.

Fischer, Claude. "20th-Year Assessment of the Subcultural Theory of Urbanism." *American Journal of Sociology* 101 (1995): 543–77.

FitzGerald, Frances. *Cities on a Hill: A Journey through Contemporary American Cultures.* New York: Simon and Schuster, [1981] 1986.

FitzGibbon, Carole. "Gay Day Official Responds to Dissidents." *Bay Area Reporter,* June 5, 1980, 1.

Fligstein, Neil. "The Cultural Construction of Political Action: The Case of the European Community's Single Unitary Market Program." Paper presented at the American Sociological Association annual meeting, Miami, 1993.

———. "Markets as Politics: A Political Cultural Approach to Market Institutions." *American Sociological Review* 61 (1996): 656–73.

———. "Social Skill and the Theory of Fields." Unpublished paper, Department of Sociology, University of California, Berkeley, 2001.

———. *The Transformation of Corporate Control.* Cambridge: Harvard University Press, 1990.

Fligstein, Neil, and Doug McAdam. "A Political-Cultural Approach to the Problem of Strategic Action." Unpublished paper, Department of Sociology, University of California, Berkeley, 1995.

Fortunato, John. *AIDS: The Spiritual Dilemma.* New York: Harper and Row, 1987.

Foucault, Michel. *The History of Sexuality.* Vol. 1: *An Introduction.* Translated by Robert Hurley. New York: Vintage, 1978.

Freedberg, Louis, and Christopher Heredia. "Mixed Feelings about Gay March." *San Francisco Chronicle,* April 10, 2000, A2.

Freeman, Jo. *The Politics of Women's Liberation.* New York: McKay, 1975.

Friedland, Roger, and Robert R. Alford. "Bringing Society Back In: Symbols, Practices, and Institutional Contradictions." In *The New Institutionalism in Organizational Analysis,* edited by Walter W. Powell and Paul J. DiMaggio, 232–63 (Chicago: University of Chicago Press, 1991).

Friedman, Debra, and Doug McAdam. "Collective Identity and Activism: Networks, Choices, and the Life of a Social Movement." In *Frontiers in Social Movement Theory,* edited by Aldon D. Morris and Carol McClurg Mueller, 156–73 (New Haven: Yale University Press, 1992).

Gagnon, John H., and William Simon. "Homosexuality: The Formulation of a Sociological Perspective." In *Social Perspectives in Lesbian and Gay Studies: A Reader,* edited by Peter M. Nardi and Beth E. Schneider, 59–67 (London: Routledge, [1967] 1998).

Gamson, Joshua. "The Gay Movement's Long-Simmering Tensions Erupt in a High-Stakes Mud Fight: Whose Millennium March?" *Nation,* April 17, 2000, 16.

———. "Must Identity Movements Self-Destruct? A Queer Dilemma." In *Social Perspectives in Lesbian and Gay Studies: A Reader,* edited by Peter M. Nardi and Beth E. Schneider, 589–604 (London: Routledge, [1995] 1998).

———. "Silence, Death, and the Invisible Enemy: AIDS Activism and Social Movement 'Newness.'" *Social Problems* 36 (1989): 351–67.

Gamson, William. *The Strategy of Social Protest.* 2d ed. Belmont, Calif.: Wadsworth, 1990.

Garber, Eric. *A Historical Directory of Lesbian and Gay Establishments in the San Francisco Bay Area.* San Francisco: San Francisco Lesbian and Gay History Project, 1986.

Garfield, Charles. *Sometimes My Heart Goes Numb: Love and Caregiving in a Time of AIDS*. San Francisco: Jossey-Bass, 1995.

"Gay 'Guerillas' Picket Drag Ball." *San Francisco Free Press*, November 1, 1969, 1.

"Gay Freedom Week: 1981." *Bay Area Reporter*. June 18, 1981, 8.

Gay Revolution Party Women's Caucus. "Realesbians and Politicalesbians." In *Out of the Closets: Voices of Gay Liberation*, edited by Karla Jay and Allen Young, 177–81 (New York: New York University Press, [1972] 1992).

Gelman, David. "A Perilous Double Love Life." *Newsweek*, July 13, 1987, 44.

George, Perry A. "The Gay Revolution (?) and S.I.R.?" *Vector*, January 1970, 11, 28.

Gitlin, Todd. *The Sixties: Years of Hope, Days of Rage*. New York: Bantam, 1987.

———. *The Twilight of Common Dreams: Why America Is Wracked by Culture Wars*. New York: Holt, 1995.

Gomez, Jewelle. "Out of the Past." In *The Question of Equality: Lesbian and Gay Politics in America since Stonewall*, edited by David Deitcher, 18–65 (New York: Scribner, 1995).

Gould, Deborah. "Sex, Death, and the Politics of Anger: Emotions and Reason in ACT UP's Fight against AIDS." Ph.D. diss., Department of Political Science, University of Chicago, 2000.

Gould, Roger V. *Insurgent Identities: Class, Community, and Protest in Paris from 1848 to the Commune*. Chicago: University of Chicago Press, 1995.

Greene, Beverly, ed. *Ethnic and Cultural Diversity among Lesbians and Gay Men*. Vol. 3: *Psychological Perspectives on Lesbian and Gay Issues*. Thousand Oaks, Calif.: Sage, 1997.

Griffin, Jean Latz. "The Pain and Gain of Being Gay: Reflections on a Cause That Came Out of the Closet 20 Years Ago." *Chicago Tribune*, June 26, 1989, 1.

Hammonds, Donald. "Where Do We Go from Here?" *Pittsburgh Post-Gazette*, May 10, 2000, A15.

Hannan, Michael T. "The Ecology of Organizational Mortality: American Labor Unions, 1836–1985." *American Journal of Sociology* 94 (1988): 25–52.

Hannan, Michael T., and John Freeman. "Density Dependence in the Growth of Organizational Populations." In *Ecological Models of Organizations*, edited by Glenn R. Carroll, 7–31 (Cambridge: Ballinger, 1988).

———. *Organizational Ecology*. Cambridge: Harvard University Press, 1989.

———. "The Population Ecology of Organizations." *American Journal of Sociology* 82 (1977): 929–64.

Harris, Paul. "New Leadership Needed at the HRC." *Harvard Gay and Lesbian Review* 6, no. 2 (1999): 5.

Harry, Joseph, and William B. DeVall. *The Social Organization of Gay Males*. New York: Praeger, 1978.

Haveman, Heather A., and Hayagreeva Rao. "Structuring a Theory of Moral Sentiments: Institutional and Organizational Coevolution in the Early Thrift Industry." *American Journal of Sociology* 102 (1997): 1606–51.

Hayden, Tom. *Reunion: A Memoir*. New York: Random House, 1988.

Heller, Karen S. "Silence Equals Death: Discourses on AIDS and Identity in the Gay Press, 1981–1986." Ph.D. diss., Department of Medical Anthropology, University of California, San Francisco, 1993.

Herrell, Richard K. "The Symbolic Strategies of Chicago's Gay and Lesbian Pride Day Parade." In *Gay Culture in America: Essays from the Field*, edited by Gilbert Herdt, 225–52 (Boston: Beacon, 1992).

Highleyman, Liz A. "Identity and Ideas: Strategies for Bisexuals." In *Bisexual Politics: Theories, Queries, and Visions*, edited by Naomi Tucker, 73–92 (New York: Haworth, 1995).

Hippler, Mike. "20 Years of Parade Memories." *San Francisco Lesbian/Gay Freedom Day Parade and Celebration Magazine,* June 25, 1989, 17–23, 44–45.

Hoagland, Sarah H., and Julia Penelope, eds. *For Lesbians Only: A Separatist Anthology.* London: Onlywomen, 1988.

Hooker, Evelyn. "Male Homosexuals and Their Worlds." In *Sexual Inversion: The Multiple Roots of Homosexuality,* edited by Judd Marmor, 83–107 (New York: Basic, 1965).

Humphreys, Laud. "New Styles in Homosexual Manliness." *Trans-Action* 8 (March–April 1971): 38–66.

———. *Out of the Closets: The Sociology of Homosexual Liberation.* Englewood Cliffs, N.J.: Prentice-Hall, 1972.

Hutchins, Loraine, and Lani Kaahumanu, eds. *Bi Any Other Name: Bisexual People Speak Out.* Boston: Alyson, 1991.

Inglehart, Ronald. *The Silent Revolution: Changing Values and Political Styles among Western Publics.* Princeton: Princeton University Press, 1977.

Irkin, Michael Francis. "The Homosexual Liberation Movement: What Direction?" *San Francisco Free Press,* December 7, 1969, 8–9.

Isserman, Maurice. *If I Had a Hammer: The Death of the Old Left and the Birth of the New Left.* New York: Basic, 1987.

Jasper, James M. *The Art of Moral Protest.* Chicago: University of Chicago Press, 1997.

Jay, Karla, and Allen Young, eds. *Out of the Closets: Voices of Gay Liberation.* 20th-anniversary ed. New York: New York University Press, 1992.

Jenkins, J. Craig. "Foundation Funding of Progressive Social Movements." In *The Grant Seekers Guide,* edited by Jill Shellow, 7–17 (Nyack, N.Y.: Glenmeade, 1985).

———. "Nonprofit Organizations and Policy Advocacy." In *The Nonprofit Sector: A Research Handbook,* edited by Walter Powell, 296–318 (New Haven: Yale University Press, 1987).

———. *The Politics of Insurgency: The Farm Worker Movement in the 1960s.* New York: Columbia University Press, 1985.

Jenkins, J. Craig, and Craig M. Ekert. "Channeling Black Insurgency." *American Sociological Review* 51 (1986): 812–29.

Jepperson, Ronald L. "Institutions, Institutional Effects, and Institutionalism." In *The New Institutionalism in Organizational Analysis,* edited by Walter W. Powell and Paul J. DiMaggio, 143–63 (Chicago: University of Chicago Press, 1991).

Johnson, David K. " 'Homosexual Citizens': Washington's Gay Community Confronts the Civil Service." *Washington History,* fall/winter 1994–95, 44–63, 93–96.

Johnston, Jill. "Are Lesbians 'Gay'?" *Ms.,* December 1975, 85.

———. *Lesbian Nation: The Feminist Solution.* New York: Simon and Schuster, 1973.

Jonsen, Albert R., and Jeff Stryker, eds. *The Social Impact of AIDS in the United States.* Washington: National Academy, 1993.

Joseph, Stephen C. *Dragon within the Gates: The Once and Future AIDS Epidemic.* New York: Carrol and Graf, 1992.

Julien, Isaac, and Kobena Mercer. "True Confessions: A Discourse on Images of Black Male Sexuality." In *Brother to Brother,* edited by Essex Hemphill, 167–73 (Boston: Alyson, 1991).

Kanter, Rosabeth Moss. *Commitment and Community: Communes and Utopias in Sociological Perspective.* Cambridge: Harvard University Press, 1972.

Kauffman, L. A. "The Anti-politics of Identity." *Socialist Review* 20, no. 1 (1990): 67–80.

Kayal, Philip M. *Bearing Witness: Gay Men's Health Crisis and the Politics of AIDS.* Boulder: Westview, 1993.

Kennedy, Elizabeth Lapovsky, and Madeline D. Davis. *Boots of Leather, Slippers of Gold: The History of a Lesbian Community.* New York: Routledge, 1993.

King, Mary. *Freedom Song: A Personal Story of the 1960s Civil Rights Movement.* New York: Morrow, 1987.

Kinsella, James. *Covering the Plague: AIDS and the American Media.* New Brunswick: Rutgers University Press, 1989.

Kissack, Terrence. "Freaking Fag Revolutionaries: New York's Gay Liberation Front, 1969–1971." *Radical History Review* 62 (1995): 104–34.

Kitschelt, Herbert. "New Social Movements in West Germany and the United States." *Political Power and Social Theory* 5 (1985): 273–324.

Klages, Ellen. "When the Bar Was the Only Place in Town." *San Francisco Lesbian and Gay Freedom Parade and Celebration Magazine,* 1984, 39–41.

Kleidman, Rob, Dan Cress, and Ann Mische. "CBSM Workshop Proposal." *Critical Mass Bulletin: Newsletter of the Section on Collective Behavior and Social Movements, American Sociological Association,* spring 2001.

Laurence, Leo. "Gay Revolution." *Vector.* April 1969, 11, 25.

———. "My Boss Knows: Gay-Is-Good at Work, Too!" *Vector,* January 1969, 13, 29.

——— [Gary Patterson, pseud.]. "Gay Is Good." *Vector,* November 1968, 5, 27.

Lee, Yong. "A Question of Political Styles: A Comparison of Gays and Lesbians of Color in Inclusive and Ethnic Organizations." Senior thesis, Department of Sociology, University of California, Berkeley, 1994.

Leishman, Katie. "Heterosexuals and AIDS." *Atlantic,* February 1987, 39–58.

Levy, Dan. "Queer Nation in S.F. Suspends Activities/Racism, Sexism Issues Spur Membership Vote." *San Francisco Chronicle,* December 27, 1991, A21.

Lichterman, Paul. *The Search for Political Community: American Activists Reinventing Commitment.* Cambridge: Cambridge University Press, 1996.

"The Life Style of the Homosexual Succeeds." *Vector,* December 1968, 34, 40.

Linden, Robin Ruth, Darlene R. Pagano, Diana E. H. Russell, and Susan Leigh Star, eds. *Against Sadomasochism: A Radical Feminist Analysis.* San Francisco: Frog in the Well, 1982.

Littlejohn, Larry. "President's Column." *Vector,* January 1970, 10, 27.

———. "The President's Corner." *Vector,* November 1968, 9.

Lobel, Kerry. "Fuzzy Goals, Rising Costs Plague Millennium March." *Harvard Gay and Lesbian Review* 6, no. 3 (1999): 4.

Lorch, Paul. "Gay Men Dying: Shifting Gears, Part 1." *Bay Area Reporter,* March 31, 1983, 6.

Lorde, Audre. *Sister Outsider: Essays and Speeches by Audre Lorde.* Freedom, Calif.: Crossing, 1984.

Lounsbury, Michael, and Marc J. Ventresca. Introduction to *Social Structure and Organizations Revisited,* edited by Michael Lounsbury and Marc J. Ventresca (Oxford: JAI, forthcoming).

Ly, Phuong. "March Shows Gays Taking Different Roads." *Washington Post,* March 29, 2000, B01.

"Marching in the Pride Parade? Here's How to Find Your Contingent. . . ." *San Francisco Bay Times,* June 15, 1995, 8.

Marcus, Eric. *Making History: The Struggle for Gay and Lesbian Equal Rights, 1945–1990, An Oral History.* New York: HarperCollins, 1992.

Marotta, Toby. *The Politics of Homosexuality.* Boston: Houghton Mifflin, 1981.

Martin, Del. "Columnist Resigns, Blasts Male Chauvinism." *Vector,* October 1970, 35–37, 53.

Martin, Del, and Phyllis Lyon. *Lesbian/Woman.* 20th-anniversary ed. Volcano, Calif.: Volcano, 1991.

Mass, Lawrence D. "Early Warnings." In *Long Road to Freedom: The Advocate History of the Gay and Lesbian Movement,* edited by Mark Thompson, 211–12 (New York: St. Martin's, 1994).

Maupin, Armistead. *Tales of the City.* New York: HarperPerennial, 1978.

McAdam, Doug. *Freedom Summer*. New York: Oxford University Press, 1988.

———. *Political Process and the Development of Black Insurgency, 1930–1970*. Chicago: University of Chicago Press, 1982.

McAdam, Doug, John D. McCarthy, and Mayer N. Zald, eds. *Comparative Perspectives on Social Movements: Political Opportunities, Mobilizing Structures, and Cultural Framings*. Cambridge: Cambridge University Press, 1996.

McAdam, Doug, and W. Richard Scott. "Organizations and Movements." Department of Sociology, Stanford University, 2001.

McAuliffe, Kathleen, Joseph Carrey, Stacy Wells, Barbara E. Quick, and Muriel Dobbin. "AIDS: At the Dawn of Fear." *U.S. News and World Report*, January 12, 1987, 60–70.

McCarthy, John D., David W. Britt, and Mark Wolfson. "The Institutional Channeling of Social Movements by the State in the United States." *Research in Social Movements, Conflicts, and Change* 13 (1991): 45–76.

McCarthy, John D., and Mayer N. Zald. "Resource Mobilization and Social Movements: A Partial Theory." *American Journal of Sociology* 82 (1977): 1212–41.

Meeker, Martin. " 'I Wanted to Be at the Gay Center of the Universe': Exploring Motivations among Gay and Lesbian Migrants: 1945–1992." Unpublished paper, Department of History, University of Southern California, 1995.

Melucci, Alberto. *Nomads of the Present: Social Movements and Individual Needs in Contemporary Society*. Philadelphia: Temple University Press, 1989.

———. "The Symbolic Challenge of Contemporary Movements." *Social Research* 52 (1985): 789–816.

"A Message about Gay Power." *San Francisco Chronicle*, May 2, 2000, A20.

Mendenhall, George. "The Editor Comments." *Vector*, June 1971, 4.

Methered, Fred R. "I Love a Parade." *Bay Area Reporter*, June 18, 1981, 6.

Meyer, David S., and Douglas R. Imig. "Political Opportunity and the Rise and Decline of Interest Group Sectors." *Social Science Journal* 30, no. 3 (1993): 253–70.

Meyer, John W., and Brian Rowan. "Institutionalized Organizations: Formal Structure as Myth and Ceremony." In *The New Institutionalism in Organizational Analysis*, edited by Walter W. Powell and Paul J. DiMaggio, 41–62 (Chicago: University of Chicago Press, [1977] 1991).

Meyer, John W., and W. Richard Scott. *Organizational Environments: Ritual and Rationality*. Beverly Hills: Sage, 1983.

Michael, M. "Alternate Prophylaxis" (letter). *New York Native*, October 21, 1985, 5.

Michels, Robert. *Political Parties*. Glencoe: Free Press, [1911] 1962.

Miller, James. *Democracy Is in the Streets: From Port Huron to the Siege of Chicago*. New York: Simon and Schuster, 1987.

Minkoff, Debra. *Organizing for Equality: The Evolution of Women's and Racial-Ethnic Organizations in America, 1955–1985*. New Brunswick: Rutgers University Press, 1995.

Mohr, John. "Community, Bureaucracy, and Social Relief: An Institutional Analysis of Organizational Forms in New York City, 1888–1917." Ph.D. diss., Department of Sociology, Yale University, 1992.

Moore, Kelly, and Michael P. Young. "Social Movements and Organizations." Unpublished paper, Barnard College, Department of Sociology, 2000.

Moraga, Cherríe, and Gloria Anzaldúa, eds. *This Bridge Called My Back: Writings by Radical Women of Color*. New York: Kitchen Table/Women of Color, 1983.

Morris, Aldon. *The Origins of the Civil Rights Movement: Black Communities Organizing for Change*. New York: Free Press, 1984.

Murray, Stephen O. *American Gay*. Chicago: University of Chicago Press, 1996.

Nagel, Joane. "American Indian Ethnic Renewal: Politics and the Resurgence of Identity." *American Sociological Review* 60 (1995): 947–65.

North American Man/Boy Love Association. *An Introduction to The North American Man/Boy Love Association.* San Francisco: North American Man/Boy Love Association, 1995.

Nungesser, Lon G. *Epidemic of Courage: Facing AIDS in America.* New York: St. Martin's, 1986.

Oberschall, Anthony. "The Decline of the 1960s Social Movements." *Research in Social Movements, Conflicts and Change* 1 (1978): 257–89.

Olson, Mancur. *The Logic of Collective Action.* Cambridge: Harvard University Press, 1965.

Olzak, Susan. *The Dynamics of Ethnic Competition and Conflict.* Stanford: Stanford University Press, 1992.

Olzak, Susan, and Elizabeth West. "Ethnic Conflict and the Rise and Fall of Ethnic Newspapers." *American Sociological Review* 56 (1991): 458–74.

Overseth, Marcus. "Grows Rapidly: What Kind of People?" *San Francisco Free Press,* December 7, 1969, 6.

Padgug, Robert A., and Gerald M. Oppenheimer. "Riding the Tiger: AIDS and the Gay Community." In *AIDS: The Making of a Chronic Disease,* edited by Elizabeth Fee and Daniel M. Fox, 245–78 (Berkeley and Los Angeles: University of California Press, 1992).

Paul, Jay P., Robert B. Hayes, and Thomas J. Coates. "The Impact of the HIV Epidemic on U.S. Gay Male Communities." In *Lesbian, Gay, and Bisexual Identities over the Lifespan: Psychological Perspectives,* edited by Anthony R. D'Augelli and Charlotte J. Patterson, 347–97 (New York: Oxford University Press, 1995).

Paul, William. "Minority Status for Gay People: Majority Reaction and Social Context." In *Homosexuality: Social, Psychological, and Biological Issues,* edited by William Paul, James D. Weinrich, John C. Gonsiorek, and Mary E. Hotvedt, 351–70 (Beverly Hills: Sage, 1982).

Paxton, Pamela. "Is Social Capital Declining in the United States? A Multiple Indicator Assessment." *American Journal of Sociology* 105 (1999): 88–127.

Penelope, Julia, and Susan Wolfe, eds. *Lesbian Culture: An Anthology.* Freedom, Calif.: Crossing, 1993.

———, eds. *The Original Coming Out Stories.* Freedom, Calif.: Crossing, 1989.

Pennington, Greg L. "A Parade Almanac." *San Francisco Lesbian/Gay Freedom Parade and Celebration Magazine,* June 25, 1989.

Perrow, Charles, and Maurio F. Guillen. *The AIDS Disaster.* New Haven: Yale University Press, 1990.

Pichardo, Nelson A. "New Social Movements: A Critical Review." *Annual Review of Sociology* 23 (1997): 411–30.

Poirier, Paris (director). *Pride Divide* (film). New York: Filmakers Library, 1997.

Polletta, Francesca, and James M. Jasper. "Collective Identity and Social Movements." *Annual Review of Sociology* 27 (2001): 283–305.

Powell, Walter W., and Paul J. DiMaggio, eds. *The New Institutionalism in Organizational Analysis.* Chicago: University of Chicago Press, 1991.

Press, Eyal, and Jennifer Washburn. "The Kept University." *Atlantic,* March 2000, 39–52.

Putnam, Robert D. *Bowling Alone: The Collapse and Revival of American Community.* New York: Simon and Schuster, 2000.

Quam, Michael, and Nancy Ford. "AIDS Policies and Practices in the United States." In *Action on AIDS: National Policies in Comparative Perspective,* edited by Barbara A. Misztal and David Moss, 25–50 (New York: Greenwood, 1990).

Radicalesbians. "The Woman-Identified Woman." In *Out of the Closets: Voices of Gay Liberation,* edited by Karla Jay and Allen Young, 172–77 (New York: New York University Press, [1972] 1992).

Raeburn, Nicole. "The Rise of Lesbian, Gay, and Bisexual Rights in the Corporate Work-place: The Impact of Employee Mobilization." Paper presented at the Pacific Sociological Association meeting, San Francisco, 1998.

Rao, Hayagreeva, Calvin Morrill, and Mayer N. Zald. "Power Plays: How Social Movements and Collective Action Create New Organizational Forms." *Research in Organizational Behaviour* 22 (2000): 239–82.

Reagon, Bernice Johnson. "Coalition Politics: Turning the Century." In *Home Girls: A Black Feminist Anthology,* edited by Barbara Smith, 356–68 (New York: Kitchen Table/Women of Color, [1981] 1983).

Rich, Adrienne. "Compulsory Heterosexuality and Lesbian Existence." In *Powers of Desire: The Politics of Sexuality,* edited by Ann Snitow, Christine Stansell, and Sharon Thompson, 177–205 (New York: Monthly Review, 1983).

Rist, Darrell Yates. "AIDS as Obsession: The Deadly Cost of an Obsession." *Nation,* February 13, 1989, 181–83.

Roberts, Matthew. "Gay Identities and Social Movement Formation in the Developing World: The AIDS Crisis as Catalyst." *Alternatives* 20 (1995): 243–64.

Robertson, Marie. "We Need Our Own Banner." In *Flaunting It!,* edited by Ed Jackson and Stan Persky, 177–78 (Vancouver: New Star, 1982).

Rofes, Eric E. "Gay Groups vs. AIDS Groups: Averting Civil War in the 1990s." *Out/Look: National Lesbian and Gay Quarterly* 8 (spring 1990): 8–17.

Rossinow, Doug. *The Politics of Authenticity.* New York: Columbia University Press, 1998.

Roszak, Theodore. *The Making of a Counter-culture: Reflections on the Technocratic Society and Its Youthful Opposition.* New York: Doubleday, 1969.

Rotello, Gabriel. *Sexual Ecology: AIDS and the Destiny of Gay Men.* New York: Dutton, 1997.

Rubin, Gayle. *The San Francisco Leather Community* [tentative title]. Chicago: University of Chicago Press, forthcoming.

———. "Thinking Sex: Notes for a Radical Theory of the Politics of Sexuality." In *Pleasure and Danger: Exploring Female Sexuality,* edited by Carole S. Vance, 267–319 (Boston: Routledge, 1984).

———. "Valley of the Kings." *Sentinel,* September 13, 1984, 10–11.

Rupp, Leila J., and Verta Taylor. *Survival in the Doldrums: The American Women's Rights Movement, 1945 to the 1960s.* Columbus: Ohio State University Press, 1990.

Russell, Sabin. "S.F. AIDS Summit Will Shift Focus as Death Rate Drops." *San Francisco Chronicle,* January 27, 1998, 1.

Sagarin, Edward. *Odd Man In: Societies of Deviants in America.* Chicago: Quadrangle, 1969.

San Francisco AIDS Foundation. Untitled brochure. San Francisco: San Francisco AIDS Foundation, 1995.

San Francisco Department of Public Health AIDS Office. *AIDS Surveillance Report: AIDS Cases Reported through December 1994.* San Francisco: San Francisco Department of Public Health, 1994.

Schartz, Ruth L. "New Alliances, Strange Bedfellows: Lesbians, Gay Men, and AIDS." In *Sisters, Sexperts, Queers: Beyond the Lesbian Nation,* edited by Arlene Stein, 230–44 (New York: Penguin, 1993).

Schmidt, Laura Anne. *The Corporate Transformation of American Health Care: A Study in Institution Building.* Princeton: Princeton University Press, forthcoming.

Schneider, Richard, Jr. "Stonewall Hits the Big 3-0." *Harvard Gay and Lesbian Review* 6, no. 3 (1999): 4.

Scott, W. Richard. "Conceptualizing Organizational Fields: Linking Organizations and Soci-

etal Systems." In *Systemrationalität und Partialinteresse,* edited by Hans-Ulrich Derlien, Uta
Gerhardt, and Fritz W. Scharph, 203–21 (Baden-Baden: Nomos, 1994).

———. *Institutions and Organizations.* Thousand Oaks, Calif.: Sage, 1995.

Scott, W. Richard, and John W. Meyer, eds. *Institutional Environments and Organizations: Structural
Complexity and Individualism.* Thousand Oaks, Calif.: Sage, 1994.

Seidman, Steven. "AIDS and the Discursive Construction of Homosexuality." In *The New
American Cultural Sociology,* edited by Philip Smith, 47–59 (Cambridge: Cambridge University Press, 1998).

———. "Identity and Politics in a 'Postmodern' Gay Culture: Some Historical and Conceptual Notes." In *Fear of a Queer Planet: Queer Politics and Social Theory,* edited by Michael Warner, 105–42 (Minneapolis: University of Minnesota Press, 1993).

Sewell, William H., Jr. "Historical Events as Transformations of Structures: Inventing Revolution at the Bastille." *Theory and Society* 25 (1996): 841–81.

———. "A Theory of Structure: Duality, Agency, and Transformation." *American Journal of
Sociology* 98 (1992): 1–29.

———. *Work and Revolution in France: The Language of Labour from the Old Regime to 1848.* New
York: Cambridge University Press, 1980.

"S.F. to Host National Conference." *Vector,* August 1966, 1, 10.

Shelley, Martha. "Gay Is Good." In *Out of the Closets: Voices of Gay Liberation,* edited by Karla Jay
and Allen Young, 31–33 (New York: New York University Press, [1972] 1992).

Shepard, Benjamin Heim. *White Nights and Ascending Shadows.* London: Cassell, 1997.

Shilts, Randy. *And the Band Played On: People, Politics, and the AIDS Epidemic.* New York: Penguin,
1987.

———. "Castro Street: Mecca or Ghetto?" In *Long Road to Freedom: The Advocate History of the
Gay and Lesbian Movement,* edited by Mark Thompson, 155–57 (New York: St. Martin's,
1994).

———. *The Mayor of Castro Street: The Life and Times of Harvey Milk.* New York: St. Martin's,
1982.

"SIR Awards Motorcycle Trophies." *Vector,* November 1966, 3.

"S.I.R.'s Statement of Policy." *Vector.* December 1964, 1.

Smith, Barbara, ed. *Home Girls: A Black Feminist Anthology.* New York: Kitchen Table/Women
of Color, 1983.

Smith, Barbara, and Beverly Smith. "Across the Kitchen Table: A Sister-to-Sister Dialogue."
In *This Bridge Called My Back: Writings by Radical Women of Color,* edited by Cherríe Moraga
and Gloria Anzaldúa, 113–27 (New York: Kitchen Table/Women of Color, 1983).

Snow, David A., and Robert D. Benford. "Ideology, Frame Resonance, and Participant Mobilization." *International Social Movement Research* 1 (1988): 197–217.

———. "Master Frames and Cycles of Protest." In *Frontiers in Social Movement Theory,* edited by
Aldon Morris and Carol McClurg Mueller, 133–55 (New Haven: Yale University Press,
1992).

Snow, David A., E. Burke Rochford, Steven K. Worden, and Robert D. Benford. "Frame
Alignment Processes, Micromobilization, and Movement Participation." *American Sociological Review* 51 (1986): 464–81.

"Special Report: C.R.H. Needs Donations." *Vector,* March 1965, 3.

Stanhope, Victoria. "NOW Lesbian Rights Summit: More Mayhem about the Millennium
March." *Off Our Backs* 29, no. 6 (1999): 6.

"State Fair Booth Cancelled." *Vector,* September 1966, 1, 9.

"State Fair Booth Cancelled: Loss or Gain to Homophile Movement." *Vector,* October 1966,
1, 5.

Stein, Arlene. *Sex and Sensibility: Stories of a Lesbian Generation.* Berkeley and Los Angeles: University of California Press, 1997.

———. "Sisters and Queers: The Decentering of Lesbian Feminism." *Socialist Review* 22, no. 1 (1992): 33–55.

Stevens. "Sir?" *San Francisco Free Press,* November 1, 1969, 7.

Stevens, Mitchell. "Kingdom of Children: Culture and Controversy in the Homeschooling Movement." Presentation, Department of Sociology, Indiana University, February 16, 2001.

———. *Kingdom of Children: Culture and Controversy in the Homeschooling Movement.* Princeton: Princeton University Press, forthcoming.

Stinchcombe, Arthur. "Social Structure and Organizations." In *Handbook of Organizations,* edited by J. G. March, 142–93 (Chicago: Rand McNally, 1965).

Stine, Gerald J. *AIDS Update 1998: An Annual Overview of Acquired Immune Deficiency Syndrome.* Upper Saddle River, N.J.: Prentice-Hall, 1998.

Stryker, Sean D. "Knowledge and Power in the Students for a Democratic Society, 1960–1970." *Berkeley Journal of Sociology* 38 (1993–94): 89–138.

Stryker, Susan. "Anatomy of a Riot: The Compton's Cafeteria Disturbance of 1966." Paper presented at American Historical Association meetings, San Francisco, 2002.

Stryker, Susan, and Jim Van Buskirk. *Gay by the Bay: A History of Queer Culture in the San Francisco Bay Area.* San Francisco: Chronicle, 1996.

Swaminathan, Anand, and James B. Wade. "Social Movement Theory and the Evolution of New Organization Forms." In *The Entrepreneurship Dynamic in Industry Evolution,* edited by C. B. Schoonhoven and E. Romanelli (Stanford: Stanford University Press, forthcoming).

Swidler, Ann. "Culture in Action: Symbols and Strategies." *American Sociological Review* 51 (1986): 273–86.

———. *Talk of Love: How Culture Matters.* Chicago: University of Chicago Press, 2001.

Tarrow, Sidney. *Power in Movement: Social Movements, Collective Action, and Politics.* Cambridge: Cambridge University Press, 1994.

Taylor, Verta, and Nancy Whittier. "Collective Identity in Social Movement Communities: Lesbian Feminist Mobilization." In *Frontiers in Social Movement Theory,* edited by Aldon D. Morris and Carol McClurg Mueller, 104–29 (New Haven: Yale University Press, 1992).

Teal, Donn. *The Gay Militants: How Gay Liberation Began in America, 1969–1971.* 2d ed. New York: St. Martin's, 1995.

Teller, Gary. "I Give You My Word as a Homosexual. . . ." *Vector,* January 1966, 1, 8.

Thompson, Mark, ed. *Long Road to Freedom: The Advocate History of the Gay and Lesbian Movement.* New York: St. Martin's, 1994.

Thornton, Patricia H., and William Ocasio. "Institutional Logics and the Historical Contingency of Power in Organizations: Executive Succession in the Higher Education Publishing Industry, 1958–1990." *American Journal of Sociology* 105 (1999): 801–43.

Thorp, Charles P. "I.D., Leadership, and Violence." In *Out of the Closets: Voices of Gay Liberation,* edited by Karla Jay and Allen Young, 352–62 (New York: New York University Press, [1972] 1992).

Tilly, Charles. *From Mobilization to Revolution.* Reading, Mass.: Addison-Wesley, 1978.

Touraine, Alan. *The Voice and the Eye: An Analysis of Social Movements.* Cambridge: Cambridge University Press, 1981.

Tucker, David J., Jitendra Singh, Agnes G. Meinhard, and Robert J. House. "Ecological and Institutional Sources of Change in Organizational Populations." In *Ecological Models of Organizations,* edited by Glenn R. Carroll, 127–51 (Cambridge: Ballinger, 1988).

Tucker, Naomi, ed. *Bisexual Politics: Theories, Queries, and Visions.* New York: Haworth, 1995.

Tuller, David. "Gays, Lesbians Head for Capital." *San Francisco Chronicle,* April 17, 1993, A14.

Vaid, Urvashi. *Virtual Equality: The Mainstreaming of Gay and Lesbian Liberation.* New York: Anchor, 1995.

Venturelli, Peter J. "Institutions in an Ethnic District." *Human Organization* 41, no. 1 (1982): 26–35.

Voss, Kim, and Rachel Sherman. "Breaking the Iron Law of Oligarchy: Union Revitalization in the American Labor Movement." *American Journal of Sociology* 106 (2000): 303–49.

Walker, Bill. "San Francisco Bay Area Gay and Lesbian Serials: A Guide to the Microfilm Collection." University of California, Berkeley, and Gay, Lesbian, Bisexual, Transgender Historical Society of Northern California, 1991.

Walker, Jack. "The Origins and Maintenance of Interest Groups in America." *American Political Science Review* 77 (1983): 390–406.

Walker, Robert S. Letter. *Vector.* August 1967, 15.

Warner, Mel. "Anxious Ingenues Await 4th Annual Coitillion." *Vector,* June 1970, 10.

Weeks, Jeffrey. *Coming Out: Homosexual Politics in Britain from the Nineteenth Century to the Present.* London: Quartet, 1977.

Weise, Elizabeth Reba, ed. *Closer to Home: Bisexuality and Feminism.* Seattle: Seal, 1992.

Weiss, Amy. "The AIDS Bereaved: Counseling Strategies." In *Face to Face: A Guide to AIDS Counseling,* edited by James W. Dilley, Cheri Pies, and Michael Helquist, 267–75 (San Francisco: AIDS Health Project, 1989).

Whittington, Gale. Letter. *Vector.* April 1970, 27.

Willer, Shirley. "The Lesbian, the Homosexual, and the Homophile Movement." *Vector,* October 1966, 8, 9.

Wittman, Carl. "A Gay Manifesto." In *Out of the Closets: Voices of Gay Liberation,* edited by Karla Jay and Allen Young, 330–41 (New York: New York University Press, [1972] 1992).

Wolf, Deborah Goleman. *The Lesbian Community.* Berkeley and Los Angeles: University of California Press, 1979.

Young, Allen. "Out of the Closets, Into the Streets." In *Out of the Closets: Voices of Gay Liberation,* edited by Karla Jay and Allen Young, 6–30 (New York: New York University Press, [1972] 1992).

Zald, Mayer N. "Taking It to the Streets in the Office: Collective Actions and Protest in Organizations." *LSAmagazine,* spring 2001, 14–21.

Zald, Mayer N., and Michael A. Berger. "Social Movements in Organizations: Coup d'Etat, Insurgency, and Mass Movements." *American Journal of Sociology* 83 (1978): 823–61.

Zinn, Howard. *SNCC: The New Abolitionists.* Boston: Beacon, 1965.

Zucker, Lynne G. "Combining Institutional Theory and Population Ecology: No Legitimacy, No History." *American Sociological Review* 54 (1989): 542–45.

INDEX

Printed in the USA
CPSIA information can be obtained
at www.ICGtesting.com
LVHW090151061023
760342LV00007B/106